OLD ENGLISH POETRY:
AN ANTHOLOGY

OLD ENGLISH POETRY:
AN ANTHOLOGY

a *Broadview Anthology of British Literature* edition

Edited and Translated by
R.M. Liuzza

With contributions by
Stephen O. Glosecki

General Editors,
Broadview Anthology of British Literature:
Joseph Black, University of Massachusetts, Amherst
Leonard Conolly, Trent University
Kate Flint, University of Southern California
Isobel Grundy, University of Alberta
Don LePan, Broadview Press
Roy Liuzza, University of Tennessee
Jerome J. McGann, University of Virginia
Anne Lake Prescott, Barnard College
Barry V. Qualls, Rutgers University
Claire Waters, University of California, Davis

broadview press

Library and Archives Canada Cataloguing in Publication

Old English poetry : an anthology / edited and translated by R.M. Liuzza ; with contributions by Stephen O. Glosecki.

(A Broadview anthology of British literature edition)
Includes bibliographical references.
ISBN 978-1-55481-157-1 (pbk.)

1. English poetry—Old English, ca. 450-1100—Translations into English. I. Glosecki, Stephen O., 1952-, contributor II. Liuzza, R. M., editor and translator of compilation III. Series: Broadview anthology of British literature.

PR1508.O43 2014   829'.1008   C2014-900108-8

Broadview Press is an independent, international publishing house, incorporated in 1985.

We welcome comments and suggestions regarding any aspect of our publications—please feel free to contact us at the addresses below or at broadview@broadviewpress.com.

North America	PO Box 1243, Peterborough, Ontario K9J 7H5, Canada
	555 Riverwalk Parkway, Tonawanda, New York 14150, USA
	Tel: (705) 743-8990; Fax: (705) 743-8353
	email: customerservice@broadviewpress.com
UK, Europe, Central Asia,	Eurospan Group, 3 Henrietta St., London WC2E 8LU, UK
Middle East, Africa, India,	Tel: 44 (0) 1767 604972; Fax: 44 (0) 1767 601640
and Southeast Asia	email: eurospan@turpin-distribution.com
Australia and New Zealand	NewSouth Books, c/o TL Distribution
	15-23 Helles Ave., Moorebank, NSW 2170, Australia
	Tel: (02) 8778 9999; Fax: (02) 8778 9944
	email: orders@tldistribution.com.au

www.broadviewpress.com

Developmental Editor: Jennifer McCue

Broadview Press acknowledges the financial support of the Government of Canada through the Canada Book Fund for our publishing activities.

PRINTED IN CANADA

Contents

COVER IMAGE

The cover shows fol. 8r of Exeter, Cathedral Library 3501, the Exeter Book of Old English poetry, written ca. 975 and housed in the Exeter Cathedral Library since at least the eleventh century. It is taken from *The Exeter Anthology of Old English Poetry (The Exeter DVD)*, ed. Bernard Muir with software by Nick Kennedy (Liverpool: Liverpool University Press, 2006) and reproduced by kind permission of the Dean and Chapter of Exeter Cathedral Library. The original manuscript of the Exeter Book is owned by the Dean and Chapter of Exeter and is held in the Cathedral Library, Exeter, UK.

The image shows the damaged beginning of "Advent" (*Christ I*); the stains and slash marks on the page suggest the precarious fate of many Old English manuscripts in the later medieval period—undecorated and unreadable, they were probably regarded as little better than waste parchment. These marks were once thought to indicate that the manuscript had been used as something like a beer mat and cheese board, but it is more likely that they are signs of scriptorium use, stains from a glue pot and knife-marks from cutting strips of parchment for binding other manuscripts. See Patrick W. Conner, *Anglo-Saxon Exeter: A Tenth-Century Cultural History* (Woodbridge: Boydell Press, 1993), 237-38.

Introduction

About 30,000 lines of Old English poetry survive, most of it in six manuscripts.[1] One of these, Paris, Bibliothèque Nationale MS 8824 (the "Paris Psalter"), contains verse versions of Psalms 51-150; another, London, BL Cotton Otho A.vi, contains versified portions of the English translation of Boethius's *Consolation of Philosophy*.[2] The remaining four manuscripts are better known: London, BL Cotton Vitellius A.xv, the "Beowulf Manuscript" or "Nowell Codex," contains *Beowulf* and *Judith*; Oxford, Bodleian Library MS Junius 11, the "Junius manuscript," contains *Genesis, Exodus, Daniel*, and *Christ and Satan*; Vercelli, Biblioteca Capitolare MS CXVII, the "Vercelli Book," contains six poems including *The Dream of the Rood, Elene*, and *Andreas*; and Exeter, Cathedral Library, Dean and Chapter MS 3501, the "Exeter Book," contains a large collection of short and long poems on various subjects, among them *The Wanderer, The Seafarer*, and the Old English *Riddles*. Almost all Old English poems are preserved in only a single copy, often in a damaged or incomplete state— in other words, they have barely survived.

With the exception of the Paris Psalter, which is somewhat later, all the manuscripts containing Old English poetry are from the second half of the tenth century, but the poetry they contain may be older, in some cases much older. Most scholars agree that Old English poetry grew out of a literary tradition of performance, with poetry being sung in public or private gatherings. The poems performed would have been perhaps partly memorized, partly improvised from a store of common lines and metrical formulae that filled a given poetic

---

1   Poems also survive in the manuscripts of the *Anglo-Saxon Chronicle*, the Old English version of Bede's *Ecclesiastical History*, and elsewhere; a few poems, such as *The Battle of Maldon* and *The Fight at Finnsburh*, survive only in modern transcriptions. Most of the corpus of Old English poetry is edited in G.P. Krapp and E.V.K. Dobbie, *The Anglo-Saxon Poetic Records*. 6 vols. (New York: Columbia University Press, 1931-53; abbreviated *ASPR*). Some of Krapp and Dobbie's texts have been superseded by more recent editions; these are mentioned in the notes to individual poems.

2   The former is edited by G.P. Krapp, *The Paris Psalter and the Meters of Boethius*. ASPR V (New York: Columbia University Press, 1932); the latter is edited by Malcolm Godden and Susan Irvine, *The Old English Boethius: An Edition of the Old English Versions of Boethius's De Consolatione Philosophiae*. 2 vols. (Oxford: Oxford University Press, 2009).

need—praising a king, naming a hero, giving thanks, expressing sorrow, introducing a speech, setting a scene, describing an action, and so on. These formulae would have been variable within certain limits and probably recognizable to the audience; the artistry of the singer/poet would have been displayed in how well he or she wove together traditional language for each new occasion, and improvised new constellations of images and ideas from familiar poetic elements. The practice of composing and performing poetic songs long predated the introduction of writing and the development of literacy; poetry was part of the deep cultural inheritance of the English, brought from the continent by the Germanic Angles and Saxons who migrated to Britain in the fifth century.

When the pagan English were converted to Christianity in the seventh century, the traditional craft of verse-making was adapted to incorporate the new ideas of Christian culture, and to embrace new subjects and situations such as a saint's life or the monastic cell. Likewise the oral and performative art of poetic composition was adapted to the written page and the new practices of reading introduced along with the new religion. The Old English poetry that has survived is a hybrid form, with old and new elements mixed together, each informing and supporting the other. Older modes of composition and performance which reflected and underwrote older values and social structures are still visible in the language, but new content, new audiences, and new reading situations inflect this old material in new ways. Even a traditional celebration of heroic military might like *The Battle of Brunanburh* acknowledges its place in the pages of a written prose chronicle; even the devotional verses of the Old English psalms use poetic formulae and techniques crafted through centuries of performance.

Because most Old English poems are anonymous, untitled, and undated in their manuscripts, it is all but impossible to reconstruct the literary history of Old English poetry—what came first and what came later, which poems were influential and which were idiosyncratic, who borrowed from whom, who read what. There are only a few facts from which we might build an understanding of the origins and development of Old English poetry. Cædmon's *Hymn* can probably be dated to the time of Cædmon in the late seventh century; if the portions of the *Dream of the Rood* carved on the Ruthwell Cross are not a later addition, then that part of the poem existed in the early eighth century. *The Battle of Maldon* was obviously written after the battle occurred in 991, and the poems in the *Anglo-Saxon Chronicle* after the events they describe. Metrical prefaces and epilogues to some prose works from the time of King Alfred were most likely written around the same time as the works they accompany. But these facts are not much, and for the longer poems in Old English—*Genesis, Exodus, Andreas, Christ,* and above all *Beowulf*—we know neither their dates of composition nor their relative chronology. Some educated guesses about chronology can be made based on assumptions about meter and language, but these are just guesses and assumptions.[1] Moreover, if poets did in fact draw on a pre-existing body of traditional formulae and themes, as the prevailing theory of poetic composition in Old English studies believes, then any line found in more than one poem is not necessarily a sign that one poet has influenced another; it might rather indicate that both poets drew from the same storehouse of traditional verse elements. So even the internal evidence for literary history is uncertain. Finally, to all this uncertainty about the history of Old English poetry we must add the fact that we know nothing about the range of poetic style in Anglo-Saxon England. The poems that survive probably represent only a small fraction of the poetry that once existed—much of it was probably never written down, and not all that was written down has survived. Did all Old English poetry aspire to the high formality of *Beowulf,* or were there levels of style reflecting different audiences and occasions, informal folk genres and popular forms, bodies of looser or less formal poetry—lullabies, love songs, laments—that for one reason or another did not get copied into manuscripts? And what influence, if any, did these unknown bodies of poetry have on the poems that *did* get written down?

Despite all this uncertainty, there are some things we can infer about Old English poetry simply by reading it. Common ideas, images, and phrases abound; certain familiar notes are sounded again and again no matter what the subject at hand. Eventually we can build up a sense of the things that must have mattered to the Anglo-Saxons because they kept returning to them in their poetry. At the

---

1   The best of these are in R.D. Fulk, *A History of Old English Meter* (Philadelphia: University of Pennsylvania Press, 1991), and, among many other works, "Old English Meter and Oral Tradition: Three Issues Bearing on Poetic Chronology," *JEGP* 106 (2007): 304-24.

same time any reader of Old English literature must be struck by the broad range and diversity in the works that have survived, from heartbreaking sorrow to wide-eyed wonder, from the wisdom of old age to the hot blood of battle to the deepest and most poignant loneliness. There is breathless storytelling and ponderous cataloguing; there is fervent religious devotion and playful teasing. The poems translated here are meant to provide a sense of some of this range and diversity, but while they do so they also offer significant portions of three of the important manuscripts of Old English poetry—the Vercelli Book, the Junius Manuscript, and the Exeter Book.

As a way of thinking about some major areas of common poetic interest in Old English, the poems translated here are divided into four main headings—Elegies, Wisdom, Faith, and Fame—containing, respectively, poems about mutability and time, poems about the world and its wonders, poems about God and His saints, and poems about heroes and battles. These groupings are somewhat traditional, but they are really fairly arbitrary. Other headings might have been devised, and most poems would fit equally well under more than one heading. The *Dream of the Rood*, for example, is as heroic as it is pious; *The Seafarer* is as pious as it is elegiac; *Widsith* is a poem of wisdom as well as fame; and so on—almost every poem shares some elements with poems in other categories One alternative might be to read all the poems in one manuscript, looking for threads that link the Exeter Book *Advent* to the elegies to the wisdom poems to the Riddles. In many respects the labels we place on these poems, beginning with their titles (which are all invented by modern editors, not medieval authors or scribes), place unfair limits on our experience of them; they can shape our expectations in ways that we must work to overcome. But labels and categories can also be useful ways to focus a first reading of an unfamiliar body of poetry, so I have chosen to use them to organize this collection. But please remember that the groupings presented here are meant to suggest only one of many ways to experience these poems, not the only way or even the best way to read them.

One kind of diversity that a reader might be surprised *not* to find in Old English poetry is a diversity of verse forms. A modern anthology of English poetry would contain a wild menagerie of forms—from sonnets and limericks to free verse and prose-poems; certain forms are associated with certain content, and it would be as difficult to write a heartfelt love limerick as it would be to write a heroic haiku (difficult, though certainly not impossible). All Old English poetry, however, is written in essentially the same meter.[1] This meter is stressed rather than counted, and alliterative rather than rhymed. In other words, while a line of modern English metrical poetry generally has a fixed number of syllables and stresses (for iambic pentameter, this would be ten syllables and, in theory, five stresses), an ordinary line of Old English poetry contains four stressed syllables—thought of as two half-lines of two stresses each—and a variable number of unstressed syllables whose placement conforms to a limited number of verse types. And while lines of modern English poetry might form rhymed couplets or tercets or quatrains in various patterns (with four rhyming lines represented *abab*, *abba*, etc.), lines of Old English poetry are linked internally by alliteration (the two half-lines are represented as *aa:ax*, *xa:ax*, etc.) and are not linked to one another by rhyme or any other device.[2]

The simplest way to understand the form of Old English verse is to see an example of it; here is Cædmon's *Hymn* in Old English:[3]

Nu sculon herian   heofonrices weard,
Metodes meahta   ond his modgeþanc,
weorc wuldorfæder,   swa he wundra gehwæs,
ece Drihten,   or astealde.
He ærest scop   ielda bearnum   5
heofon to hrofe,   halig Scieppend;

---

1   There are a few exceptions—*Seasons for Fasting* is divided into regular stanzas, and *Deor* into irregular ones; a few poems have refrains, or repeated lines that are almost refrains; a poem in the Exeter Book called *The Rhyming Poem* does just that. Some poems contain irregular patches of hypermetric verses containing more than two stresses in each half-line; others have isolated half-lines that may be deliberately done for effect (and not accidentally created by a scribe's omission). And within the one Old English alliterative verse form there appears to have been some range in formality and strictness.

2   There are a number of additional rules regarding which syllables may be stressed, limiting the position of partly-stressed syllables, allowing two short syllables to play the role of one long syllable, and so on, but for most beginning readers these are not as important as the fundamental rules of four stressed syllables, at least two of them alliterating. An interesting introduction to the study of Old English meter can be found in Thomas Bredehoft, "What are Old English Metrical Studies For?" *Old English Newsletter* 39.1, 25-36, online at http://www.oenewsletter.org/OEN/pdf/bredehoft39_1.pdf.

3   For a translation of the poem see below, p. 19.

þa middangeard   manncynnes weard,
ece Drihten,   æfter teode,
firum foldan   Frea ælmihtig.

The pattern of alliteration is clearly seen in the second line _Metodes meahta ond his modgeþanc_; the fourth line _ece Drihten or astealde_ indicates both that any vowel can alliterate with any other vowel and that both stressed syllables in the first half of the line do not need to alliterate.

Cædmon's _Hymn_ also contains good examples of some of the important stylistic features of Old English poetry. Most notable—and noticeable—among these is repetition with variation, a kind of turning and returning around a name or quality to denominate it several times over. This style has been called _appositive_,[1] after the grammatical practice of setting two nouns or phrases that refer to the same thing next to another, as in Shakespeare's "This royal throne of kings, this scepter'd isle, / This earth of majesty, this seat of Mars, / ... This blessed plot, this earth, this realm, this England" (_Richard II_ Act II Scene i). Cædmon's _Hymn_ is a virtuoso exercise in apposition and in naming and renaming; the poem is largely a list of the names and attributes of God, who in nine lines is called _heafonrices weard_ "guardian of the heavenly kingdom," _metod_ "Maker," _wuldorfæder_ "Father of glory," _ece Drihten_ "eternal Lord," _halig scieppend_ "holy Creator," _mancynnes weard_ "guardian of mankind," and _frea_ "Lord." Another notable stylistic feature is the use of formulae. God is called _heofonrices weard_ in line 1 and _manncynnes weard_ in line 7; in other poems appear the expressions _rodera weard_ ("guardian of the skies," _Genesis_ 1), _sigora weard_ ("guardian of victories," _Andreas_ 987), _sumera weard_ ("guardian of summer," _Seafarer_ 53), and _beahhorda weard_ ("guardian of a ring-treasure," _Beowulf_ 921), among many others. The metrical formula in this half-line might be expressed as "/xx _weard_" (with / indicating a stressed syllable and x an unstressed one); the first word varies depending on the sense of the poem and the needs of alliteration. Not all formulae need variation; God is called _ece Drihten_ "eternal Lord" twice in the poem's nine lines. The presence of repetitive

---

1   Best explained in F.C. Robinson, _Beowulf and the Appositive Style_ (Knoxville: University of Tennessee Press, 1985).

lines and phrases and of formulaic expressions drawn from a common poetic repertoire does not indicate some lapse in creative energy or some failure of editing; such repetitions and variations are part of the traditional art of the Old English poet. The same principles of repetition-with-variation, adaptation of old expressions to new contexts, linking of lines and ideas by sound and suggestion, can be found on the largest scale across the whole body of Old English poetry.

FURTHER READING:
INTRODUCTIONS TO OLD ENGLISH LITERATURE AND POETRY

Amodio, Mark. *The Anglo-Saxon Literature Handbook*. Chichester: Wiley-Blackwell, 2006.

Donoghue, Daniel. *Old English Literature: A Short Introduction*. Chichester: Wiley-Blackwell, 2006.

Fulk, R.D., and Christopher Cain. *A History of Old English Literature*. 2nd ed. Chichester: Wiley-Blackwell, 2013.

Godden, M.R., and Michael Lapidge, eds. *The Cambridge Companion to Old English Literature*. 2nd ed. Cambridge: Cambridge University Press, 2013.

Greenfield, Stanley B., and Daniel G. Calder. *A New Critical History of Old English Literature*. New York: New York University Press, 1986.

Momma, Haruko. "Old English Poetic Form: Genre, Style, Prosody." *The Cambridge History of Early Medieval English Literature*. Ed. Clare A. Lees. Cambridge: Cambridge University Press, 2013. 278-308.

Stodnick, Jacqueline A., and Renée R. Trilling, eds. *A Handbook of Anglo-Saxon Studies*. Chichester: Wiley-Blackwell, 2013.

Note

The poems are presented with short introductions, either for a group of poems such as the elegies or for individual poems in other sections. These introductions note manuscript sources and edited texts, and include a few suggestions for further reading for anyone interested in a deeper exploration of the style, meaning, and context of these works. Some of the translations and the accompanying introductions have appeared, in a different form, in *The Broadview Anthology of British Literature*; they have all been revised for this volume. I am grateful to

Don LePan for his encouragement and advice, and to Natalie Grinnell, Robin Norris, and Andrew Scheil, who read a first draft of the manuscript, for many points of advice and suggestions for improvement. All errors that remain are, of course, my own.

Stephen Glosecki, scholar, teacher, and poet, died in 2007; I am grateful to his wife Karen Reynolds for permission to include his translations of *Judith* and the Old English metrical charms. His style of translation is very different from mine;[1] I hope readers will enjoy hearing once again his unique and powerful voice.

---

1   I have discussed my own ideals of translating Old English poetry in the introduction to my translation of *Beowulf* 2nd edition (Peterborough: Broadview Press, 2013), 36-43.

Preface—The Birth of Poetry

Bede, *Ecclesiastical History* IV.24
The Story of Cædmon

Bede "the Venerable," the most learned writer of the Anglo-Saxon period, was born in Northumbria around 673. At the age of seven he entered the twin monastery of Wearmouth-Jarrow and remained there, except for a few short excursions, until his death. Under the Abbot Ceolfrith, Bede received a thorough education in grammar, rhetoric, mathematics, music, natural science, and the study of Scripture; he was ordained a deacon at 19 and a priest at 30. In a brief autobiographical note appended to his *Ecclesiastical History* he describes himself in this manner: "Amid the observance of the discipline of the Rule [of St. Benedict] and the daily task of singing in the church, it has always been my delight to learn or to teach or to write." Over the course of his fairly long life—he died in 735— Bede produced a body of writing that remains impressive for its clarity, intelligence, range, and devotion. His works, which survive in hundreds of manuscripts, were deeply influential and widely copied throughout the Middle Ages. Apart from a brief and enigmatic Old English poem called "Bede's Death Song" and a lost translation of the Gospel of John that he is said to have been writing on his deathbed, all Bede's works were written in Latin, which was at that time the international language of scholarship and of the Church.

Benedict Biscop, founder of Jarrow monastery, had traveled extensively and assembled an impressive library; during Bede's lifetime this remote outpost on the northeastern coast of England—founded about the year Bede was born, scarcely 50 years after the rulers of Northumbria had converted to Christianity—was perhaps the most learned monastic center in all of Europe. Bede's writings include works of Scriptural commentary, homilies, handbooks on meter and orthography, lives of saints, books of poetry and hymns, and treatises on cosmology and timekeeping. He was deeply interested in time and its measurement, a matter of some urgency in his lifetime because the Irish and Roman churches had different methods for calculating the date of Easter. In some years the two churches celebrated the feast on different days, which to Bede was a shocking sign of disunity. In his works promoting the Roman method of reckoning Easter he also helped establish the foundations of medieval astronomy and chronology; Bede is primarily responsible for popularizing the western "BC" and "AD" system of reckoning dates using the *anno domini* or "year of (the birth of) the Lord" as the dividing principle.

It is Bede's historical works, however, that are best known today. His *Ecclesiastical History of the English People* (*Historia Ecclesiastica Gentis Anglorum*), completed in 731, is an extensive history of England which takes as its theme the conversion of the Anglo-Saxon invaders who had displaced the native Britons. The *Ecclesiastical History* imagines an "English" people united not so much by culture or language or geography as by faith, the Roman Christianity brought to the island by Augustine of Canterbury and other missionaries sent by Pope Gregory the Great in 597. This work still provides the foundation for much of our knowledge of England in the fourth, fifth, and sixth centuries. Bede was able to take multiple sources—documents, memorials of abbots and holy men, histories, local oral traditions and legends—and weave them together into a coherent narrative. Writing very much from the Northumbrian point of view, Bede tells how the English are gradually and inevitably brought into the happy embrace of the Roman church, triumphing against the bitterness and treachery of the native Britons, the well-meaning but deluded zeal of the Irish missionaries, and the temporizing and backsliding of one pagan king after another. It is a tribute to Bede's great literary talent that the story he crafted from whatever meager evidence was available to him is still regarded by many as a fundamentally accurate account.

By far the most well-known episode in the *Ecclesiastical History* is Bede's story of the poet Cædmon. According to Bede, Cædmon is a layman cowherd at the monastery of Whitby who receives a miraculous talent for poetic composition and becomes, without any previous training, a great composer of religious verse in English. The story of Cædmon is both a myth (a way of explaining the origins of something) and a miracle (a dramatic intervention of God into the everyday world); Bede insists that Cædmon was the first English Christian poet, and that he did not learn any part of his art from other, more secular poets. Modern critics have pointed out that Cædmon's *Hymn* makes use of the same formulaic diction as most other poems in Old English and it is likely that Cædmon, if he really existed, was adapting an existing body of poetic practice to express the new ideas of Christian history and doctrine.

The story of Cædmon sets in opposition two different worlds—the monastery and the cowshed, the literate reader and oral singer, the religious and secular life—whose contact changes both worlds. It is important to notice, however, that this contact has little to do with literacy and the technology of writing—nobody teaches Cædmon to read the Bible or to write down the songs he makes. For Bede, the world of English poetry—even Christian poetry—is parallel to but separate from the monastic world of books and written learning. Still his poetry must have been known beyond the immediate circle of his listeners; Bede reports Cædmon's miraculous poem in a Latin paraphrase, but scribes of two early manuscripts of Bede's work added a short English verse text in the margins as a kind of footnote to Bede's story, and when Bede's work was translated into Old English in the ninth century the English poem replaced Bede's Latin paraphrase.

SOURCE/EDITION

The standard edition of the *Historia Ecclesiastica*, with a modern English translation, is Bertram Colgrave and R.A.B. Mynors, eds., *Bede's Ecclesiastical History of the English People* (Oxford: Oxford University Press, 1969). This translation relies heavily on that work, as well as the earlier work of L. Stevens (London: J.M. Dent; New York: E.P. Dutton, 1910) and J.M. Wallace-Hadrill's *Bede's Ecclesiastical History of the English People: A Historical Commentary* (Oxford: Clarendon Press, 1991).

FURTHER READING

Frantzen, Allen J., and John Hines, eds. *Cædmon's Hymn and Material Culture in the World of Bede*. Medieval European Studies 10. Morgantown, WV: West Virginia University Press, 2006.

O'Brien O'Keeffe, Katherine. "Orality and the Developing Text of Cædmon's *Hymn*." *Speculum* 62 (1987): 1-20.

O'Donnell, Daniel Paul, ed. *Cædmon's Hymn: A Multi-Media Study, Archive and Edition*. With the assistance of Dawn Collins et al. Cambridge: D.S. Brewer in association with SEENET and The Medieval Academy, 2005.

Orchard, Andy. "Poetic Inspiration and Prosaic Translation: The Making of Cædmon's *Hymn*." *Studies in English Language and Literature*. "*Doubt Wisely*": *Papers in Honour of E.G. Stanley*. Ed. M.J. Toswell and E.M. Tyler. London and New York: Routledge, 1996. 402-22.

In the monastery of this abbess[1] was a certain brother specially marked by the grace of God, who used to make pious and religious verses, so that whatever he learned from the holy Scriptures through interpreters, he soon afterwards turned into poetry in English—which was his native language—of great sweetness and humility. By his verses the minds of many were often inspired to despise the world and to long for the heavenly life. After him other Englishmen tried to compose religious poems, but none could ever compare with him, for he did not learn the art of poetry from men or through a man,[2] but received the gift of song freely by divine grace. For this reason he never could compose any trivial or foolish poem, but only those which were concerned with devotion and were fitting for his pious tongue to utter.

He had lived in the secular life until he was well advanced in years, and had never learned any verses; therefore sometimes at feasts, when it was agreed for the sake of entertainment that all present should take a turn singing, when he saw the harp coming towards him, he would rise up from the table in the middle of the feast, go out, and return home. On one occasion when he did this, he left the house of feasting and went to the stable, where it was his turn to take care of the animals that night. In due time he stretched out to rest; a person appeared to him in his sleep, called him by name, and said, "Cædmon, sing me something." Cædmon answered, "I cannot sing; that is why I left the feast and came here, because I could not sing." The man who was talking to him replied, "Nevertheless, you must sing to me."[3] "What shall I sing?" he asked. "Sing about the beginning of created things," he replied. At that, Cædmon immediately began to sing verses which he had never heard before in praise of God, whose general sense is this:

> Now let us praise Heaven-kingdom's guardian,
> the Maker's might and his mind's thoughts,
> the work of the glory-father—of every wonder,

---

1 *abbess*   Hild, abbess of Whitby (c. 614-80). Bede recounts her remarkable life in the *Ecclesiastical History* IV.23.

2 *from men or through a man*   See Galatians 1.1.

3 *Nevertheless ... sing to me*   Or more gently, "you *can* sing to me." The Latin is *mihi cantare habes.*

eternal Lord, He established a beginning.
He first shaped for men's sons   5
Heaven as a roof, the holy Creator;
then middle-earth mankind's guardian,
eternal Lord, afterwards prepared
the earth for men, the Lord almighty.[1]

This is the sense but not the actual order of the words he sang in his sleep, for poetry, no matter how well composed, cannot be literally translated from one language into another without losing much of its beauty and dignity. Awaking from his sleep, Cædmon remembered all that he had sung in his dream, and soon added more verses in the same manner, praising God in a worthy style.

In the morning he went to the steward, his master, and told him of the gift he had received; the steward led him to the abbess, who ordered him, in the presence of many learned men, to recount his dream and repeat his poem, so that they might all decide what it was and where it had come from. It was clear to all of them he had received a gift of heavenly grace from our Lord. Then they explained to him a passage of sacred history or doctrine, and ordered him, if he could, to turn it into verse. He undertook this task and went away; when he returned the next morning he repeated it to them, composed in excellent verse.

At this the abbess, recognizing the grace of God in this man, instructed him to renounce the secular habit and take up the monastic life; when this was done she joined him to the rest of the brethren in her monastery and ordered that he should be taught the whole course of sacred history. He learned all that he could by listening, and turning it over in his mind like a clean beast chewing the cud,[2] turned it into the most harmonious verse, and recited it so sweetly that his teachers became in turn his audience. He sang of the creation of the world, the origin of the human race, and all the history of Genesis; and made many verses on the departure of the children of Israel from

---

1   *Now let us praise ... the Lord almighty*   Bede gives only a Latin paraphrase; in two manuscripts of Bede's Latin *Historia* a poem in the Northumbrian dialect of Old English is added in the margins. When Bede's work was translated into Old English at the end of the ninth century and the translators substituted a version of this poem for Bede's paraphrase, the disclaimer that follows it was omitted. For the Old English of the poem, see the Preface.

2   *He learned ... the cud*   See Leviticus 11.3; Deuteronomy 14.6.

Egypt, and their entry into the Promised Land, and many other stories from the holy Scriptures; of the Incarnation, Passion, and Resurrection of our Lord, and of His Ascension into heaven, of the coming of the Holy Spirit and the teaching of the apostles, also of the terror of future judgment, the horror of the pains of hell, and the joys of the kingdom of heaven, and many more songs about the divine mercies and judgments by which he tried to turn all men away from the love of vice and to inspire in them the love and practice of good works. He was a very devout man, humbly submissive to the discipline of the monastic rule, but full of zeal against those who behaved otherwise; for this reason his life had a lovely ending.

When the hour of his departure drew near, for fourteen days he was afflicted with a bodily weakness which seemed to prepare the way, yet mild enough that he could talk and walk the whole time. Nearby was the house to which the sick and dying were carried. As evening fell on the night he was going to depart this life, he asked his attendant[1] to prepare a place for him there so he could take his rest. The attendant wondered why he should desire that, because there seemed to be no sign of his dying soon, but did what he had asked. They went there and were talking pleasantly and joyfully with the people who were already in the house; when it was past midnight he asked them whether they had the Eucharist there. They answered, "Why do you need the Eucharist? You are not likely to die, since you talk so merrily with us, just as though you were in perfect health." "Nevertheless," he said, "bring me the Eucharist." When he had taken it into his hand he asked whether they were all in charity with him, without any complaint or quarrel. They answered that they were all in perfect charity, and free from anger; and likewise asked him whether he felt the same towards them. He answered at once, "My sons, I am in charity with all the servants of God." Then strengthening himself with the heavenly viaticum, he prepared for his entrance into the next life; he asked how near it was to the time when the brothers had to awaken to sing their nightly praise of our Lord. They answered, "It is not far off." He said, "Good; let us wait until then," and signing himself with the sign of the holy cross, he laid his head on the pillow and fell into a slumber,

---

1   *his attendant* Older monks were attended by young novices who took care of them.

and so ended his life quietly. And so it happened that, just as he had served God with a simple and pure mind and quiet devotion, so now he departed into His presence and left the world by a quiet death, and his tongue, which had composed so many holy words in praise of the Creator, uttered its last words while he was in the act of signing himself with the cross, and commending his spirit into God's hands; and from what has been said, it seems he had foreknowledge of his death.

1. Elegies—Complaint and Consolation

The manuscript known as Exeter Cathedral Library, Dean and Chapter MS 3501 is a large anthology of secular and religious poems. The book was given to the Cathedral library at Exeter by the bishop Leofric some time before his death in 1072 CE (and has remained there ever since), but it was written probably a century earlier, somewhere in the south of England. Because some pages have been lost from the manuscript, we cannot say how many poems it originally contained, and we do not know the reasons behind its compilation. But the Exeter Book is a fascinating collection whose contents range from serious religious poetry on the Advent and Ascension of Christ, to verse lives of St Guthlac and Juliana, to a reworking of a Latin poem on the Phoenix, to a collection of almost 100 verse riddles which are sometimes comical or obscene. The poems are probably by many different authors; a poet named Cynewulf encoded his own name (in runes) in two poems, *Juliana* and *Christ II*, but all others are anonymous and untitled.

The Exeter Book includes a number of short philosophical poems, differing from one another in style and outlook but similar in tone, which have come to be known as "elegies": these are *The Wanderer*, *The Seafarer*, *Deor*, *Wulf and Eadwacer*, *The Wife's Lament*, and *The Ruin* (a short poem called *The Husband's Message* and two fragmentary poems called *Resignation A* and *B*, not translated here, are also generally considered elegies). All these titles, it must be remembered, are modern inventions, and not always the most reliable guides to the content or meaning of the poem. Likewise the modern label "elegy" is potentially misleading: in Greek and Latin literature the term refers to a particular metrical form, and since the sixteenth century the word has been used in English literature to describe a poem of mourning (the most famous examples of classic English elegies include Milton's *Lycidas*, Shelley's *Adonais*, and Tennyson's *In Memoriam*). But the term "elegy" is sometimes used more loosely to describe any serious meditative lyric poem, and it is in this broad sense that these Old English poems should be considered "elegies," and can be read and studied together.

The Old English elegies are not grouped together in the Exeter Book and are all, as far as we know, by different authors, but they share certain themes and concerns—the passage of time and the transience of earthly things, the pain of exile and separation, the ache of absence and longing—as well as certain images and scenes such as ruined or abandoned buildings, desolate landscapes, storms at sea, darkness, and the chill of winter. These themes, and the traditional language in which they are presented, are found in other Old English poems—certain passages of *Beowulf* are "elegiac," if not outright "elegy"—and the contemplation of earthly mutability sometimes seems almost obsessive in Old English literature. The tone and language of elegy may have roots deep in the traditions of Germanic poetry, but it is also influenced by late classical works such as Boethius's *Consolation of Philosophy*; the recognition that the world under the heavens is a place of tragic impermanence would probably have been regarded as equally good Christian doctrine and worldly wisdom.

Most of the Old English elegies are monologues spoken by an unidentified character whose situation is unclear but who seems to be cut off from human society and the comforts of home and companionship. But even though they share the poetic language of exile and longing, each poem has its own shape and purpose, and each makes its own statement about the problems and possibilities of earthly life. *The Wanderer* laments the passing of a whole way of life, the heroic world of the warrior's hall; *The Wife's Lament* and *Wulf and Eadwacer* are poems of intense personal longing for an absent husband or lover, even if their expressions of erotic desire are largely framed in the heroic language of lordship and loyalty. *Deor* stays close to the secular world of heroic legend; *The Seafarer* is explicitly and even aggressively homiletic and Christian. *The Ruin* is more detached and dispassionate about the scene it describes (it is the only poem without a first-person narrator) and its moral judgments, if any, are implicit and indirect.

Each of the poems presented here has some structural and interpretive difficulties. *The Wanderer* is a dramatic monologue with a prologue and epilogue, but the beginnings and endings of speeches are not indicated in the manuscript and can only be guessed at. *The Seafarer* switches tone so radically that many readers (including Ezra Pound, who translated the poem) have simply rejected the second, more homiletic half. These poems develop philosophical arguments and present evidence and conclusions, but Old English poetic language is not necessarily congenial to the demands of precise reasoning; sentence boundaries and relationships between clauses are often uncertain. Other sorts of interpretive difficulties accompany the elegies. The legends and stories alluded to in *Deor*, though they may once have been familiar to its audience, are now obscure, and have to be explained by reference to other literary works in other languages, some of which are almost equally uncertain. *The Wife's Lament* is obscure more by virtue of its language than its structure—a number of the poem's key terms have more than one meaning, and there is no indication which of several ways each of them ought to be translated. And the pages of the Exeter Book containing *The Ruin* have been damaged, leaving the poem to crumble into incoherence.

Among these difficult and enigmatic poems, the brief *Wulf and Eadwacer* stands out as one of the most obscure poems in Old English. It is, along with *The Wife's Lament*, one of the few poems in Old English in the voice of a woman—though whether its author was in fact a woman cannot be known—and its unusual structure may offer a tantalizing glimpse of a lost body of looser traditional poetry, love lyrics or laments with stanzas and refrains and more relaxed meter, very different from the formal heroic mode of *Beowulf*. Its real mystery, however, lies in its unknown backstory. Like the other elegies, the poem is a lyric, capturing an outpouring of emotion in a particular moment in time. The force of its emotional logic depends, like many lyrics, on an embedded narrative explaining who the speaker is—in this case a woman whose identity is unknown—and how she came to be in her situation. The importance of this implied narrative can be seen in many Old English lyrics; the philosophical insights of the Wanderer, for example, seem to flow from some catastrophic personal loss (perhaps the burial of his lord) and keep returning to that event even as the narrator moves forward intellectually. *Deor* is nothing more than a series of such narrative vignettes, each depicting a moment of lyric crisis analogous in some way to the speaker's personal devastation, and each dependent on our knowing the story leading up to and beyond the lyric moment. In *Wulf and Eadwacer*, however, we have no idea what the story is; we can only guess from the poem itself. This has naturally given rise to many theories on the meaning of the poem, some more plausible than others.

Some few things are generally agreed on. The speaker is a woman—the statement that a bold warrior enfolded the speaker in his arms (line 11) suggests this, and the use of a feminine adjective form for *reotunga* "weeping" (line 10) confirms it. The speaker is pining for someone named Wulf, but is kept apart from him on an island by someone named Eadwacer, presumably the same as the "bold warrior" in line 11, so perhaps her husband (his name means something like "property-watcher," which is a good name for a jealous husband). There is some hostility between Eadwacer's people and Wulf. The "cub" (OE *hwelp*) in the last lines is presumably the speaker's child, and the "wolf" that bears it away may be her lover Wulf—perhaps also the child's biological father. But this is only speculation.

All these poems (with the exception of *The Ruin*) are first-person accounts of individual emotion and experience; they seem to speak across the ages in voices whose pain often strikes a reader as vividly authentic and intimate. But their expression of individual subjectivity takes shape from deep within literary conventions, forms, and images that anchor their personal voices in a shared cultural tradition. This tension between the individual and the tradition may be an important part of the work of the Old English elegies; they dramatize the moment when an individual recognizes the universality of his or her experience, when one turns from loneliness and isolation to accept, even embrace, the shared suffering of the human condition. And despite their interpretive problems—which are found to some degree in all early literature—the Exeter Book elegies are among the most moving and powerful poems in Old English; their vision of life as both infinitely precious and inevitably transitory still strikes a responsive chord in the minds of many readers.

SOURCE

Exeter, Cathedral Library, Dean and Chapter MS 3501: *The Wanderer* fols. 76v-78r, *The Seafarer* fols. 81v-84v, *Deor* fols. 100rv, *Wulf and Eadwacer* fols. 100v-101r, *The Wife's Lament* fols. 115rv, *The Ruin* fols. 123v-124v.

EDITION

Bernard J. Muir, *The Exeter Anthology of Old English Poetry*. Revised 2nd ed. Exeter: University of Exeter Press, 2000.

FURTHER READING

Conner, Patrick W. "The Old English Elegy: A Historicization." *Readings in Medieval Texts: Interpreting Old and Middle English*

Literature. Ed. David F. Johnson and Elaine Treharne. Oxford: Oxford University Press, 2005. 30-45.

Dailey, Patricia. "Questions of Dwelling in Anglo-Saxon Poetry and Medieval Mysticism: Inhabiting Landscape, Body, and Mind." *New Medieval Literatures* 8. Ed. Rita Copeland, David Lawton, and Wendy Scase. Turnhout: Brepols, 2006. 175-214.

Davis, Joshua. "The Literary Languages of Old English: Words, Styles, Voices." *The Cambridge History of Early Medieval English Literature.* Ed. Clare A. Lees. Cambridge: Cambridge University Press, 2013. 257-77.

Davis, Kathleen. "Old English Lyrics: A Poetics of Experience." *The Cambridge History of Early Medieval English Literature.* Ed. Clare A. Lees. Cambridge: Cambridge University Press, 2013. 332-56.

Green, Martin, ed. *The Old English Elegies: New Essays in Criticism and Research.* London and Toronto: Associated University Presses, 1983.

Harbus, Antonina. "The Medieval Concept of the Self in Anglo-Saxon England." *Self and Identity* 1 (2002): 77-97.

Klein, Stacy S. "Gender and the Nature of Exile in Old English Elegies." *A Place to Believe in: Locating Medieval Landscapes.* Ed. Clare A. Lees and Gillian R. Overing. University Park, PA: Pennsylvania State University Press, 2006. 113-31.

Klinck, Anne L. *The Old English Elegies: A Critical Edition and Genre Study.* Montreal: McGill-Queen's University Press, 1992.

Niles, John D. *Old English Enigmatic Poems and the Play of the Texts.* Studies in the Early Middle Ages 13. Turnhout: Brepols, 2006.

O'Brien O'Keeffe, Katherine, ed. *Old English Shorter Poems: Basic Readings.* New York: Garland Publishing, 1994.

Shippey, T.A. "*The Wanderer* and *The Seafarer* as Wisdom Poetry." *Companion to Old English Poetry.* Ed. Henk Aertsen and Rolf H. Bremmer, Jr. Amsterdam: VU University Press, 1994. 145-58.

The Wanderer

Always the one alone longs for mercy,[1]
the Maker's mildness, though, troubled in mind,
across the ocean-ways he has long been forced
to stir with his hands the frost-cold sea,
and walk in exile's paths. *Wyrd*[2] is fully fixed.   5

    Thus spoke the Wanderer, mindful of troubles,
of cruel slaughters and dear kinsmen's downfall:[3]
"Often alone, in the first light of dawn,
I have sung my lament. There is none living
to whom I would dare to reveal clearly   10
my heart's thoughts. I know it is true
that it is a nobleman's lordly nature
to closely bind his spirit's coffer,
hold fast his treasure-hoard, whatever he may think.
The weary mind cannot withstand *wyrd*,   15
the troubled heart can offer no help,
and so those eager for fame often bind fast
in their breast-coffers a sorrowing soul,
just as I have had to take my own heart—
often wretched, cut off from my own homeland,   20
far from dear kinsmen—and bind it in fetters,
ever since long ago I hid my gold-giving friend
in the darkness of earth, and went wretched,
winter-sad, over the ice-locked waves,

---

1   *longs for mercy*   The Old English word *gebidan*, translated "longs for," can also mean "awaits" or "experiences." The word *ar* "mercy" can also mean "prosperity" in an earthly sense.

2   *Wyrd*   Old English word for Fate, a powerful but not quite personified force. It is related to the verb *weorthan*, meaning roughly "to occur." Its meanings range from a neutral "event" to a prescribed "destiny" to a personified "Fate"; it is useful to think of *wyrd* as "what happens," usually in a negative sense. In a poem so preoccupied with puzzling over the nature and meaning of *wyrd*, it seemed appropriate to leave the word untranslated.

3   *Always the one ... kinsmen's downfall*   Old English manuscripts do not use quotation marks, and there are no clear indications of where one speech begins and ends in this poem; we are not sure whether lines 1-5 are spoken by the same character that speaks the following lines, or whether they are the narrator's opinion on the general situation of the Wanderer.

sought, hall-sick, a treasure-giver,   25
wherever I might find, far or near,
someone in a meadhall who might know my people,
or who would want to comfort me, friendless,
accustom me to joy. He who has come to know
how cruel a companion is sorrow   30
for one with few dear friends, will understand:
the path of exile claims him, not patterned gold,
a winter-bound spirit, not the wealth of earth.
He remembers hall-holders and treasure-taking,
how in his youth his gold-giving lord   35
accustomed him to the feast—that joy has all faded.

    And so he who has long been forced to forego
his lord's beloved words of counsel will understand:
when sorrow and sleep both together
often bind up the wretched exile,   40
it seems in his mind that he clasps and kisses
his lord of men, and on his knee lays
hands and head, as he sometimes long ago
in earlier days enjoyed the gift-throne.[1]
But when the friendless man awakens again   45
and sees before him the fallow waves,
seabirds bathing, spreading their feathers,
frost falling and snow, mingled with hail,
then the heart's wounds are that much heavier,
longing for his loved one. Sorrow is renewed   50
when the memory of kinsmen flies through the mind;[2]
he greets them with great joy, greedily surveys
hall-companions—they always swim away;
the floating spirits bring too few
familiar voices. Cares are renewed   55

---

1   *lays hands and head ... enjoyed the gift-throne*   The description seems to be some sort of
     ceremony of loyalty, charged with intense regret and longing.
2   *the memory of kinsmen flies through the mind*   Old English *þonne maga gemynd mod geond-*
     hweorfeð could also mean "when the mind surveys the memory of kinsmen."

for one who must send, over and over,
a weary heart across the binding waves.[1]

And so I cannot imagine for all this world
why my spirit should not grow dark
when I think through all this life of men,   60
how suddenly they gave up the hall-floor,
mighty young retainers. Thus this middle-earth
droops and decays every single day;
and so a man cannot become wise, before he has weathered
his share of winters in this world. A wise man must be patient,   65
neither too hot-hearted nor too hasty with words,
nor too weak in war nor too unwise in thoughts,
neither fretting nor fawning nor greedy for wealth,
never eager for boasting before he truly understands;
a man must wait, when he makes a boast,   70
until the brave spirit understands truly
where the thoughts of his heart will turn.

The wise man must realize how ghastly it will be
when all the wealth of this world stands waste,
as now here and there throughout this middle-earth   75
walls stand blasted by wind,
beaten by frost, the buildings crumbling.
The wine halls topple, their rulers lie
deprived of all joys; the proud old troops
all fell by the wall. War carried off some,   80
sent them on the way, one a bird carried off
over the high seas, one the gray wolf
shared with death—and one a sad-faced man
covered in an earthen grave. The Creator
of men thus destroyed this walled city,   85
until the old works of giants[2] stood empty,
without the sounds of their former citizens.

---

1   *greets them with great joy ... the binding waves*   The grammar and reference of this intense,
    almost hallucinatory scene is not entirely clear; the translation reflects one commonly-
    proposed reading.
2   *old work of giants*   Ruined buildings are called "the work of giants" (*enta geweorc*) in several
    places in Old English literature.

He who deeply considers, with wise thoughts,
this foundation and this dark life,
old in spirit, often remembers   90
so many ancient slaughters, and says these words:
'Where has the horse gone? where is the rider? where is the
      giver of gold?
Where are the seats of the feast? where are the joys of the hall?
O the bright cup! O the brave warrior!
O the glory of princes! How the time passed away,   95
slipped into nightfall as if it had never been!
There still stands in the path of the dear warriors
a wall wondrously high, with serpentine stains.
A storm of spears took away the warriors,
bloodthirsty weapons, *wyrd* the mighty,   100
and storms batter these stone walls,
frost falling binds up the earth,
the howl of winter, when blackness comes,
night's shadow looms, sends down from the north
harsh hailstones in hatred of men.   105
All is toilsome in the earthly kingdom,
the working of *wyrd* changes the world under heaven.
Here wealth is fleeting, here friends are fleeting,
here man is fleeting, here woman is fleeting,
all the framework of this earth will stand empty.'"   110

So said the wise one in his mind,[1] sitting apart in meditation.
He is good who keeps his word,[2] and the man who never too
      quickly
shows the anger in his breast, unless he already knows the remedy
a noble man can bravely bring about. It will be well for one who
      seeks mercy,
consolation from the Father in heaven, where for us all stability
      stands.   115

---

1   *the wise one in his mind*   Old English *snottor on mode* could also mean "the one who was
    wise in mind."
2   *keeps his word*   Or "keeps faith." These last lines offer an answer to the Wanderer's unre-
    solved melancholy—the wisdom of self-control and the hope of Christian salvation.

The Seafarer

I can sing a true song of myself,
tell of my journeys, how in days of toil
I've often suffered troubled times,
endured hard heartache, come to know
many of care's dwellings on the keel of a ship,   5
terrible tossing of the waves, where the anxious
night-watch often held me at the ship's stem
when it crashes against the cliffs. Pinched with cold
were my feet, bound by frost
in cold fetters, while cares seethed   10
hot around my heart, and hunger gnawed
my sea-weary mind. That man does not know,
he whose lot is fairest on land,
how I dwelt all winter, wretched with care,
on the ice-cold sea in the paths of exile,   15
deprived of dear kinsmen,[1]
hung with icicles of frost while hail flew in showers.
I heard nothing there but the noise of the sea,
the ice-cold waves; the wild swan's song
sometimes served for music, the gannet's call   20
and the curlew's cry for the laughter of men,
the seagull's singing for mead-drink.
Storms beat the stone cliffs; the tern answered,
icy-feathered, the eagle screamed,
dewy-feathered—no sheltering family   25
could bring consolation to my desolate soul.

---

1   *deprived of dear kinsmen*   A half-line may be missing here. There is no break in the manu-
script or in the sense of the poem, but the line has only two stresses instead of the expected
four.

And so[1] he who has tasted life's joy in towns,
suffered few sad journeys, scarcely believes,
proud and puffed up with wine, what I, weary,
have often had to endure in my seafaring.   30
The night-shadow darkened; snow came from the north,
frost bound the ground, hail fell on earth,
coldest of grains. And so[2] they compel me now,
my heart-thoughts, to try for myself
the high seas, the tossing salt streams;[3]   35
my heart's desire urges my spirit
time and again to travel, so that I might seek
a foreign land somewhere far from here.

And so no man on earth is so proud in spirit,
nor so gifted in grace nor so keen in youth,   40
nor so bold in deeds, nor so beloved of his lord,
that he never has sorrow over his seafaring,
when he sees what the Lord might have in store for him.
He has no thought of the harp or the taking of rings,
nor the pleasures of woman nor joy in the world,   45
nor anything else but the tumbling waves—
he who hastens to sea always has longing.
The groves take blossom, the cities grow fair,
the fields brighten, the world rushes on;
all these urge the eager-hearted   50
spirit to travel, when one intends

---

1 *And so* The repeated connecting word *forþon* is notoriously difficult in this poem—it
  points forwards and/or backwards, meaning either "therefore" or "thus" or "because." In a
  poem whose logical progression is by no means clear or easy to follow this is a significant
  source of ambiguity. I have chosen to render it with the vague "and so," hoping to preserve
  some of the loose connection and interpretive difficulty found in the original.

2 *And so* The disjunction between what has come before and what comes after this line is so
  great that it has been proposed that a second speaker is introduced here (there are no quota-
  tion marks in the manuscript that might clarify this ambiguity). Though this "two-speaker"
  theory is no longer widely accepted, it reflects the difficulty many critics have reconciling
  the conflicting attitudes presented in the poem—sea voyage as terrible suffering, sea voyage
  as longed-for escape (as in the opening of Melville's *Moby-Dick*), sea-voyage as metaphor for
  spiritual pilgrimage, or even for life itself.

3 *they compel me ... salt streams* Or "and yet my heart-thoughts are pressing me, now that I
  myself might explore the high seas and tossing salt waves."

to journey far over the flood-ways.
Even the cuckoo urges with its sad voice,
summer's guardian announces sorrow
bitter in the breast-hoard. He does not know,   55
the man blessed with ease, what those endure
who walk most widely in the paths of exile.

    And so now my thought flies out from my breast,
my spirit moves with the sea-flood,
roams widely over the whale's home,   60
to the corners of the earth, and comes back to me
greedy and hungry; the lone flier cries out,
incites my heart irresistibly to the whale's path
over the open sea—because hotter to me
are the joys of the Lord than this dead life,   65
loaned, on land.[1] I will never believe
that earthly goods will endure forever.
Always, for everyone, one of three things
hangs in the balance before its due time:
illness or age or attack by the sword   70
wrests life away from one doomed to die.
And so for every man the praise of posterity,
those coming after, is the best eulogy—
that before he must be on his way, he act
bravely on earth against the enemies' malice,   75
do bold deeds to beat the devil,
so the sons of men will salute him afterwards,
and his praise thereafter live with the angels
forever and ever, in the joy of eternal life,
delight among heaven's host.

                The days are lost,   80
and all the pomp of this earthly kingdom;

---

1   *this dead life, loaned, on land* At this point the sea-voyage is revealed to be a journey of
spiritual discovery, as in the Hiberno-Latin *Voyage of St Brendan*. The hermit-monks of
Ireland had a particular penchant for taking to small boats and trusting in God for their
safety. Some reached Iceland; some are rumored to have reached the Americas; many others,
no doubt, found rest at the bottom of the sea.

there are now neither kings nor emperors
nor gold-givers as there once were,
when they did the greatest glorious deeds
and lived in most lordly fame.   85
All this noble host is fallen, their happiness lost,
the weaker ones remain and rule the world,
laboring and toiling. Joy is laid low,
the earth's nobility grows old and withers,
like every man throughout middle-earth.   90
Old age overtakes him, his face grows pale,
the graybeard grieves; he knows his old friends,
offspring of princes, have been given up to the earth.
When his life fails him, his fleshly cloak will neither
taste the sweet nor touch the sore,   95
nor move a hand nor think with his mind.
Though a brother may wish to strew his brother's
grave with gold, bury him among the dead
with heaps of treasure to take with him,
that gold will be useless before the terror of God   100
for any soul that is full of sin,
the gold he had hidden while here on earth.

    Great is the terror of God, before which the earth trembles;
He established the sturdy foundations,
the earth's solid surface and the high heavens.   105
Foolish is he who dreads not the Lord; death will find him
        unprepared.
Blessed is he who lives humbly; mercy from heaven comes to him,
the Maker strengthens his spirit, for he believes in His might.
A man must steer a strong mind and keep it stable,
steadfast in its promises, pure in its ways;   110
every man must hold in moderation
his love for a friend and his hatred for a foe,
though he may wish him full of fire ...[1]
                    ... or his friend consumed

---

1 *full of fire* Something is missing here, though there is no gap in the manuscript; the trans-
    lation is conjectural and makes as little sense as the original.

on a funeral pyre. Fate is greater,
the Maker mightier than any man's thoughts.

Let us consider[1] where we should have our home,
and then think how we might come there,
and let us also strive to reach that place
of eternal peace, unending blessedness,
where life is found in the love of the Lord,
hope in heaven. Thanks be to the holy one
that he has so honored us, ruler of glory,
eternal Lord, throughout all time. Amen.

---

1   *Let us consider*   The tone of these last lines, different in many respects from the rest of the
poem, seems to place the poem finally in a homiletic setting—the exhortation of a preacher
rather than the confession of a weathered Ancient Mariner.

Deor

Wayland learned suffering from snares[1]—
that strong-minded earl endured misery,
with care and sorrow as companions,
and ice-cold exile; he found ample woe
after Nithhad laid hard restraints on him,   5
supple sinew-bonds on the better man.[2]
    That passed away; so can this.[3]

To Beadohild, her brother's death was not
so sore in her heart as her own situation,
once she came clearly to see   10
that she carried a child; she could never
think through how that might turn out.[4]
    That passed away; so can this.

We have heard many things of Mæthhild—
her desire for Geat was so deep, boundless,   15
that her sorrowful love stole all sleep.[5]
    That passed away; so can this.

---

1 *from snares* Old English *be wurman* means either "by sorrow" or "by worms"—the latter does not make much sense, though many critics have tried; the emendation *be wearnum* "by hindrances" is translated here.

2 *on the better man* Wayland (Old English *Weland*, ON *Volundr*) was the famous smith of Northern legend; his story is told in the Old Norse *Volundarkviða* in the *Poetic Edda* and, in a somewhat different form, in the twelfth- or thirteenth-century Norse *Thidrekssaga*. King Nithhad (ON *Niðuðr*) is so greedy for Wayland's work that he cuts the smith's hamstrings to prevent his escape. In revenge (as we read in the next stanza) Wayland kills the king's sons—he fashions bowls out of their skulls, gems from their eyeballs, and brooches from their teeth, and presents these to the king; he then rapes and impregnates the king's daughter Beadohild and escapes by means of a flying coat made of feathers.

3 *That passed away; so can this* The Old English line *þæs ofereode; þisses swa mæg* is almost passive: "it passed away with respect to that; so may it with respect to this."

4 *how that might turn out* In the world of legend, at least, it turned out better than you might expect; Beadohild and Wayland were reconciled, and their child Widia (Old English *Wudga*, ON *Viðga*) became famous as one of Dietrich von Berne's warriors (see the note to line 19, below) in the Norse *Thidrekssaga*.

5 *stole all sleep* In fact nothing is known of Mæthhild, or the story to which this stanza alludes, and the translation is conjectural.

For thirty winters Theodoric held
the Mæring's stronghold; many knew that.[1]
   That passed away; so can this.   20

We have heard of Eormanaric's
wolfish wit; he ruled far and wide
in the Gothic kingdom—a grim king.
Many a warrior sat wrapped in sorrow,
expecting woe, often wished   25
that his kingdom would be overcome.[2]
   That passed away; so can this.

If a man sits sorrowing, bereft of joy,
his spirit darkens, and it seems to him
that his share of troubles is endless.   30
He may then think that throughout this world
the Lord in his wisdom often works changes,
to many a man He shows mercy
and certain fame, and to some a share of woe.

Concerning myself I will say this: 35
that once I was the Heodenings' *scop*,[3]
dear to my lord, and Deor was my name.[4]

---

1 *many knew that* Theodoric (ON *Thidrek*), king of the Ostrogoths who ruled from 493-526, became the legendary Dietrich of Berne; he is said to have lived in exile at the court of Attila the Hun for thirty years. The identity of "the Mæring's stronghold" (Old English *Mæringa burg*) is unknown, and it is not clear whether we are supposed to sympathize with Theodoric or the city he ruled/oppressed.

2 *would be overcome* Eormanaric, king of the Goths (died around 375), is, in legend, the uncle of Theodoric, and the one who drove him out of Berne and into exile. He had a widespread reputation for outrageous cruelty.

3 *scop* Singer/poet.

4 *Deor was my name* A *scop* is a singer/poet. The character Deor (the name means either "beloved" or "wild beast") is otherwise unknown. The *Heodenings* would be a tribe founded by Heoden. The Norse *Skáldskaparmál* (*Prose Edda* ch. 49) tells how king Hedin (ON *Heðinn*) of the Hjaðnings (equivalent to the Old English *Heodenings*) kidnaps Hild, daughter of Högni. The Middle High German heroic epic *Kudrun* tells a somewhat different version of this tale, in which King Hettel (MHG *Hetele*) plans to steal the beautiful Hild from her father Hagen. Among his helpers in this adventure is a minstrel named Horant (equivalent to the Old English *Heorrenda*). Somewhere behind or among these tales may lie the story implied here.

Many winters I held this high-ranking post,
with a noble lord, until now Heorrenda,
a man skilled in song, has snatched the estate   40
that the protector of warriors had once given to me.
    That passed away; so can this.

Wulf and Eadwacer

It's as if someone should give a gift[1] to my people—
they will kill him[2] if he comes to the troop.
It is otherwise for us.

Wulf is on an island, I on another.
Fast is that island, surrounded by fen.   5
The men on the island are murderous and cruel;
they will kill him if he comes to the troop.
It is otherwise for us.

I felt far-wandering hopes[3] for my Wulf,
as I sat weeping in the rainy weather,   10
when the bold warrior's arms embraced me—
it was sweet to me, yet I also despised it.

Wulf, my Wulf! My wanting you
has made me sick—your seldom coming,
my mourning heart, not lack of meat.   15

Do you hear, Eadwacer?[4] A wolf bears away
our wretched cub to the woods.
One can easily split what was never united,
the song of the two of us.

---

1   *a gift*   The Old English word *lac* "gift" can also mean "battle."
2   *kill him*   The Old English word *apecgan*, translated "kill," can also mean "receive, accept" or "devour, destroy."
3   *felt far-wandering hopes*   The word translated here as "felt" is Old English *dogode*. It is found nowhere else in Old English and is probably a scribal mistake (I have assumed the correct form is *hogode*, "thought" or "intended") but the similarity with the Old English *docga* "dog" (itself found very rarely in written Old English, but presumably used in popular speech as an informal synonym of the more commonly-attested *hund* "hound") has led some readers, almost irresistibly, to imagine a hypothetical verb *dogian* "to follow like a dog," which would certainly be appropriate in a poem about a man named "wolf."
4   *Eadwacer*   The name—if it is in fact a proper name—means roughly "guardian of property." It seems an appropriate name for a jealous husband.

The Wife's Lament

I make this song of myself, deeply sorrowing,
my own life's journey. I am able to tell
all the hardships I've suffered since I grew up,
but new or old, never worse than now—
ever I suffer the torment of my exile.   5

   First my lord left his people
over the tumbling waves; I worried at dawn
where on earth my leader of men might be.
When I set out myself in my sorrow,
a friendless exile, to find his retainers,   10
that man's kinsmen began to think
in secret that they would separate us,
so we would live far apart in the world,
most miserably, and longing seized me.

   My lord commanded me to live here;[1]   15
I had few loved ones or loyal friends
in this country, which causes me grief.
Then I found that my most fitting man
was unfortunate, filled with grief,
concealing his mind, plotting murder   20
with a smiling face. So often we swore
that only death could ever divide us,
nothing else—all that is changed now;
it is now as if it had never been,
our friendship. Far and near, I must   25
endure the hatred of my dearest one.

   They forced me to live in a forest grove,
under an oak tree in an earthen cave.[2]

---

1 *to live here* Or, "to take up a dwelling in a grove" or "to live in a (pagan) shrine." The precise meaning of the line, like the general meaning of the poem, is a matter of dispute and conjecture.

2 *in an earthen cave* Or even "in an earthen grave or barrow."

This earth-hall is old, and I ache with longing;
the dales are dark, the hills too high,   30
harsh hedges overhung with briars,
a home without joy. Here my lord's leaving
often fiercely seized me. There are friends on earth,
lovers living who lie in their beds,
while I walk alone in the first light of dawn   35
under the oak tree and through this earth-cave,
where I must sit the summer-long day;
there I can weep for all my exiles,
my many troubles; and so I can never
escape from the cares of my sorrowful mind,   40
nor all the longings that seize me in this life.

    May the young man always be sad-minded[1]
with hard heart-thoughts, yet let him have
a smiling face along with his heartache,
a crowd of constant sorrows. Let to himself   45
all his worldly joys belong! Let him be outlawed
in a far distant land, so that my friend sits
under stone cliffs chilled by storms,
weary-minded, surrounded by water
in a sad dreary hall! My beloved will suffer   50
the cares of a sorrowful mind; he will remember
too often a happier home. Woe to the one
who must wait with longing for a loved one.

---

1   *May the young man always be sad-minded*   These difficult lines have been read as a particular reflection, imagining the mental state of her distant beloved, or as a general reflection on the double-faced nature of the world; here, following the reading of some critics, they are taken as a kind of curse, wishing upon the beloved all the suffering and sorrow felt by the speaker.

The Ruin

Wondrous is this wall's foundation—*wyrd*[1] has broken
and shattered this city; the work of giants crumbles.
The roofs are ruined, the towers toppled,
frost in the mortar has broken the gate,
torn and worn and shorn by the storm,   5
eaten through with age. The earth's grasp
holds the builders, rotten, forgotten,
the hard grip of the ground, until a hundred
generations of men are gone.

                        This wall, rust-stained
and covered with moss, has seen one kingdom after another,   10
stood in the storm, steep and tall, then tumbled.
The foundation remains, felled by the weather,
it fell.....[2]
grimly ground up....
     ......cleverly created....   15
...... a crust of mud surrounded ...
..... put together a swift
and subtle system of rings; one of great wisdom
wondrously bound the braces together with wires.

    Bright were the buildings, with many bath-houses,   20
high noble gables and a great noise of armies,
many a meadhall filled with men's joys,
until mighty *wyrd* made an end to all that.
The slain fell on all sides, plague-days came,
and death destroyed all the brave swordsmen;   25
the seats of their idols became empty wasteland,
the city crumbled, its re-builders collapsed
beside their shrines. So now these courts are empty,

---

1   *wyrd* On this Old English word, see the note to line 5 of *The Wanderer*.
2   *it fell* Several lines are lost here; the translation tries to make sense of a few surviving
words.

and the rich vaults of the vermilion roofs
shed their tiles. The ruins toppled to the ground, 30
broken into rubble, where once many a man
glad-minded, gold-bright, bedecked in splendor,
proud, full of wine, shone in his war-gear,
gazed on treasure, on silver, on sparkling gems,
on wealth, on possessions, on the precious stone,[1] 35
on this bright capital of a broad kingdom.

    Stone buildings stood, the wide-flowing stream
threw off its heat; a wall held it all
in its bright bosom where the baths were,[2]
hot in its core, a great convenience. 40
They let them gush forth.....
the hot streams over the great stones,
under ...
    until the circular pool.... hot ...
      .....where the baths were. 45
Then....
    ..... that is a noble thing,
how.... the city....[3]

---

1   *the precious stone*   The singular form *eorcanstan* here is unexpected; it may be nothing more
than a collective noun, meaning something like "the mass of precious stones."

2   *where the baths were*   This description has led many readers to assume the poem is describing the actual ruins of the Roman temple complex at Aqua Sulis in the modern city of Bath.

3   *the city*   The poem, appropriately, trails off into incoherent decay.

2. Wisdom—The Order of Wonder

The Cotton Maxims (Maxims II)

This collection of proverbs is found in an eleventh-century manuscript now in the British Library (London, BL Cotton Tiberius B.i). It is copied there between a poetic list of liturgical feasts called the *Menologium* and a version of the *Anglo-Saxon Chronicle*; the arrangement creates a progression from the cycle of the Christian year, to the eternal truths of nature and society, to the flow of historical events.

The loosely-linked collection of gnomic observations is a poetic genre as old as Hesiod's *Works and Days* and the biblical book of Proverbs. Modern culture tends to look down on proverbs and clichés; in Shakespeare's *Hamlet*, Polonius's sententious advice to Laertes such as "neither a borrower nor a lender be" (*Hamlet* 1.3.75) is one sign of his age and foolishness. But such "wisdom-literature" was well respected in the ancient and medieval world, and survived well into the modern age in such works as Benjamin Franklin's *Poor Richard's Almanack*. Maxims point to universal facts of life ("fish gotta swim, birds gotta fly," as a later poet would write) or norms of behavior (e.g., the fish "shall be" in the water spawning, and the king in his hall giving out rings, lines 25-27—the implication being that a king in his hall is as natural as a fish in water, and ring-giving generates life as abundantly as a fish spawns fry). In Old English literature, proverbial statements are often recognized by their use of the word *sceal* "shall" or "must," which in this context implies a general tendency (here it is usually translated as "must" or "belongs," or with the simple present tense, as in the first line).

Though *The Cotton Maxims* may seem like, and in places may actually be, a disorganized jumble of random observations, some common threads can be perceived, and if the reader lets go of the demand for paragraph-style unity he or she can appreciate the concatenation of associations, similitudes, and contrasts that make up the poems' structure. Reading in this spirit, one can also notice a number of recurring themes that would be perfectly at home in a more widely-appreciated literary work like *The Wanderer*: delight in the manifold and various harmonies in the diversity of the world, acknowledgment of God's power and mystery in establishing and ordaining the world, and recognition of the need for wisdom to balance the destructive forces of human desire.

SOURCE

London, BL Cotton Tiberius B.i, fols. 115rv

EDITION

E.V.K. Dobbie, *Anglo-Saxon Minor Poems*. Anglo-Saxon Poetic Records VI. New York: Columbia University Press, 1942.

FURTHER READING

Deskis, Susan E. "Exploring Text and Discourse in the Old English Gnomic Poems: The Problem of Narrative." *JEGP* 104 (2005): 326-44.

Hansen, Elaine Tuttle. *The Solomon Complex: Reading Wisdom in Old English Poetry*. McMaster Old English Studies and Texts 5. Toronto: University of Toronto Press, 1988.

Hill, Thomas D. "Wise Words: Old English Sapiential Poetry." *Readings in Medieval Texts: Interpreting Old and Middle English Literature*. Ed. David F. Johnson and Elaine Treharne. Oxford: Oxford University Press, 2005. 166-82.

Larrington, Carolyne. *A Store of Common Sense: Gnomic Theme and Style in Old Icelandic and Old English Wisdom Poetry*. Oxford: Clarendon Press; New York: Oxford University Press, 1993.

A king controls his realm. Cities are clear from afar,
ancient ingenious giant-works on the earth,
wondrous work, stone foundations. In the sky wind is swiftest,
thunder loudest in its time. Great are the glories of Christ,
wyrd is most powerful. Winter is coldest,   5
Lent most frosty, and longest cold,
summer most sun-lovely, its sunshine hottest,
autumn most bountiful—it brings to men
the fruits of the seasons, sent from God.
Truth is trickiest, golden treasure most costly   10

to every man; old folks are wisest,
having known many years and endured much—
woe is wondrously clinging,[1] but the clouds glide past.
Good comrades encourage a young nobleman
in battle and in bestowing rings.   15
In the nobleman, courage; the blade endures combat
against the helmet. The hawk belongs on the glove,
though wild; the wolf belongs in his den,
a wretched loner; in the woods the boar,
strong with great tusks; a good man belongs at home,   20
striving for fame. The spear belongs in the hand,
adorned with gold, and gems in a ring,
standing broad and high. Streams in the waves
shall mingle with the flood; the mast stands on a ship,
the sailyard hanging heavy. The sword belongs in the lap,   25
a lordly iron; the dragon belongs in his barrow,
old, proud of his finery; the fish in the water,
spawning his own kind, the king in his hall,
handing out rings. The bear belongs on the heath,
old and frightening; down from the hills flows   30
a river, sea-grey. An army must stand together,
a troop firm in glory; trust must be in a nobleman,
wisdom in a man. The woods on the earth
must blossom with leaves, a barrow must stand
green on the ground, and God in his heaven,   35
judging our deeds. The door in the hall
is a broad building-mouth; the boss on the shield
a firm finger-protector. The bird belongs above,
sailing on the wind, the salmon in the water,
gliding with the trout. Tempests from the heavens   40
come into this world, churned by the wind.
A thief goes out in murky weather; a monster dwells in the fens
alone in the land; a young lady must visit her lover
with secret cunning, if she does not want people to think

---

1   *woe is wondrously clinging*   The manuscript reads *weax* "wax" rather than *wea* "woe," but
    the emendation is irresistible.

she can be bought with rings.[1] The waves surge salty,   45
misty clouds and ocean flood flow around every land,
and mountain streams; cattle must breed
and multiply on the earth; the star must shine
bright in the heavens, just as the Maker commanded.
Good against evil, youth against old age,   50
life against death, light against darkness,
army against army, enemies against each other,
foe against foe—all must fight to gain ground,
accuse the other of sin. A wise man must always consider
the contentiousness of the world—the criminal hangs,   55
rightly pays for the crime he has committed
against mankind. The Maker alone knows
where his soul must travel afterwards;
and all those spirits who travel to God
after their death-day await judgment   60
in the Father's embrace. The shape of the future
is hidden and secret; the Lord alone knows,
the redeeming Father. No one returns
here under the firmament who will truly
say to men what sort of thing God's creation is,   65
the thrones of the triumphant, where He himself dwells.

---

1   *she can be bought with rings*   I.e., if she does not want it to be rumored that she is a pros-
    titute. This reading, offered by Joseph A. Dane, "*On folce gepeon*: Note on the Old English
    Maxims II Lines 43-5," *Neuphilologische Mitteilungen* 85 (1984), 61-64, is only one possible
    interpretation of a difficult passage which apparently alludes to social norms we no longer
    understand. The idea of "buying with rings" may refer to the custom of giving a "bride-
    price" as part of a marriage; the woman's "secret cunning" (*dyrne cræft*) may be an allusion to
    the alleged affinity of women for magical charms and spells. The implication may be that a
    woman must seek out her own lover by magical means if she wants to have any control over
    her marriage plans at all. Another possible translation is "a lady, a woman, must find a lover
    by secret means so that she may be married, if she does not have a good reputation among
    her people." See Audrey L. Meaney, "The *ides* of the Cotton Gnomes," *Medium Ævum* 48
    (1979), 23-39. These are just two of several plausible readings.

The Gifts of Men

The Gifts of Men celebrates the diversity of talents and abilities that make up the human community, and praises the moderation of the Creator in distributing such gifts with a fairly even hand. The poem is similar to a passage in the Exeter Book *Christ II* and to *The Fortunes of Men*, also in the Exeter Book. The list of accomplishments may seem a bit haphazard and even repetitive to a modern reader, and it seems compiled without any clear order. But this apparent lack of hierarchy or organization may be the point—to celebrate diversity one must embrace diversity, not try to organize it under a single principle or in some kind of order, whether it be order of importance or alphabetical order.

The author emphasizes the wisdom of God—so much so that the poem's recent editor suggests that we change the title to *God's Gifts to Humankind*—but he need not have been a priest or monk to express such an opinion. It is not a homiletic poem, though like many Old English poems its language does tend that way in its conclusion; nor is it a philosophical reflection, though there is some room for that as well. The source of the poem has been sought in the Biblical Parable of the Talents (Matthew 25.14-30; Luke 18.11-27), and in patristic writings such as the homilies of Gregory the Great or his *Pastoral Care*; various cross-cultural analogues for its catalogue-like style have been proposed. But it may be that the diversity of human talents—and the desire to list them—is a universal feature of the poetry of wisdom, and the various rhetorical structures used to develop this theme in the poem, especially anaphora (repetition of grammatical structures) and antithesis (contrast) are, given the subject matter, practically inevitable.

All the accomplishments listed are, in one way or another, admirable qualities, and are the attributes of kings and heroes in various Norse poems and sagas. It encompasses nearly all aspects of the aristocratic life—skill in hunting, fighting, poetry; wisdom, strength, agility—but also the Christian virtues of piety, devotion, and patience. Heroic skills like military prowess or political leadership stand alongside more ordinary, though not more common, skills like carpentry, music, and acrobatics. These are not, in other words, simply different ways of earning a living, or physical characteristics like beauty or strength, but the diverse skills and interests that make up a community.

SOURCE

Exeter, Cathedral Library, Dean and Chapter MS 3501, fols. 78r-80r.

EDITION

Bernard J. Muir, Jr., *The Exeter Anthology of Old English Poetry*, 2nd ed., 2 vols. Exeter: University of Exeter Press, 2000.

FURTHER READING

Howe, Nicholas. *The Old English Catalogue Poems.* Anglistica 23. Copenhagen: Rosenkilde and Bagger, 1984.

Russom, Geoffrey R. "A Germanic Concept of Nobility in *The Gifts of Men* and *Beowulf.*" *Speculum* 53 (1978): 1-15.

Many are the fresh gifts of men on earth,
easily seen by anyone with spirit—
men carry them in their minds as the mighty Creator,
the God of Hosts, sees fit to grant them,
gives out His special gifts far and wide,   5
dispenses prosperity so that each person
among the people receives a portion.
No one in the world is so woebegone,
no man so meager in achievement,
so small-minded or slow-witted   10
that the Giver of gifts would completely deny him
some skills of the mind or strength of deeds,
wisdom or wit or a way with words,
lest he should despair in whatever works
he might bring about in this worldly life,   15
or in every gift. God never decrees
that anyone should ever become so wretched.
Likewise, no one ever in this life
gains so much glory among the nations
through his own cleverness that mankind's Guardian   20
would send to him here through His holy gift
wise thoughts and worldly skills—
place everything under one person's power—

lest the strong-minded man, full of splendid gifts,
might turn from moderation and grow proud,   25
and then despise those more poorly endowed;
but He, in His power of discernment, bestows
variously throughout this middle-earth
human skills and abilities to land-dwellers.

    To some here on earth He lends possessions,   30
wealth in the world. One is unfortunate,
a hapless hero, and yet he is wise
in the mind's skills; one receives greater
physical strength; one is fair in figure,
nobly handsome; one is a poet,   35
richly gifted in songs. One is ready of speech;
one is enriched with success in the chase
and hunting of beasts; one is beloved
by a wealthy man; one is war-hardened,
skilled in battle when shields crash together.   40
One can deliberate on public law
in the assembly of scholars in council,
when groups of wise men gather together.
One can devise a clever construction,
any high-timbered thing; his hand is trained—   45
wise and controlled, as befits a craftsman—
to build a hall; he knows how to brace the broad
building securely against sudden collapse.
One can take up the harp in his hands,
and guide the quick sounds of the glee-wood.   50
One is a swift runner,[1] one a sure shot;
one skilled in singing, one in sprinting,
fleet-footed; one steers over the fallow waves
the ship's stern, knows the sea-roads well,
captains his crew across the open ocean   55
when sea-brave sailors with stalwart might
pull their oars against the outer planks.

---

1 *a swift runner* The Old English word *rynig* "swift runner" may in fact mean "skilled in
counsel" or "good at advising."

One is a swimmer, one is very skillful
with gold and gems, when a guardian of men
commands him to craft a jewel for his own glory.   60
One is a skillful smith, knowing how to shape
powerful weapons, potent in war,
when he makes for the use of men in battle
a helmet or hip-sword or coat of mail,
a shining blade or the boss of a shield,   65
fixed firmly against the flight of a spear.
One is firm in faith and open in almsgiving,
pious and moral; one is appointed to serve
in the mead-hall; one is a master of horses,
skilled handler of steeds; one with self-control   70
can patiently meet whatever he must endure.
One knows the law, where lordly men gather
to deliberate judgment. One loves the dice,
one keeps his wits at wine-drinking,
a good beer-keeper;[1] one is a builder,   75
good at raising a roof; one is a commander,
a bold campaigner; one is a public counselor;
one is a thane whose thoughts grow bolder
at his prince's need; one has patience,
a firm and steadfast spirit; one is a fowler,   80
skilled with hawks; one is handy with horses;
one is graceful, agile in games,
light and limber, whose tricks raise a laugh
among noblemen. Another one is lovable,
attractive to people in his thoughts and words.   85
One here earnestly keeps his spiritual good
foremost in mind, and chooses for himself
the favor of God above all earthly goods;
one is bold-minded in the battle against the devil,
in the struggle against sin he is always ready;   90
one is skillful in churchly services,
loudly he can extol the Lord of life
in hymns of praise, with his pure and bright

---

1   *a good beer-keeper*   The modern idiom might be "holds his beer well."

singing voice; one is versed in books,
a teacher and scholar; one has a talent   95
for writing down deep mysteries in words.

   There is no man now living across the earth
so skillful in mind, so mighty in strength,
that all these gifts are ever granted to one alone,
prepared for one person, lest pride injure him,   100
or his heart grow haughty because of his greatness
if he alone, above all other men,
has beauty and wisdom and success in his works;
but He diversely directs the races of mankind
away from pride, and dispenses his gifts—   105
to some virtue, skill to others,
to some fair appearance, to others battle-prowess,
to one man He gives a merciful heart,
a mind fixed on virtue; another is faithful to God.
In this worthy way the Lord scatters   110
His gifts far and wide. Glory be to Him forever,
and luminous praise; He gives us this life
and makes His merciful mind known to the people.

The Fortunes of Men

The Fortunes of Men is another Exeter Book catalogue poem listing various possible endings, generally unfortunate, for a human life, followed by some of the skills and abilities of various occupations. The deaths it depicts are particularly gruesome, generally involving the total consumption of the body—by wolves, by fire, by birds, by decay. This horror at the fragmentation and desecration of the corpse after death brings the poem into dialogue with a whole tradition of Christian "Soul and Body" poems and with the Christian belief in the resurrection of the body at the Last Judgment.

Poems which are composed of lists are particularly easy to add to or continue as they are recited and retold, copied and circulated in manuscript. In light of this we might expect such a poem to contain both older and newer material, traditional ideas and innovative re-considerations of these ideas. The poem may not reflect a single unified point of view or set of values—notice, for example, how the talents of a "wise scholar" (*bocere ... wisfæste*) is sandwiched between skill at board games and the skills of a goldsmith. This does not mean, however, that it does not have its own kind of coherence and meaning. On an even larger scale, the catalogue of grisly deaths seems to have little to do with the catalogue of talents and skills—physical prowess, musical talent, a way with wild birds, and so on, a catalogue which seems to belong rather to *The Gifts of Men*. Though it might lack the sort of unity expected of a more formal or modern composition, its four parts—introduction, misfortunes, good fortunes, and conclusion—are linked by theme and image and parallel language. It may be that the poem seeks to balance the disorder of death with the order of society, the sorrow of misfortune with the solace of diverse talents, the existential horror of the apparent randomness of disaster with some Christian consolation over the ultimate wisdom of God, who has "directed the destiny" (*gesceapo ferede* 95) of mankind. It is in this sense—the balance between terror at the random violence of death and wonder at the many pleasures of life—that the poem might be considered an example of "wisdom" poetry.

SOURCE

Exeter, Cathedral Library, Dean and Chapter MS 3501, fols. 87r-88v.

EDITION

Bernard J. Muir, Jr., *The Exeter Anthology of Old English Poetry*, 2nd ed., 2 vols. Exeter: University of Exeter Press, 2000.

FURTHER READING

DiNapoli, Robert. "Close to the Edge: *The Fortunes of Men* and the Limits of Wisdom Literature." *Text and Transmission in Medieval Europe*. Ed. Chris Bishop et al. Newcastle upon Tyne: Cambridge Scholars, 2007. 127-47.

Drout, Michael D.C. "Possible Instructional Effects of the Exeter Book 'Wisdom Poems': A Benedictine Reform Context." *Form and Content of Instruction in Anglo-Saxon England in the Light of Contemporary Manuscript Evidence: Papers Presented at the International Conference, Udine, 6–8 April 2006*. Ed. Patrizia Lendinara, Loredana Lazzari, and Maria Amalia D'Aronco. Turnhout: Brepols, 2006. 447-66.

Jurasinski, Stefan. "Caring for the Dead in *The Fortunes of Men*." *Philological Quarterly* 86 (2007): 343-63.

Often by the grace of God it comes to pass
that into the world a man and woman
give birth to a child; they clothe him in colors,
nurture and teach him[1] until the time comes,
with the passing of years, that the young limbs,   5
sturdy members, become strong.
His father and mother carry and feed him,
cherish and guide him—but God alone knows
what the years will hold for him as he grows.

For one unfortunate man it happens   10
that his end comes too quickly in early youth,
a woeful fate. The wolf will devour him,
grey walker of the wasteland; his mother mourns
his tragic journey—but cannot change it.

---

1   *nurture and teach him*   The words *tennaþ ond tætaþ* are not found elsewhere in Old English; they are usually translated "cheer and cherish," and their sense is conjectured from context. My translation assumes instead that the phrase is an error for *temiaþ and tæcaþ*, "discipline and instruct."

Hunger will waste one, storm sweep one away,   15
the spear will spill one, one war will destroy.
One must endure his life without light,
feel about with his hands; one lame in foot,
stricken in his sinews, must groan at his fate,
mourn the Maker's decrees with a troubled mind.   20
One will fall from a high forest tree[1]—
wingless, yet flying—flailing at the air,
sailing through space until there are no more
branches to break his fall; then he lies senseless
among the roots, robbed of his soul,   25
he falls to the ground, his spirit flies away.

One must wander in ways remote,
forced, foot-sore, his provisions in a pack,
to tread a damp trail in dangerous territories
and foreign lands; he has few living   30
who might help him—everyone hates
a friendless man because of his misfortunes.
One must hang on the high gallows,
swing there in death until his soul-hoard,
his bloody corpse, is broken to pieces.   35
There the dark-plumed raven will pluck out
the eyes in his head, and shred his soulless carcass;
his hands cannot hold off that hateful scavenger,
fierce bird of prey; his life has fled,
and senseless, hopeless, pallid and stark,   40
he awaits his fate on that wooden beam,
in a fog of death—his name is damned.
Flames will enfold one on the funeral pyre,
a doomed man devoured by greedy fire;
swiftly and suddenly his life is stripped away   45
by the wild red blaze. The woman weeps
who sees the flames so enfold her child.
The edge of a blade on the mead-bench

---

1 *fall from a high forest tree* Some readers interpret this section as describing a hanging, a
   ritual sacrifice; I have translated it as an accidental death, since a more obvious hanging is
   described elsewhere in the poem.

takes the life of one, an angry ale-drinker,
a wine-drunk brawler too bold with his words. 50
The cup-bearer's hand makes one beer-drinker
a drunken sot; he doesn't know how
to govern his mouth with his mind in due measure,
but he will lose his life most wretchedly,
suffer catastrophe, cut off from joy— 55
suicide, self-killer, men will call him,
and tell tales of the drunkard's intemperance.
One, with God's power, will put an end
to all his hardships while he is still young,
and be blessed with success again in later years 60
living days of delight, indulging in wealth,
treasures and mead-cups in the midst of his family,
as much as any man might hold on to them.

So the Lord Almighty allots to all men
diversely over the face of the earth, 65
appoints, decrees, controls their destinies—
to one wealth, to one a share of woe,
to one gladness in youth, to one glory in war,
successful battles, to one shooting or throwing,
shining fame; to one skill at *tæfl*, 70
cunning at the chessboard.[1] One becomes
a wise scholar. Wonderful talents
are given to one as a gold-smith;
often he tempers and trims with adornments
a mighty king's mail-coat; and he in return 75
receives broad lands, and accepts them happily.
One will amuse men at a gathering, and cheer
those who sit down to beer on their benches,
great merriment for the men who drink there.
One will be found sitting at his lord's feet, 80
harp in hand; he takes hold of his payment,

---

1   *chessboard*   Old English *bleobord*, not otherwise recorded, literally means "colored board."
The game of *tæfl*, which held something like the place of chess in Germanic society, is some-
what similar to the Latin game *latrunculi* and is played on a board divided into an uneven
number of squares by two players with unequal forces.

sharp and shrill he will pluck the strings,
let the plectrum sing loud as it leaps about,
making sweet music, to much delight.
One will tame the proud wild bird,   85
a hawk to his hand, until the fierce bird
becomes gentle; he makes him jesses,
and feeds the feather-proud bird in fetters,
gives the swift flier little scraps of food
until the wild creature becomes humble,   90
obeys his master in looks and behavior,
trained and tamed to the young man's hand.

    So, wonderfully, the Savior of multitudes
shaped and determined the skills of men,
directed the destiny of every one   95
of humankind throughout the earth.
Therefore let each one now say thanks to Him
for that which He in his Mercy ordains for men.

Vainglory

Vainglory is a short poem of moral instruction, a Christian warning against pride and excess, particularly excess of drink and the drunken boasting to which it can lead. It contrasts the better and worse paths, the stronger and weaker person, the "true son of God" (6) and "the devil's child" (47). While this is not exactly groundbreaking theology—it is a commonplace of patristic writing and of the many homilies and spiritual guidebooks derived from them—it does cast an interesting light on the sorts of feasting, drinking, and boasting depicted in a heroic poem like *Beowulf* or remembered so fondly in *The Wanderer*. While scholars have pointed out the ways the poem uses biblical or homiletic thought and structure, it is equally notable that the poem expresses these themes in the same language of heroic fame and feasting, and military attack and defense, found in secular poems. By viewing this heroic world through the lens of Christian morality, *Vainglory* exposes the darker side of this culture of violent self-assertion and sensual gratification. And by depicting the struggle against sin and evil as a *psychomachia* or internal battle, the poet is able to make use of the rich and evocative language of heroic poetry to valorize the Christian life. Perhaps in this way the poem tries to speak to a secular audience in language and images it can understand, depicting the ascetic Christian life of moral struggle on a par with the heroic life of violent activity. The poem is also notable for its diction, containing some dramatic plays on words, along with a relatively large number of rare words and compounds, which suggests a high degree of poetic invention on the part of its author.

SOURCE

Exeter, Cathedral Library, Dean and Chapter MS 3501, fols. 83r-84v.

EDITION

Bernard J. Muir, Jr., *The Exeter Anthology of Old English Poetry*, 2nd ed., 2 vols. Exeter: University of Exeter Press, 2000.

FURTHER READING

McKinnell, John. "A Farewell to the Old English Elegy: The Case
of *Vainglory*." *Parergon* n.s. 9.2 (1991): 67-89.

Regan, Catherine A. "Patristic Psychology in the Old English *Vain-
glory*." *Traditio* 26 (1970): 324-35.

Listen! An old advisor told me long ago,
wise messenger, of many marvels:
he opened his word-hoard, the prophets' wisdom,
the old sayings of the saints, this scholarly man,
so that afterwards I might truly recognize   5
by these sayings the true son of God,
a welcome guest, and the weaker one too
I might discern, cut off by his sins.[1]

    Every man can easily understand this,
who does not let a lecherous mind   10
mar his reason in this fleeting world
or drunkenness drown all his days:
when many men meet in the assembly,
proud warmongers in their cities of wine,[2]
they sit at the feast singing old songs,   15
exchanging words, and try to determine
what field of strife may find its dwelling
among the men in the hall, when wine whets
their thoughts. The clamor rises,
a din in the company; in discord   20
they shriek their words. So the minds of men
are differently divided; men of honor
are not all alike. One in his arrogance
vaunts his glory, within him swells
an immoderate mind—there are too many like this!   25
He is entirely filled with envy,

---

1 *cut off by his sins* The Old English *scyldum bescyrede* can also mean "deprived of his shield,"
i.e., exposed and defenseless.

2 *proud warmongers in their cities of wine* The Old English *wlonce wigsmiþas winburgum in*
can also mean "proud makers of idols in their cities of strife."

the flying darts and schemes of the devil;
he shouts and belches, boasts of himself
much more than does a better man,
thinks that his ways will seem to everyone   30
utterly unblemished. It will turn out otherwise
when he sees the result of that wickedness.
He shifts and he cheats and imagines deceits,
so many snares,[1] shoots his mental darts,
lets them fly in showers. He feels no guilt   35
for the crimes he has committed, hates the better
man with envy, lets the arrows of malice
break the castle wall which his Maker commanded
him to protect, that place of battle.
He sits proud at the feast, foggy with wine,   40
with wily cunning he lets a word
slip out in provocation, leavened with pride,
inflamed with envy, glutted with vainglory,
malice and treachery. Now you can know
if you should meet such a thane   45
living in the dwellings—learn from these
few declarations that this is the devil's child
incarnate, with a corrupt life,
his spirit bound for hell, empty of God,
the King of Glory.

            The prophet sang of this,   50
ready of speech, and spoke this verse:
"He who exalts himself in arrogance,
advances himself in an evil time
in haughty pride, he will be humbled,
brought down after his journey of death   55
to dwell in torments, entangled in serpents."[2]

---

1   *snares*   The Old English word *hinderhoca* suggests a kind of barbed hook like a fishhook.
2   *He who exalts himself ... entangled by serpents*   This is not a direct quotation from any par-
     ticular biblical passage; it is most similar to Isaiah 2.17 *et incurvabitur sublimitas hominum
     et humiliabitur altitudo virorum et elevabitur Dominus solus in die illa* "And the haughtiness
     of man shall be humbled, and the pride of men shall be brought low; and the Lord alone
     will be exalted in that day."

It was long ago in the Kingdom of God
that pride arose among the angels,
a notorious struggle; they raised up strife,
a hard campaign, polluted heaven,   60
betrayed their better when they tried with treason
to steal the kingdom and the King of Glory's
royal throne—as was not right—
and then to occupy just as they pleased
the fair land of glory. The Father of creation   65
stopped them in battle—too bitter was the fight for them.

   It will be unlike that for the other one,
who lives his life humbly here on earth,
and always keeps with all his neighbors
peace in the land, and loves his enemy,   70
though he has often done him offense
willfully in this world. In wonderful joy
he may ascend hence from the earth
to the land of the angels. Not so the other one,
who in his pride and wicked deeds   75
lives in his sins; the reward will not be the same
from the King of Glory. Keep this in mind,
if you meet a modest prince,
a thane in the nation—to him is always
joined as a guest God's own son,   80
delight of the world, if the prophet did not lie.
Therefore always considering the counsel of salvation,
we must remember at every moment
the truest good, the God of victories. Amen.

The Order of the World

The Order of the World—also called The Wonder of Creation—is situated somewhere between homiletic poetry and Germanic wisdom. It is a poem about creation both material and poetic, with God's fashioning of the cosmos parallel to the poet's work of capturing such wonders in words. It is notable among wisdom poems for the strict and explicit logic of its construction; like the God he praises, the poet's control of his work is rigorous and methodical.

Like Cædmon, whom Bede places at the very beginning of the tradition of English Christian poetry, the poet sings of the Creation. The first section (lines 1-37) praises poets and their art, and introduces a *herespel* or "praise-song" based, to some extent, on Psalm 18 (Ps 19), *Caeli ennarant gloriam Dei, Et opera manuum eius annuntiat firmamentum* "The heavens declare the glory of God, and the firmament shows forth the works of His hands." The poem is not so much a translation of the Psalm, however, as a recreation of it in the vernacular poetic style.

SOURCE

Exeter, Cathedral Library, Dean and Chapter MS 3501, fols. 92v-94v.

EDITION

Bernard J. Muir, Jr., *The Exeter Anthology of Old English Poetry*, 2nd ed., 2 vols. Exeter: University of Exeter Press, 2000.

FURTHER READING

DiNapoli, Robert. "The Heart of the Visionary Experience: *The Order of the World* and Its Place in the Old English Canon." *English Studies* 79 (1998): 97-108.

Huppé, Bernard F. *The Web of Words: Structural Analysis of the Old English Poems* Vainglory, The Wonder of Creation, The Dream of the Rood, *and* Judith. Albany: State University of New York Press, 1970.

Wehlau, Ruth. "Rumination and Re-Creation: Poetic Instruction in *The Order of the World.*" *Florilegium* 13 (1994): 65-77.

Eager warrior, will you greet a stranger,
share a word with a wise scholar,
ask this far-flung traveler about fate,
question him about this vast creation,
the subtle forces that stir in living things   5
which every day, through God's decree,
bring miracles and wonders to the race of men?
It is an obvious sign to each and all
of the thoughtful ones wise enough to know
how to hold the whole world in their hearts,   10
for long ago men often made lays,
displayed their skill in the art of song,
resolute warriors who could speak rightly;
always inquiring, always speaking,
they wove a web of deep mysteries,   15
of the whole race of men they knew most of all.
Therefore he who lives bravely and thoughtfully
must inquire after the secrets of creation,
inscribe it in his mind with the word-hoard's skill,
secure it in his spirit and consider it well;   20
nor must it weary a warrior of courage
to wisely complete his worldly ways.

    Learn these lessons! I will gladly speak
to you about the majesty of the Maker,
more than you can comprehend in your mind,   25
no matter how clever. His might is too vast—
it is beyond the ability of any earthly man
to inquire with his mind into God's high works
any further than the Lord allows him
to understand his own commands.   30
But we should thank the splendid prince
forever and ever for that which the eternal King
wishes to grant us in the soul's great beauty,
so that we might more easily ascend
to the celestial kingdom, if we have enough spirit   35
and are willing to keep the decrees of Heaven's King.
Now hear this praise-song and set it in your mind.

Lo! In the beginning the Father almighty,
high guardian of treasure, formed heaven and earth,
the wide depths of the sea and the visible world,   40
all myriad things which, through the Lord's hand,
now exalt and extol his holy abundance.
And likewise he linked them, one to another,
as he well knew how; all must hold
a strict course, at the Helmsman's command,   45
in diverse measures through this vast world.

So they bear forth beauty into the world,
the glory of God and his generous deeds,
shining praise through length of days;
they faithfully perform the Lord's eternal word   50
in their ancient seats where the Lord set them,
bright guardian of Heaven; they hold firmly
their great circuit.[1] His power propels
heaven's candle and the high waves with it,
the Lord of life beckons, and brings   55
all creation into his own vast embrace.
And so forever and ever glory is his,
the gentlest of judges and the most fitting,
who made this life for us, and this bright light
that comes over the misty cliffs each morning   60
traversing the waves adorned with wonders,
and at break of day dawns in the east,
joyous and lovely to the generations of men;
it bears forth its light for every living thing,
brightest of brands, and anyone on earth   65
can enjoy it, if the true King of victories
has seen fit to give sight to his eyes.
Departing with wonder into the western sky,
the most glorious star goes traveling in a troop,
until in the evening it treads the edge   70
of the outer ocean, and summons another gloom;

---

1   *they hold firmly their great circuit*   The Old English might mean "the seas zealously keep
within their boundaries"; the translation here seems to suit the context better.

night comes afterwards, held by the constraint
of the holy Lord. Heaven's bright clear light
hastens, shining, wandering star,
under the bosom of earth by God's decree. 75
There is no man alive with the wisdom to know
its secret origin through his own power,
how the gold-bright sun passes beyond the horizon
into murk and gloom under the mass of waters,
or what earthly beings might enjoy that light 80
once it departs over the edge of the sea.

    And so he knit together—as he well knew how—
day with night, depth with height,
the sky with the sea, the shore with the streams,
land and water, fishes and waves. 85
That work never weakens, he holds it all well;
it stands firm, stoutly girded
with great bonds of might in the majestic power
by which Heaven and earth have been raised.
Those who abide in that place are blessed, 90
a hopeful hearth-troop. That is the greatest of hosts,
innumerable blessed bands of angels.
Always they see their own King,
gaze with their eyes, and have enough of everything.
They lack for nothing, those who see 95
the King of glory above; theirs is joy and bliss,
eternal, unending, consolation to the blessed.

    And so a man should strive to obey the Maker,
every child of men should abandon idle lusts,
life's fleeting fancies, and hurry to true bliss, 100
abandon every hateful enmity, set aside
old sinful deeds, and set out for that better realm.

Exeter Book *Riddles*

The Exeter Book ends with two groups of verse riddles. The manuscript is damaged and it is impossible to know how many riddles were in the original collection, but there may have been 100, following the model of the popular Latin *Enigmata* of Aldhelm and Symphosius. But apart from this speculation, there are few similarities between the Latin and English versions of this popular poetic genre. The *Enigmata* of Aldhelm were apparently used as classroom examples of the principles of Latin versification; it is unlikely (though not impossible) that the English Riddles would have served such a purpose for apprentice English poets. Moreover, very few of the English Riddles depend on the sort of deliberate obscurity common in the *Enigmata*—no. 86 is a rare example, but it is closely modeled on one of the Latin Riddles of Symphosius.

Apart from one Riddle which is found in an earlier version, there is little evidence for the origins and audience of the Riddles, either individually or collectively. Many of the Exeter Book Riddles echo one another's language, especially in the repeated closing line *saga hwæt ic hatte* "say what I am called," but it is unlikely that the whole collection was written by one person. A number of the Riddles seem to come from a bookish milieu, probably monastic (see nos. 26 and 47), and others are somewhat philosophical in tone (no. 43), but the presence of about a dozen riddles whose obscene double meanings seem out of place in a monastic setting (see no. 44 and 45 below) still raises a few eyebrows. Unlike the Latin riddles, which give away their solution in their title, some of the Old English riddles are apparently meant to be genuinely puzzling and difficult to solve—in fact a few (such as no. 95 below) continue to baffle readers to this day.

In many cases, however, the pleasure of the Riddles seems to lie not in obscurity but in observation—they are in essence short lyric poems which show the world at a slightly odd angle, and bring the material and the natural world to new life through metaphor, analogy, wordplay, and misdirection. In the Riddles creatures speak, things express their point of view, everyday objects perform heroic deeds, and innocent household items become obscene projections of human desire. The playful language of the Riddles is a kind of lens through which the wonder, poignancy, and wild energy of the world are brought into focus. Whether they were written for education, inspiration, or amusement, the delight of the Riddles lies in their gift for seeing familiar things with fresh eyes, and compressing these insights in a few short lines which draw the listener into the process of that perception; they help remind us that the poetic landscape of Old English literature was not as gloomy, as pious, or as bloody as is sometimes thought.

SOURCE

Exeter, Cathedral Library, Dean and Chapter MS 3501, fols. 101r–114v; fols. 124v-130v.

EDITION

Bernard J. Muir, Jr., *The Exeter Anthology of Old English Poetry*, 2nd ed., 2 vols. Exeter: University of Exeter Press, 2000.

FURTHER READING

Dailey, Patricia. "Riddles, Wonder and Responsiveness in Anglo-Saxon Literature." *The Cambridge History of Early Medieval English Literature*. Ed. Clare A. Lees. Cambridge: Cambridge University Press, 2013. 451-72.

Niles, John D. *Old English Enigmatic Poems and the Play of the Texts*. Studies in the Early Middle Ages 13. Turnhout: Brepols, 2006.

Orchard, Andy. "Enigma Variations: The Anglo-Saxon Riddle-Tradition." *Latin Learning and English Lore: Studies in Anglo-Saxon Literature for Michael Lapidge*. Ed. Katherine O'Brien O'Keeffe and Andy Orchard. 2 vols. Toronto: University of Toronto Press, 2005. I:284-304.

Tigges, Wim. "Snakes and Ladders: Ambiguity and Coherence in the Exeter Book Riddles and Maxims." *Companion to Old English Poetry*. Ed. Henk Aertsen and Rolf H. Bremmer, Jr. Amsterdam: VU University Press, 1994. 95-118.

Wilcox, Jonathan. "'Tell Me What I Am': The Old English Riddles." *Readings in Medieval Texts: Interpreting Old and Middle English Literature*. Ed. David F. Johnson and Elaine Treharne. Oxford: Oxford University Press, 2005. 46-59.

Williamson, Craig. *A Feast of Creatures: Anglo-Saxon Riddle-Songs*. Philadelphia: University of Pennsylvania Press, 1982 (Rept. 2011).

[NOTE: Solutions to the Riddles are given at the end of the section; though some of these are virtually certain, they all represent scholarly guesses, not definite answers, and careful close reading may yet produce better or more satisfying solutions.]

Riddle 1[1]

What man is so bold in mind and so clever
that he can say who drives me on my way?
When I rise up strong and savage,
with a roar of thunder I wreak havoc,
I go about the earth fiercely, burning halls,   5
ravaging buildings; the reek of smoke rises
grey over the rooftops, clamor and terror
fall among men. When I shake the forest,
I fell the trees bright with ripe fruit;
roofed with water, I am hurled on my way,   10
driven far and wide by mighty forces.
What once protected people on land
I bear on my back, bodies and souls
tossed in the sea. Say what shrouds me,
or what I am called, who carries such cargo?   15

(Riddle 2)

At times I travel under the thronging waves,
where no one sees me, seek the depths
of the ocean floor. The sea is angry,
flecked with foam,[2]
the whale's home roars and howls.   20

---

1   *Riddle 1*   Riddles 1–3 are printed as three separate Riddles in Krapp and Dobbie and in
    Muir, but in the manuscript they are treated as one text in three parts—or perhaps two texts
    (Riddle 1 and Riddles 2/3) in three parts—and are generally regarded as one long riddle by
    modern editors.
2   *flecked with foam*   There is no gap in the manuscript here, but a half-line seems to be miss-
    ing.

Streams beat the shore, hurling waves
of stone and sand and sea and seaweed
onto the steep shingle, when I struggle
beneath the waves, stirring the bottom
of the broad sea-bed. I cannot break free   25
from the sea's protection until He permits it,
my guide in all my journeys. O wise man,
say who draws me from the sea's embrace,
when the streams again grow still
and the waves calm that once covered me.   30

(Riddle 3)

Sometimes my lord constrains me closely,
pushes me down under the deep bosom
of the broad plain, and brings me to bay,
presses my mighty power into a dark hole,
cramped and small, where the earth sits   35
hard on my back.[1] I have no escape
from that terror, even though I could shake
the very pillars of the earth—make palaces
tremble, buildings totter, walls tumble down
crashing on their heads. The air seems calm   40
across the earth, the sea quiet and still,
until I come heaving up out of the ground,
just as He guides me, who in the beginning
first put me in bondage, fastened
fetters and chains; I can never break free   45
from the power that points out my path.

Sometimes I swoop down and stir up
the sea from above, drive to the shore
the flint-grey flood; the foaming waves
batter the wall, black dunes rise   50
from the deep; dark in its tracks

---

1   *where the earth sits hard on my back*   This passage reflects the widespread early belief that
    earthquakes were caused by subterranean winds.

comes another surge, driven by the sea,
until together they rush against the high ridges
along the shoreline, with the groans of ships
and the cries of sailors. The steep stone crags   55
silently await the battering storms,
the crash of arms, when the crushing sea
crowds the cliffs. A boat can expect
bitter struggle, if the sea catches it
in that grim season with all souls on board,   60
until it comes, driven out of control,
ransacked of life, to ride the foam
on the waves' back. I bring terror
to the race of men, when I rampage[1]
on my savage way. Who will stop me?   65

   Sometimes I rush, the dark rain-clouds
riding on my back; I scatter them wide,
sea-soaked, then let them slip
back together again. Great is the roar,
a mighty scream bellowing from the cities,   70
when the clouds crash sharp together,
scraping edge upon edge. Shadowy spirits
hurrying spew sparks of flames
over the earth, clashing clamor
spreads dark over men with a dire din,   75
goes forth fighting, and lets fall
the dim, pounding, drumming deluge
from its belly. The battle rages on,
a great and terrible troop of horsemen,
a mighty fear rises in the hearts of men,   80
panic in the cities, when that sliding demon
shoots his sharp gleaming arrows.
Only a fool does not fear those deadly spears—
and yet he too dies, if the true Creator
lets fly his fiery darts from the whirlwind,   85
straight from above, sends his arrows

---

1   *to the race of men, when I rampage*   This line lacks alliteration in the original and is probably
    corrupt, or else something is missing here.

through the slashing rain. Few survive
who are touched by the tempest's deadly weapon.

    I start that strife and stand at its head,
when I set my course in the crowded clouds,   90
move my mighty strength through the throng
over the breast of the sea. Crowding in battle,
the high storm bursts when I bend down again
close to the ground under the covering of the sky,
and load on my back the burden I must bear   95
commanded by the Creator's almighty power.

    And so, a mighty servant, I struggle—
at times under the earth, at times I dive deep
below the waves, at times above the sea
I stir up the streams, at times I ascend   100
and trouble the clouds, I travel widely,
violent and swift. Say what I am called,
or who raises me when I cannot rest,
or who steadies me when I become still.

Riddle 7

My garment is silent when I tread the ground,
or dwell in towns, or stir the seas,
Sometimes my raiment raises me up
and the high air, over the homes of men,
and when the strength of the wind sends me far   5
above mankind, my adornments
resound in song, ring out loudly,
sing out clear when I am untouched
by land or sea, a traveling spirit.

Riddle 14

I once was a warrior's weapon, but now
a young man has wound me in twisted wires
of gold and silver. Sometimes men kiss me;

sometimes I summon willing companions
to battle; sometimes a steed bears me   5
across the borders; sometimes a sea-horse
brings me, bright treasure, over the ocean.
Sometimes a woman adorned with rings
fills my bosom; sometimes on the boards
I lie—hard, headless, and plundered.   10
Sometimes I hang shining on a wall,
decorated and adorned, where men drink—
noble war-gear. Sometimes the warriors
take me on horseback, and then treasure-clad,
I breathe in the breath of a soldier's breast.   15
Sometimes my song summons proud warriors
to share wine; sometimes in anger
my voice saves what is stolen,
puts foes to flight. Say what I am called.

Riddle 26

Some strong enemy snatched my life,
deprived me of strength and soaked me,
drenched me in water, dragged me away,
set me in the sun, where I soon lost
all the hair I had. The hard edge,   5
clean-ground blade of a knife cut me,
then fingers folded, then the bird's delight
with swift drops darting again and again
over the dark brim swallowed wood-dye,
streamed across me and stopped again,   10
left a dark path. Protecting boards
were wrapped around me, stretched with skin,
gleaming gold; there glittered upon me[1]
the splendid work of smiths, fine-woven wire.
Now the adornments and the red dye   15
and the precious settings widely proclaim

---

1   *glittered upon me*   The Old English word *gliwedon* literally means "played" like a musical
    instrument. Some editors see a metaphor here—the sparkle of sunlight on gold like the
    sound of music—while others want to emend to *glisnedon*, "glittered."

the Protector of men—the fool cannot fault it.[1]
If the sons of men will make use of me
they will be safer and more certain of victory,
bolder in heart, happier in mind,   20
wiser in spirit; they will find more friends,
nearer and dearer, truer, more devoted,
kinder and more loyal, who will increase
honor and wealth, give them generously
all benefits, and in a loving embrace   25
clasp them close. Say what I am called,
needful to men; my name is glorious,
a help to heroes, and holy in myself.

Riddle 43

I know a noble guest within the gates,
whom great men love. Grim hunger
cannot harm him, nor hot thirst,
nor illness or age. If the servant
treats him well, who must go with him   5
on his journey, then food and joy
they will find ready for them at home—
but countless children of sorrow, if the servant
obeys his lord and master badly
on the journey. A brother ought not   10
fear his brother—that harms them both,
when they both spring from the same bosom
of one kinswoman, keen and bright,
mother and sister. Let the man who wishes
reveal with noble words how the guest   15
and servant I speak of here are called.

---

1 *the fool cannot fault it* The Old English says *nalas dolwite*, which might mean "not at all the
    pain of a wound" (i.e., the object is decorated like a hero, not wounded and scarred like a
    shield, another leather-covered wooden object). The translation assumes the reading is *nalas
    dol wite*, "by no means should a fool find fault."

Riddle 44

A marvelous thing hangs by a man's thigh,
under his tunic. There's a hole at the tip;
it's stiff and strong and set in a good place.
When a young lord lifts his cloak
over his knees, there's a well-known hole   5
he hopes to greet with the head of his dangler,
one he has often filled with its full length.

Riddle 45

Something's swelling over in the corner,
rising and standing, raising its cover.
A haughty bride grabbed that boneless thing
with her hands, and the prince's daughter
slipped that swelling thing under a cloth.   5

Riddle 47

A moth ate words. A marvelous fate
it seemed to me, when I heard of that wonder,
that a worm could swallow some man's song,
a thief in the dark, tales of glory
and their firm foundation. That thieving guest   5
was none the wiser for swallowing those words.

Riddle 85

My hall is not silent, but I am not loud
around ... the Lord shaped us[1]
for the same journey. I am swifter,
sometimes stronger; he is more lasting.
Sometimes I rest while he runs on;   5
as long as I live I dwell in him,
if we are separated, my death is certain.

---

1   *around ... the Lord shaped us*   There is no gap in the manuscript, but something is missing
    here.

Riddle 86

A creature came to a council of men
where many sat, wise in mind.
He had one eye and two ears,
two feet, twelve hundred heads,
a back and belly and two hands,   5
arms and shoulders, one neck,
and two sides—say what I'm called.

Riddle 95

I am a noble thing, known to men,
often I rest with rich and wretched,
world-renowned. I roam widely,
and on me—once foreign, now friendly—
rests the ravager's joy. If I am to have   5
joy in the cities or shining success,
men of wisdom most dearly love
my society; I will show
wisdom to many, with no words
spoken at all. Though the sons of men   10
who dwell on earth eagerly seek
my trail, I hide my tracks
from time to time from every man.

(Solutions to riddles: 1 Wind/Storm; 7 Swan; 14 Horn; 26 Bible; 43 Soul
and Body; 44 Penis or Key; 45 Penis or Dough; 47 Book-Moth; 85 Fish
and River; 86 A One-Eyed Seller of Garlic; 95 Book? Moon? Riddle?)

Old English Metrical Charms
TRANSLATED BY STEPHEN O. GLOSECKI

Modern scholars often give the name "charm" to a sort of language, often rhythmical or in verse, that is used for magical purposes. Most Old English charms were accompanied by some form of physical action, whether a significant gesture, writing words on an object, or the preparation of a medicinal compound. The precise relation between the words and the action are debatable and probably indefinable. Charms, like prayers, were a sort of insurance against the uncertainties of everyday life—they might be performed to ward off disease, protect livestock, increase crops, find lost or stolen objects, and so on. The "charms" below are all intended to do good—settle a swarm of bees or cure a disease—but presumably charms and other magical practices could be used for evil purposes as well, though no examples have survived.

The cultural place of such texts, and their role in the medical and religious practice of the Anglo-Saxons, have generated a great deal of controversy. Hundreds of pages of medical literature have survived from Anglo-Saxon England, most of them containing translations from late-classical sources in Latin (which in turn were translated from medical works in Greek). Manuscripts collecting and organizing medical recipes attest to the sophistication and professionalization of the practice of medicine among the Anglo-Saxons. On the other hand, most people lived without access to any literate or professional medical practitioners; they must have relied on traditional remedies and traditional beliefs about the causes and cures of disease. Only a few works in surviving manuscript appear to preserve native Germanic practices and beliefs; these have attracted a great deal of attention for the information they might reveal about the religion of the pre-Christian Anglo-Saxons. They represent only a small fraction of the medical literature of the period, but they have a great deal to tell us about the way health and sickness were imagined in the early Middle Ages.

These texts are complicated from any perspective, medical or spiritual, and their cultural significance is easily mistaken. Although some charms—and many prose medical remedies in Old English—involve the use of plants which have been shown to have some therapeutic value,[1] it should be emphasized that the plants in a given remedy were not recommended for their chemical properties but because of other qualities, such as those evident in the "Nine Herbs Charm." Modern herbal remedies, even when they are outside the mainstream of modern medicine, are used, at least ostensibly, within the theoretical frameworks supplied by chemistry, physiology, and pharmacology; Old English charms are not.

Moreover, although the charms retain traces of pre-Christian thought and belief such as the mention of the god Woden in the "Nine Herbs Charm," it should not be thought that they are "pagan" or antithetical to Christianity. The efficacy of the "dwarf" charm, for example, depends upon the ready availability of communion wafers, and calls upon the power of the Seven Sleepers of Ephesus, a group of early Christian saints. Many other charms involve Latin prayers and Christian sacramental practices such as the sign of the Cross or the saying of Mass; the "Nine Herbs Charm" invokes the power of Christ more often than that of Woden. The grey area between authorized Christian practice and condemned "magic" was apparently considerably broader in the early Middle Ages than it is today. The charms may be a more "popular" version of religious practice, but they depend upon the same elements—ritual speech and gesture, invocation of divine aid, knowledge of proper verbal formulas, performance of actions with implied spiritual power—as more orthodox religion in the Middle Ages. Like liturgical or devotional prayers, charms are a kind of poetic language in action, recited to bring about desired effects in the material world.

SOURCES

The first text is found in Cambridge, Corpus Christi College MS 41; the others are preserved in London, British Library, MS Harley 585, in a text known as the *Lacnunga*, a collection of medical recipes and prayers from around the year 1000; see Edward Pettit, *Anglo-Saxon Remedies, Charms, and Prayers from British Library MS Harley 585: "The Lacnunga"* 2 vols. New York: Edwin Mellen Press, 2001.

---

1   See M.L. Cameron, *Anglo-Saxon Medicine* (Cambridge: Cambridge University Press, 1993).

EDITIONS

E.V.K. Dobbie, ed., *The Anglo-Saxon Minor Poems*. Anglo-Saxon Poetic Records VI. New York: Columbia University Press, 1942.

FURTHER READING

Jolly, Karen Louise. *Popular Religion in Late Saxon England: Elf Charms in Context*. Chapel Hill: University of North Carolina Press, 1996.

Olsan, Lea. "The Inscription of Charms in Anglo-Saxon Manuscripts." *Oral Tradition* 14 (1999): 401-19.

Glosecki, Stephen O. "Stranded Narrative: Myth, Metaphor, and the Metrical Charm." *Myth in Early Northwest Europe*. Ed. Stephen O. Glosecki. Arizona Studies in the Middle Ages and the Renaissance 21. Tempe, AZ: ACMRS in collaboration with Brepols, 2006. 47-70.

For a Swarm of Bees

Against a swarm of bees[1] take earth, cast it with your right hand
    under your right foot, and say:

> I seize it under foot: I've found it now.
> Lo! earth has might   over all creatures
> and against malice   and over mindlessness
> and over the mighty man   with his mighty tongue.

And thereupon, when they swarm, throw gravel over them and say:

> Victory-wives! sit:[2]   sink to earth now!
> Never to the woodland   wild may you fly!
> Be as mindful   of my fortune
> As folks all are   of food and home.

---

1 *Against a swarm of bees* Presumably to make a swarm of bees settle into a *skep* or manmade hive.

2 *Victory-wives! sit* The meaning of the line *sitte ge sige-wif sigað to eorþan* is much debated. It may be that the word(s) *sige-wif*, translated "victory-wives," is actually an imperative verb, and the line should be translated "sit you down, settle, women, sink to the earth."

Against a Dwarf

Against a dwarf[1] take seven little wafers like those one offers [at mass], and write these names on each wafer: Maximianus, Malchus, Iohannes, Martimianus, Dionisius, Constantinus, Serafion.[2] Then one should sing the charm that follows here, first in the left ear, then in the right ear, then over the person's crown. And then have a virgin go in and hang it[3] around his neck; and do so for three days, and he will soon be well.

Spider creature   came right in here—
had his harness in hand: you're his horse, he claimed!
and to your neck tied reins!   Then they began to rise
               from the land.
As they left the land   their limbs grew cool.
Then in she dashed—   the dwarf's sister![4]   5
Then she ended it all   and oaths she swore:
no hurt would come   to harm the sick
nor whoever gets the lore   and learns this charm
and knows how to chant   this charm as well. Amen. *Fiat.*[5]

---

1   *dwarf*   Originally, perhaps, a night demon of some sort; in Old English prose texts translated from Latin medical treatises, however, the word seems to mean nothing more than "fever" (Latin *febrem*), and it is not certain that the word signified much more than a particular kind of disease, just as modern doctors speak of "malaria" and "influenza" without believing that these are caused by bad air (Italian *mala aria*) or the malign influence of the stars (Italian *influenza*). The vivid poem that accompanies this charm, however, certainly suggests some sort of personified agent of illness, in which the patient is the steed and the evil dwarf—the "spider creature"—is the rider.

2   *Maximianus ... Serafion*   Since the dwarf attacks sleeping victims, the charm opens with sympathetic appeal to the Seven Sleepers of Ephesus, an early Christian legend similar to the Rip van Winkle story. Seven young Christian men of Ephesus, fleeing persecution by the Emperor Decius (249-51), took refuge in a cave, where they were walled in while sleeping. Nearly two hundred years later, after the Roman Empire had officially converted to Christianity, the cave was opened and the Sleepers awoke. Thinking they had been asleep only one night, they went into the city of Ephesus, causing much confusion; eventually the miraculous truth is revealed, whereupon the young men die or return to sleep, praising God. The Seven Sleepers were often invoked in medieval prayers against insomnia and fever.

3   *hang it*   Presumably the seven wafers.

4   *the dwarf's sister*   The manuscript reads "the animal's sister"—i.e., the spider's?

5   *Fiat*   Latin: So be it.

For a Sudden Stitch

For a sudden stitch,[1] feverfew and the red nettle that grows in the grain, and plantain; boil in butter.

.Loud were they[2]—real loud!   when they rode down mound;
resolute they were   when over land they rode.
Shield yourself now: you can shake this attack.   5
Out! little spear!   if inside here!
Under linden[3] I stood,   under lambent shield
where those mighty women   wielded power:
and screaming spears   they sent our way!
Now I'll send them   another one back—   10
flying arrow   forth against them!
Out! little spear,   if inside here!
Sat that smith[4] there,   smacked little knife,
[world's best iron][5]   with wonder-punch.[6]
Out! little spear,   if inside here!   15
Six smiths sat there,   slaughter-spear forging.
Out, spear!   Not in, spear!

---

1 *a sudden stitch* The Old English word *færstice* appears only here; considering the serious-
ness of the invocations, "stabbing pain" might be a better translation. The charm protects
against a pain visualized as being caused by a "little spear" (l. 6) shot either by "gods" (Old
English *esa*, whose meaning is not entirely certain), "elves" (Old English *ylfa*) or "witches"
(Old English *hægtessan*; in German, lower back pain or lumbago is still called *Hexenschuss*).
Elves were thought to cause pains in humans and cattle by shooting projectiles at them;
they were often equated with devils and lesser demons in the Christian imagination. This
charm combines a medical recipe and a chant, perhaps meant to be recited when the salve
was applied to the affected area.

2 *Loud were they* It is not clear who "they" are, elves or devils or the "mighty women" of l. 8
(who may or may not be the same as the witches mentioned later in the charm), or where
the "mound" (Old English *hlæw*, which usually denotes a pre-Christian burial mound) is.

3 *linden* Shield of lime-wood.

4 *that smith* In many cultures smiths are perceived as ambivalent, often malevolent or half-
magical figures; it is not known who this smith is supposed to be, or the "six smiths" men-
tioned in l. 16.

5 *world's best iron* Here and in other half-lines in brackets, there is no gap in the manuscript
to indicate a loss, but something seems missing in the meter or sense of the poem. The lines
supplied are conjectural.

6 *wonder-punch* Old English *wundum swiðe* can also mean "powerful in wounding."

If within here be   an iron bit—
wicked witch-work,   away must it melt!
If you were shot in skin   or shot in flesh   20
or shot in blood   [or shot in bone]
or shot in limb: never let your life be harmed.
If it were old gods' shot[1]   or elfin shot
or hag-witch shot,   I'll help you now.
This your cure for old gods' shot!   This your cure for
elfin shot!   25
This your cure for hag-witch shot!   I'll help for sure!
Fly off, [dart-point!]   far to cliff-head!
May God help you.   Health be with you.

Then take the knife; put it in the potion.[2]

---

1   *old gods' shot*   The meaning of Old English *esa* is not really known; it is assumed to be the genitive plural of *os*, also unknown, which is assumed to mean "(pagan) god."

2   *the potion*   Presumably the buttery stew of feverfew, nettle and plantain prescribed at the beginning of the text. Stephen Glosecki, in *Shamanism and Old English Poetry* (New York: Garland Press, 1989), p. 139, notes a parallel in the Renaissance custom (called the "weapon salve") of curing a wound by putting medicine on the weapon that made it. It is also possible, however, that the terse instructions (in Old English *ado on wætan*) mean that the knife is to be smeared with the salve and then placed, wet, on the part of the body afflicted by the pain.

The Nine Herbs Charm[1]

Mind you, mugwort,   how much you showed,
what you arranged   at Rainmelding.[2]
Eldest of herbs,   "Una"[3] we call you.
You have might against three,   might against thirty,
might against all venom   and against onfliers;[4]   5
you have might against the foe   who fares through the land.

And you, plantain,   plant-tribes' mother,
eastward open,   inward mighty:
over you carts clattered;   over you queans[5] rode;
over you brides clamored;   over you bulls snorted: 10
all this you withstood   and struck against,
just as you withstand them all: onfliers, venom,
and the loathsome foe   who fares through the land.

This herb's called "Stunner,"[6]   on stone well grown:
she stands against poison;   she'll stun your pain.   15
"Valiant" we call her—   venom she allays;
she casts out venom,   overcomes evil.
This is the plant   that pummeled the worm:
she has might against all venom,   she has might against
                                     onfliers,

---

1 *The Nine Herbs Charm* This translation has been adapted from Stephen Glosecki, ""Blow these vipers from me": Mythic Magic in *The Nine Herbs Charm*," in L. C. Gruber, ed., *Essays On Old, Middle, Modern English and Old Icelandic: In Honor of Raymond P. Tripp, Jr.* (Lewiston, NY: Edwin Mellen Press, 2000), 117-19. The text of the charm is corrupt, its context obscure, and its meaning unclear. The recitation of charms over herbs was expressly condemned in some Anglo-Saxon homilies and law codes; Christian prayers were recommended instead. Such prayers and blessings over plants are not uncommon in Anglo-Saxon medicine, but the botanical animism of this charm is remarkable.

2 *Rainmelding* Or, "what you brought about at the Great Proclamation."

3 *Una* I.e., "one" (Latin).

4 *onfliers* Flying or airborne diseases.

5 *queans* Women.

6 *Stunner* Old English *stune*. From the recipe that follows the poem, this is apparently lamb's cress.

she has might against the foe   who fares through the
                                       land.   20

Launch them now, cock's-spur: lesser lash bigger;
bigger lash lesser   till both be healed.

Mind you, mayweed,[1]   how much you showed:
the end you achieved   at Alorford:
never will airborne illness   end a lifetime   25
if one make a meal   from mayweed now.

Known as nettle,   the next herb here—
a seal sent it   over sea ridges
to undo anger   and other venom.

These nine have might   against nine venoms.   30
+ Snake[2] came stealing—   he stung someone![3]
Then Woden grabbed   nine glory-twigs,
knocked that adder   into nine pieces!
There it ended: apple and venom:
never would it slither   inside a house!   35
+ Chervil and fennel,   both full of might:
herbs created   by the all-wise Lord,
holy in heaven,   while hanging there;[4]
He set them and sent them   into seven worlds

---

1 *mayweed* Mayweed is presumably chamomile.

2 *+ Snake* The small crosses in the manuscript at lines 31, 36, 45, and 58 may indicate
   sectional divisions, or instructions to make the sign of the cross, or something else whose
   meaning is no longer clear.

3 *someone* The manuscript reads *nan* "no one." Along with the *Sudden Stitch* charm, this is
   the only reference to non-Christian gods in Anglo-Saxon medical literature, and the only
   reference anywhere to Woden battling a serpent. Our knowledge of pre-Christian Anglo-
   Saxon religion is exceptionally sparse, and for all we know this passage may owe as much
   to the story of Moses and the serpent in the wilderness (Numbers 21.4-9) as to any actual
   Germanic belief.

4 *while hanging there* Woden gives way to Christ or is somehow identified with him (or
   has "Christ" been substituted for an earlier reference to Woden?) whose death on the cross
   gives rise to healing plants; folk beliefs of several cultures hold that Good Friday—the day
   of Christ's crucifixion—is a good day for planting. It may also be relevant here that in Old
   Norse legend Odin also experienced hanging on Yggdrasil, the "World Tree."

to remedy all,   the wretched and the blest.   40
They stand against pain,   they strike against venom,
They have might against three,   might against thirty,
against fiendish fist   and fast attack,
against vile creatures'   vicious witchcraft.

+ Now these nine herbs have might   against nine magic
              sendings,[1]   45
    against nine venoms   and against nine fliers—
    against the red venom,[2]   against the reeking venom,
    against the white venom,   against venom in blue,
    against the yellow venom,   against venom in green,
    against the black venom,   against the blue venom,   50
    against the brown venom,   against venom purplish,
    against worm-blister,   against water-blister,
    against thorn-blister,   against troll-blister,[3]
    against ice-blister,   against venom-blister—
    if there fly in from the east   any oncoming venom   55
    or in from the north   flying [in here now]
    or any from the west   over the world of man.

+ Christ stood over old ones—   each and every kind.[4]
    I alone fathom   a fast river
    where the nine adders   are all watching.   60
    Let all plants now   spring up from their roots!
    Let the seas divide—   all salt water—
    when I blow this poison   right past you now.

---

1 *nine magic sendings* Another possible translation of this line is that the nine herbs have might against "nine of those who fled from glory," i.e., nine demons.

2 *red venom* Presumably the various venoms and blisters listed refer to different diseases, but none of them can be identified.

3 *troll-blister* The manuscript reads *þysgeblæd*, which makes no sense. Most editors take this as an error for "thistle-blister," but it is taken here as an error for *þyrs-geblæd*, "giant (or troll) blister."

4 *Christ stood over ... every kind* The manuscript reads *Crist stod ofer alde ængan cundes*, and the meaning is unknown. Other possible emendations and translations are "Christ, whose nature was unique, overcame disease" and "Christ prevailed against every type of illness."

Mugwort,[1] plantain that is open to the east, lamb's cress, cock's-spur grass, mayweed, nettle, crabapple, chervil and fennel, old soap. Work the herbs into a powder, mix with the soap and with the pulp of an apple. Make a paste from water and ashes; take fennel, boil it in the paste, and bathe with beaten egg[2] when the salve is applied, both before and after. Sing the charm over each of the herbs, thrice before they are ground up, and also over the apple; and sing the same charm into the man's mouth and into both ears and over the wound before he applies the salve.

---

1 *Mugwort*   The dazzling and surreal poetry of the charm is followed by this rather prosaic list of ingredients and instructions. But it would be as wrong to discard the "superstition" of the charm in favor of the "rational" recipe as it would be to remove the practical elements of the cure from the "poetic" invocation that accompanies it. Both were presumably important to the readers and users of this text.

2 *bathe with beaten egg*   Or "boil with the mixture"?

3. Faith—Heaven's High King

Advent (Christ I)

This poem opens the Exeter Book and forms the first part of a three-part sequence usually known as *Christ*, consisting of this poem about Advent, a poem on the Ascension bearing the runic signature of the poet Cynewulf, and a poem on the Last Judgment. The three poems are quite different from one another and are, as far as we know, by different authors; their placement in sequence is the decision of the manuscript's compilers.

Advent is a series of meditations on the so-called O Antiphons of Advent, a group of liturgical responses found in the monastic prayers of the Divine Office for Vespers in the weeks before Christmas; they survive most famously in the Christian hymn "O Come O Come Emmanuel." It does not draw on these antiphons in sequence, or only on these alone; other and more obscure sources have been found for some sections of the poem. The poem treats its sources with a great deal of freedom and creativity, often drawing in other biblical paraphrases and allusions and the deep resonances of the formulaic language of Old English poetry—themes of darkness and light, exile and victory, joyous celebration in the bright hall, and wise contemplation of the world's mysteries. As one critic has written, "the theologically perceptive, allusive voice in the twelve didactic lyrics in fact includes an inspired mix of antiphonal and Scriptural echo, orthodox doctrine and tradition and authoritative pastoral ministry."[1]

Appropriately for a poem about Advent, the themes of Mary's virginity and Christ's incarnation are repeatedly sounded, the Old Testament prophets are invoked, and Christ is asked repeatedly to come and save His people. There is also naturally a great deal of repetition and verbal parallelism between one part of the poem and another. Not all critics agree that the twelve sections are by

---

1 Judith Garde, "*Christ I* (164-195a): The Mary-Joseph Dialogue in Medieval Christian Perspective," *Neophilologus* 74 (1990): 123.

one author,[1] but the poem gains its unity, and its appeal, not so much from authorial control, nor from its doctrinal coherence or liturgical consistency, but from the recurrence of images and ideas, and from the sort of varied repetition that is characteristic of Old English poetry at its best.

SOURCE

Exeter, Cathedral Library, Dean and Chapter MS 3501, fols. 8r-14r.

EDITION

Bernard J. Muir, Jr., *The Exeter Anthology of Old English Poetry*, 2nd ed., 2 vols. Exeter: University of Exeter Press, 2000.

FURTHER READING

Farina, Lara. "Before Affection: *Christ I* and the Social Erotic." *Exemplaria* 13 (2001): 469-96.

Irving, Edward B., Jr. "The Advent of Poetry: *Christ I*." *ASE* 25 (1996): 123-34.

Rankin, Susan. "The Liturgical Background of the Old English Advent Lyrics: A Reappraisal." *Learning and Literature in Anglo-Saxon England: Studies Presented to Peter Clemoes on the Occasion of His Sixty-Fifth Birthday.* Ed. Michael Lapidge and Helmut Gneuss. Cambridge and New York: Cambridge University Press, 1985. 317-40.

---

1   Anya Adair, "The Unity and Authorship of the Old English *Advent Lyrics*," *English Studies* 92 (2011): 823-48.

I

... the king.[1]

You are the wall-stone that the builders of old
rejected from the work. It is right and just
that you are now the head of the great hall,
and bind together the broad walls   5
in firm fastening, flint unbroken,
so that throughout the world all eyes that see
may gaze in wonder, O Lord of glory.
Show forth now your work, your subtle power,
truth-fast, triumphant; let stand there   10
wall against wall. Now the work cries out
for the craftsman to come, and the king himself,
and repair the house that now lies ruined
beneath its roof. He made the body,
these limbs of clay; now the Lord of life   15
shall rescue this wretched heap from fear,
save poor souls from terror, as he has often done.

II

O thou Ruler and righteous King,[2]
who holds the lock and opens life,
the celestial realm to the blessed soul,   20
denied to those whose works do not prosper.
Indeed, we speak these words of necessity,
beseeching Him who made mankind

---

1 *the king*   The beginning of the manuscript is lost. This section is based on the antiphon *O Rex Gentium, et desideratus earum, lapisque angularis, qui facis utraque unum: veni, et salva hominem, quem de limo formasti* ("O King of the nations, and their desire, the cornerstone making both one: Come and save the human race, whom you fashioned from clay"). It also draws upon Psalm 117.22 (also quoted in the New Testament, Matthew 21.42 / Mark 12.10 / Luke 20.17), "the stone which the builders rejected has become the cornerstone."

2 *O thou Ruler and righteous King*   This selection is based on the antiphon *O Clavis David, et sceptrum domus Israel; qui aperis, et nemo claudit; claudis, et nemo aperit: veni, et educ vinctum de domo carceris, sedentem in tenebris, et umbra mortis* ("O Key of David and scepter of the House of Israel; you open and no one can shut; you shut and no one can open: Come and lead the prisoners from the prison house, those who dwell in darkness and the shadow of death").

that He not leave us to languish, lost
in our pitiful state, as we, prisoners,   25
sit sorrowful, longing for that sun
in which the Lord of life reveals His light;
may He be to our minds a shield and protector,
and clothe our weak wits in splendor,
and make us worthy, whom He called to glory   30
when downcast, deprived of our home,
we were forced to turn to this narrow land.
And so he who speaks the truth can say
that He redeemed the race of mankind
who had gone astray.

               A sinless virgin   35
and young maiden he chose to be his mother;
it was brought about without man's embrace
that the bride came to carry a child.
Never before or since has such a thing
been merited by any woman in the world;   40
that seed was concealed, the Lord's secret mystery.
Spiritual grace spread over all regions of the earth,
and many shoots of wisdom shot up,
illuminated by the Lord of life, lasting teaching
which had long lay hidden in dark soil,   45
high songs of the prophets, when He came,
the Ruler who raises the sound of every voice
of those who wisely wish to praise
without ceasing the holy name of the Creator.

III

O sight of peace, holy Jerusalem,[1]   50
best of royal seats, city of Christ,

---

1   *O sight of peace, holy Jerusalem*   This section is based on the "added" antiphon *O Hierusa-lem, civitas Dei summi: leva in circuitu oculos tuos, et vide Dominum tuum, quia iam veniet solvere te a vinculis* ("O Jerusalem, city of the great God: lift up your eyes round about, and see our Lord, for he is coming to release you from your chains"). It refers to the common medieval explanation of the name *Jerusalem* as meaning *visio pacis* or "sight of peace" (Old English *sibbe gesihð*).

homeland of angels, in you alone
the souls of the righteous find rest forever,
rejoicing in glory. No sign of sin
is ever seen within that city's walls,   55
but all iniquity, all evil and strife,
flees far from you. You are gloriously filled
with holy hope, as your name declares.
Lift up your eyes and look all around,
survey this vast creation, the vault of heaven   60
on every hand, see how Heaven's king
Himself approaches you to seek His home,
makes His way, just as the wise prophets
foretold it long ago in words, revealed
the birth of Christ, spoke comfort to you,   65
best of cities! Now that child is born,
come to cast down the works of the Hebrews.
He brings you bliss, loosens the bonds
laid upon men. He knows their need,
how the wretched must wait for mercy.   70

IV

O joy of women beyond heavenly glory,[1]
most beautiful maiden over all the earth
that ever sea-dwellers have heard spoken of,
tell us your mystery that came down from heaven,
how you came to conceive and carried   75
a child to be born, but knew no bedfellow
in the manner of ordinary men.
Truly we have never heard of such a thing
as you received by special grace
ever coming to pass in days of old,   80
nor may we ever expect such an occurrence
in future times. Truly a noble faith

---

1   *O joy of women beyond heavenly glory*   This section is based on the antiphon *O Virgo virgi-
num, quomodo fiet istud? Quia nec primam similem visa es nec habere sequentem. Filiae Jeru-
salem, quid me admiramini? Divinum est mysterium hoc quod cernitis* ("O Virgin of virgins,
how shall this be? For before you was none like you, and there will not be after. Daughters
of Jerusalem, why do you marvel at me? The thing you behold is a divine mystery").

was in you, for in your womb you bore
the divine majesty, yet your radiant virginity
remained undefiled. All the children of men   85
sow in tears and reap the same—
they bring forth death. The blessed maid,
the sainted Mary, always full of triumph, said:
"What is this wonder at which you marvel,
and grieving that you groan with sorrow,   90
you sons and daughters of Salem?
You curiously ask how I kept my virginity,
preserved my purity, yet became the mother
of God's glorious son. Truly that secret
is not known to men, but Christ revealed   95
in David's beloved daughter
that all the guilt of Eve is wiped away,
the curse cast out, and the weaker sex
honored and exalted. Hope has arisen
that now a blessing may come for both   100
together, men and women, forever and ever
to abide in the celestial joy of angels
with the Father of truth forever."

V

O beautiful day-spring, brightest of angels[1]
sent down to earth for all mankind,   105
radiance of the sun of righteousness,
bright beyond the stars, you bring the light
your very self to all times and seasons.
As you, God from God, begotten of old,
true Son of the Father, dwell forever   110
without beginning in the glory of heaven,
so now your handiwork in its time of need
beseeches you boldly to send to us

---

1   *O beautiful day-spring, brightest of angels*   This section is based on the antiphon *O Oriens,
    splendor lucis aeternae, et sol justitiae: veni, et illumina sedentes in tenebris, et umbra mortis*
    ("O Morning Star, splendor of light eternal and sun of righteousness: Come and enlighten
    those who dwell in darkness and the shadow of death"). The "day-spring" (Old English
    earendel) is the morning star.

the bright sun; and you yourself come
to shed your light on those who for so long 115
have been covered in clouds and darkness here,
sitting in eternal night, shrouded in sin,
forced to endure the dark shadow of death.
Now, filled with hope, we believe in salvation
through the word of God brought to the world, 120
who was in the beginning God, co-eternal
with the almighty Father, and then was made
flesh without blemish, when the virgin bore him,
a solace to the sorrowful. Among us, sinless,
God was seen; together dwelled 125
the mighty Son of God and son of man
in harmony among mankind. For that we may
give thanks to the God of Victories by right,[1]
because he would to send Himself to us.

VI

O God of spirits,[2] so wisely 130
were you named rightly by that name
"Emmanuel," first by angels spoken
in the Hebrew tongue! Its hidden sense,
interpreted, is "Now God himself is with us,
guardian of the skies." So the wise ancients 135
foretold the coming of the King of Kings,
and likewise that spotless priest as well,
Melchizedek the mighty one,[3] long ago
revealed, wise in spirit, the divine glory
of the eternal Lord. He was a law bringer, 140
leader and teacher for those who had long

---

1   *by right*   Old English *bi gewyrhtum*, translated here as "by right," can also mean "for his deeds" or "through our deeds."

2   *O God of spirits*   This section is based on the antiphon *O Emmanuel, Rex et legifer noster, exspectatio Gentium, et Salvator earum: veni ad salvandum nos, Domine, Deus noster* ("O Emmanuel, our king and our lawgiver, the hope of the nations and their Savior: Come and save us, O Lord our God").

3   *Melchizedek the mighty one*   Melchizedek is mentioned only briefly and somewhat obscurely in the Old Testament (Genesis 14) but was regarded by the early church as a prefiguration of Christ himself.

hoped for His coming, as had been promised
that the son of the Creator himself would come
to cleanse the people of the earth
and visit the very depths below as well, 145
through the Spirit's power. Patiently
they sat in bondage until the Son of God
might come to the wretched; weak, tormented,
they cried out: "Come now yourself,
heaven's high king. Bring salvation and life 150
to us, weary prisoners, worn out with weeping
bitter burning tears. In you alone
is relief and remedy for our desperate need.
Come down to us captives, sick at heart;
when you hurry hence, do not leave behind 155
such a great multitude, but show us
your sovereign mercy, Christ our savior,
Prince of glory, do not leave us in the power
of the cursed one. Grant us the eternal joy
of your glory, glorious God of hosts, 160
that those whom your hands have shaped
may worship you. You remain forever
in the highest with the heavenly Father."

VII

"O my Joseph, son of Jacob,[1]
kinsman of David the mighty king, 165
must you forsake your firm friendship
and leave my love?" "Deeply troubled
I am, and all bereft of my honor,
because on your account I have heard
so many words of measureless woe, 170
taunts and scorn; they insult me
with many mocking words. I must pour out
my grieving soul's tears. God may easily

---

1 *O my Joseph, son of Jacob* This section, a dialogue in dramatic form (the earliest of its kind
in English) between Mary and Joseph, is not based on any known antiphon. It may be from
a compilation by Alcuin found in an antiphonary from York; see Thomas Hill, "A Liturgical
Source for *Christ I* 164-213 (Advent Lyric VII)," *Medium Ævum* 46 (1977): 12-15.

heal the sorrowful thoughts of my heart,
console my wretched self. O young woman, 175
maiden Mary!" "Why do you mourn,
and cry out in grief? No guilt
have I ever found in you, no fault,
no blame of sins, and yet you speak
these words as if you were full 180
of every sin and crime." "I have suffered
too much misery from this childbearing!
How can I counter their hateful words,
or find any answer at all
against my enemies? It is known to all 185
that from the glorious temple of the Lord
I readily received a pure maiden,
sinless, and now all that has changed,
I know not how. Nothing can help me now,
neither speech or silence. If I say the truth, 190
then the daughter of David must die,
stoned to death. But to hide the sin
is even worse—I would live forsworn,
despised and dishonored among all people
forever more." Then the maiden revealed 195
the true mystery, and thus she said:
"I swear truly by the Son of God,
Savior of souls, that I have never yet
had intercourse with any man
ever on earth, but in my early years 200
it was granted to me that Gabriel,
heaven's high angel, greeted me at home.
He told me truly that the spirit of heaven
would shine on me, and I would bear a son,
the Glory of life, exalted child of God, 205
bright Lord of Glory. Now I have become
his temple, without stain; the spirit of comfort
has lived within me. Now you must lay aside
all sad and sorrowful care. Give eternal thanks
to the mighty Son of God that I have become his mother, 210
yet still a maiden, and you are called his father

in the eyes of the world: indeed this prophecy
must surely be fulfilled in Himself."

VIII

O righteous ruler and peaceful,[1]
King of all Kings, Christ almighty!   215
Before all the orders of the world were formed
you were, with your Father in Glory,
a child begotten through His skill and power.
There is now no nobleman under the heavens,
no man of counsel so wise or clever   220
that he can explain to sea-dwellers
or rightly report how heaven's Guardian
took you in the beginning for his glorious Son.
That, in the beginning,[2] was first of all things
made under heaven which the race of men   225
have heard of in the nations, when wise God,
divine author of life, nobly divided
light and darkness; and the Lord of Hosts,
in dominion and judgment, ordained it thus:
"Let there be henceforth forever and ever   230
light, a shining joy to all living things
who will be born in their generations."
And it soon came about, just as it should—
a light, shining among the stars, gleamed forth
for the tribes of men in the course of time.   235
He himself ordained that you, his Son,
were co-eternal with the one Lord
before any of this ever came to pass.
You are the Wisdom who wrought all

---

1   *O righteous ruler and peaceful*   This section is based on the Christmas antiphon *O Rex
    pacifice, Tu ante saecula nate: per auream egrede portam, redemptos tuos visita, et eso illuc revoca
    unde ruerunt per culpam* ("O King of peace, born before all ages: come by the golden gate,
    visit those you have redeemed, and lead them back to the place they fell from by sin").

2   *in the beginning*   This passage recalls Genesis 1.1-3, "In the beginning, God created the
    heavens and the earth. And the earth was void and empty, and darkness was on the face of
    the abyss; and the spirit of God moved about over the waters. And God said, Let there be
    light; and there was light."

this vast and wide creation with the Ruler. 240
And so there is none so wise, so discerning,
that he can clearly recount your parentage
to the children of men. Come, Victorious Lord,
Creator of mankind, graciously make known
your mercy upon us! We must understand 245
the wonderful mystery of your mother's lineage,
we need to know, now that we cannot
recount your father's kinship any further.
Graciously bless this earth by your advent,
O savior Christ, your coming hither, 250
and the golden gates, which in bygone days
stood locked in ages long ago,
high Lord of Heaven, bid them open,
and then seek us out, yourself descending
humbly to earth. We have need of your mercy! 255
The accursed wolf, dark death-shadow,
has scattered far and wide your flock, O Lord,
driven them off. The people You redeemed
with your blood, O God, are gripped in bondage
by the Wicked One, who fiercely oppresses us 260
against our desires. O Saving Lord,
in our inmost thoughts we earnestly pray
that you come quickly, make haste to help
us weary exiles, that the wicked destroyer
may plunge headlong into the abyss of Hell; 265
and your handiwork might rise on high,
Creator of men, and come to righteousness
in the beautiful kingdom up above,
from which the dark spirit seduced and beguiled us
through our love of sin, so that, stripped of glory, 270
we must endure torments without end forever,
unless You, eternal Lord, Living God,
Shield of all creatures, might more swiftly
wish to save us from the world's enemy.

IX

O renowned woman, glory of the world,[1]   275
purest maiden that ever on earth
through these long ages have lived among men!
How rightfully do all men endowed with speech
in every realm recall your name, and say
with happy heart that you are the bride   280
of the highest and noblest Lord of heaven.
Likewise even the highest in heaven,
the thanes of Christ, proclaim and sing
that you are Lady of the heavenly legions
by holy might, and of all ranks of men   285
under the heavens, and of the hosts of hell.
For you alone of all mankind
did resolve most nobly, bold-minded,
that you would bring your maidhood to your Maker,
and offer it up without sin. No other   290
has ever come among mankind like you,
a bride adorned with rings, who brought
her shining offering with spotless mind
to its heavenly home. The Lord of Victories
commanded his high herald to fly hither   295
from his glorious majesty, and make known to you
the fullness of his power, that in pure nativity
you should bear the Son of the Lord
as a mercy to men; and you yourself, Mary,
should remain immaculate forever.   300

    We have also heard that long ago
a certain righteous prophet spoke of you

---

1   *O renowned woman, glory of the world*   This section is based on the "added" antiphon *O
mundi Domina, regio ex semine orta, ex tuo jam Christus processit alvo, tanquam sponsus de
thalamo; hic jacet in presepio qui et sidera regit* ("O mistress of the world, sprung of royal
seed: from your womb Christ went forth as a bridegroom from his chamber; here he who
rules the stars lies in the manger").

in ancient days, Isaiah,[1] who said
that he was led to where he might look upon
the abode of life in the eternal home.   305
The wise prophet gazed around that region
until his eyes came to rest upon a noble portal
fixed in place there. Precious treasure
was wrapped all around that huge door,
and wondrous bands bound it. He believed   310
indeed that no one of men could ever
raise up, in all eternity,
such firmly-fixed and massive bars,
or unlock the clasps of that city gate,
until the angel of God, with gracious purpose,   315
explained the way and said these words:
"I can tell you that it will truly come to pass
that God himself, by the spirit's power,
the Father almighty, in the fullness of time
will journey through these golden gates,   320
and through these sturdy locks will seek the earth;
and after Him they will stand forever
so tightly closed for all eternity
that no one else, except God the Savior,
will ever unlock them again."   325

What that ancient wise one there beheld
with his own eyes is now fulfilled.
You are the gate; through you the sovereign God
once ventured out upon the earth,
and thus Christ almighty came to meet you   330
adorned with power, pure and elect.
So after himself did the Prince of angels,
Giver of life, lock you again
as if with a key, completely undefiled.

---

1   *Isaiah*   In fact the passage is based on Ezechiel 44.1-2, "And he brought me back to the way
    of the gate of the outward sanctuary, which looked towards the east: and it was shut. And
    the Lord said to me: This gate shall be shut, it shall not be opened, and no man shall pass
    through it: because the Lord of Israel has entered in by it, and it shall be shut." These closed
    gates were later interpreted as Mary's virginal body, through which God entered the world.

Show us now the same mercy that the angel   335
Gabriel, God's messenger, brought to you.
Lo, as we sit in the city we pray
that you show forth your own Son
as a comfort to the people. Then with one accord
we may all rejoice in hope, now that we   340
have seen that babe lying on your breast.
Intercede for us now with eager words
that He not allow us any longer
to be drawn by error in this valley of death,
but that He carry us to the Father's kingdom,   345
where free from sorrow, we might forever
dwell in glory with the God of hosts.

X

O most holy Lord of Heaven![1]
Co-existing with the eternal Father
from ages past in that excellent home.   350
There was as yet no angel then created,
nor any of that mighty and majestic host
who keep watch over the kingdom on high
the glorious palace of the Prince and his servants,
when you, together with the eternal God,   355
first established that spacious creation,
the broad realms of earth. With you both
is the Holy Spirit, the Comforter. Christ Jesus,
with humble hearts we now call upon you,
ask that you hear the cry of these captives,   360
your bond-slaves, Savior God,
how we are harried by our own willful desires.
Hateful fiends of hell, violent spirits,
have cruelly confined us in miserable exile,
wrapped us in painful bonds. The remedy   365
lies in You alone, eternal Lord;

---

1   *O most holy Lord of Heaven*   The source of this section is not known; some sources are pro-
    posed in Simon Tugwell, "Advent Lyrics 348-77 (Lyric No. X)," *Medium Ævum* 29 (1970):
    34.

help the afflicted, so that your advent
might comfort our misery, though we
have waged war on You through our lust for sin.
Have mercy on your servants, be mindful of   370
our wretchedness, how weak-minded, we stumble,
and miserably go astray. O King of men, come,
do not delay! We need your mercy,
that you might rescue us, and in righteousness
grant us your saving grace, that henceforth   375
we may always thrive in better things,
and work Your will among the nations.

XI

O beautiful and glorious,[1] full of great honor,
high and holy heavenly Trinity,
blessed far and wide across the broad world!   380
Rightly should all endowed with speech,
poor earth-dwellers, praise You on high
with all their strength, now that the faithful Savior
has revealed God, that we might know Him.
Wherefore the righteous ranks of seraphim,   385
fervent in deeds, confirmed in judgment,
forever proclaiming with the angel hosts
in Heaven on high, never weak or tiring,
chant sweetly with clear loud voice,
fair near and far. They have a most noble   390
service before the King: Christ granted that they
might enjoy His presence before their eyes
forever and ever, and clothed in radiance,
might worship the Ruler far and wide,

---

1   *O beautiful and glorious* The source of this section is disputed; it may be based on one
    or more of several different prayers to the Trinity, and certainly it draws on the part of the
    mass known as the *Sanctus*: *Sanctus, Sanctus, Sanctus, Dominus Deus Sabaoth. Pleni sunt
    caeli et terra gloria tua. Hosanna in excelsis. Benedictus qui venit in nomine Domini. Hosanna
    in excelsis* ("Holy, holy, holy, Lord God of hosts. Heaven and earth are full of your glory.
    Hosanna in the highest. Blessed is He who comes in the name of the Lord. Hosanna in the
    highest").

and with their wings might shield the face   395
of the Lord almighty, eternal God,
and press forward around His princely throne
eager to see which of them might swoop in flight
closest to our Savior in those courts of peace.
They praise the Beloved, and in His light   400
they speak these words to Him, worshipping
the princely Author and origin of all creation:
"Holy are You, Holy, Prince of high angels,
true King of triumph, ever are You holy,
O Lord of lords! Forever lives your glory   405
on earth among men in every age,
widely honored. You are God of Hosts,
for You have filled the heavens and earth
with your glory, Shield of warriors,
Protector of all creatures. Eternal glory   410
be to You in the highest, and bright praise
on earth among men. May You live blessed,
who comes in the name of the Lord, a comfort
to wretched people. Praise eternal to You
in the highest, forever without end."   415

XII

O indeed! What a wonderful change is wrought[1]
in man's life, that the mild Creator of mankind
took flesh undefiled from a virgin,
she who knew nothing at all of men's embrace,
nor by any seed of man on earth   420
did the God of triumph come; it was greater
than any dweller on earth could understand
in its mystery, how He, Glory of the skies,

---

1   *What a wonderful change is wrought*   This section is based on the antiphon *O admirabile
    commercium*, sung in the Octave of Christmas: *O admirabile commercium, Creator generis
    humani animatum corpus sumens, de Virgine nasci dignatus est: et procedens homo sine semine,
    largitus est nobis suam deitatem* ("O admirable exchange, the Creator of the human race, tak-
    ing upon Himself a body and a soul, has vouchsafed to be born of a Virgin, and, appearing
    here below as man, has made us partakers of His Divinity").

Lord of Heaven above, brought help
to mankind through his mother's womb.   425
And so continually, the Savior of mankind,
sends forth his forgiveness each and every day
as a help to people, the Lord of Hosts.
Therefore in steadfast deeds and words we should
eagerly praise Him. That is the highest counsel   430
for every man who is mindful of past things,
that he always, most often, most inwardly,
and most earnestly honor God.
He will repay him a reward for that love,
the hallowed Savior himself,   435
in that country where he has not yet come,
in the joy of the land of the living,
where he will always dwell, forever
abiding blessed, word without end. Amen.

Seasons for Fasting

The manuscript containing this poem, London, British Library MS Cotton Otho B.xi, was destroyed in a disastrous fire of 1731 that ravaged the manuscript collection of Sir Robert Cotton; the same fire nearly consumed the *Beowulf* manuscript. The manuscript had been transcribed in 1562 by the antiquary Laurence Nowell (his transcription is now in the British Library, MS Add. 43703), but the poem was not rediscovered until 1934. The poem was already incomplete when Nowell transcribed it. One stanza of the poem (eight lines) had been copied from the manuscript and printed by the historian Abraham Whelock in 1643, and a comparison of this passage with Nowell's transcription confirms that Nowell was not always a reliable transcriber. But whatever its problems as a text, the poem is interesting for a number of reasons.

The poem deals with an important element of Christian practice in the Middle Ages, indeed of religious practice in many cultures, the abstaining from certain foods at certain times of the year. Ember weeks, abolished after the Second Vatican Council in the 1960s, were annual observances consisting of fasts (abstaining from food and drink until the ninth hour, or mid-afternoon) on Wednesdays, Fridays, and Saturdays to be observed four times a year. The four sets of Ember Days are in the first week of Lent, the week after Pentecost, the week before the Autumnal Equinox in September, and the week before Christmas. The English practice was different from the continental practice, which placed the first Ember fast in the first week of March (regardless of Lent) and the second Ember fast in the second week of June (regardless of Pentecost); the poem warns its readers to ignore such Breton and Frankish practice and keep the fasts as prescribed by Pope Gregory and practiced in England. The poem draws on a long tradition of Christian homiletic teaching about Lenten observance, as well as about fasting, gluttony, drunkenness, and the regulation of appetite. It also discusses the abuses of fasting by the clergy, and so manages to combine technical instruction with nationalistic pride and contemporary complaint in the style of a homily.

Seasons for Fasting is unusual in being divided into stanzas, mostly of eight lines each. The poem has 230 surviving lines divided into four parts: an introduction on Moses and Christ (1-38); the Ember fasts (39-102); Lent (103-83); and priestly abuses (184-230). The poet begins with the example of Moses, a spiritual leader who followed God's law. He describes the fasts of Moses, Christ in the desert, and the prophet Elijah, all examples of proper fasting and commonly cited in medieval homilies; it continues with a warning against the devil, who tries to tempt sinners as he tempted Christ in the desert. He concludes with a tirade against priests who set a poor example by eating and drinking in taverns when they should be fasting. The poem addresses lay people directly, and condemns the lax priests who do not practice the fasting and abstinence they preach. This literary trope—calling out slack clergy and urging lay people to avoid their bad example—is not common in Old English but would become much more common in Middle English, reaching its high points in Chaucer's *Canterbury Tales* and Langland's *Piers Plowman*.

The poem is probably from the later tenth century, a time of monastic reform and renewed ecclesiastical rigor; the "Frankish" calculation of the Ember Fasts which the poem warns against were introduced at this time, and other authors warn against them as well. It has some affinities with a short Latin text on the Ember fasts associated with Archbishop Wulfstan (d. 1023) called *De ieiuno quattuor temporum*. The vocabulary includes a few unusual words (e.g. *gebrefd* 45, "abridged" or "set down briefly") found elsewhere only in Byrhtferth's *Manual*, a guide to computus (the science of calculating dates for Easter and other Christian feasts) written around the turn of the millennium, and the poem seems to move in this world where Christian salvation, ecclesiastical reform, and the science of the calendar are intimately connected.

SOURCE

London, BL Cotton Otho B.xi (now lost); London, BL MS Add. 43703.

EDITION

E.V.K. Dobbie, *The Anglo-Saxon Minor Poems*. Anglo-Saxon Poetic Records VI. New York: Columbia University Press, 1942.

FURTHER READING

Hilton, C.B. "The Old English *Seasons for Fasting*: Its Place in the Vernacular Complaint Tradition." *Neophilologus* 70 (1986): 155-59.

Richards, Mary. "Old Wine in a New Bottle: Recycled Instructional Materials in *Seasons for Fasting*." *The Old English Homily: Precedent, Practice, and Appropriation*. Ed. Aaron J. Kleist. Turnhout: Brepols, 2007. 345-64.

In ancient days the people of Israel
were enlightened and instructed
by Moses the mighty teacher,
when the Lord of life, here in this life,
set him before the people by His own word,   5
Heaven's high king, to counsel men,
and Himself shared secrets with him,
how he should teach the true way to his dear nation.

Then the nation's leader followed the lore
of Heaven's high king, and the people too,   10
as they had been taught in that nation;
and if they took up some twisted work,
the God of victories sent down affliction
as a reward from heaven, and they at once
pleaded for peace, and quickly found it,   15
if they would let go of their grasp on sin.

Many are the great works which this glorious nation
carried out in its conquering warfare,
as long as they loved the Lord of life;
but their end was wretched and pitiful,   20
when they ensnared the Lord himself,
set him on a tree, and in a tomb
condemned him; there he was hidden,
and appeared to the people on the third day.

We have heard that many heroes 25
have written in their books and proclaimed
that they held four seasons of fasts,
when they offered a beast without blemish,
a lamb or calf, as a sign to the Beloved
who was himself spotless before the world.[1] 30

But the Ruler of Life proceeded to rise
from the grave, filled with glory,
and sought His home among Heaven's citizens,
a land among angels, and to us all
holds out the hope of joy, if we will 35
follow his teaching with true hearts.
None filled with evil can enter there,
nor mired in sin—he must hasten to his fate.

Now let us praise here in this life
the beloved Doer of deeds, and for Him 40
fill our count of days with gifts of alms
and works of fasting, as the wise Moses
taught long ago, and with the English
let us steadfastly keep the schedule
just as it was written by the Roman prince, 45
set down briefly by the pope of all people, Gregory.

We ought to observe that first fast
in the very first week of Lent,
in the month that men call March
all across the kingdom of the Romans, 50
and there we should read the twelve mysteries[2]
brightly arranged in the Ruler's hall,

---

1 *spotless before the world* This stanza is incomplete, probably by accident—two lines are
   missing.
2 *twelve mysteries* The "twelve mysteries" (Old English *twelfe runa*) are probably the *Sabbatum duodecim lectionem*, the "Saturday of twelve readings," the vigil mass on Saturday at the
   end of each Ember week, when six fixed readings were read (originally they were first read
   in Latin and then Greek, hence the name "twelve readings"). See P.J. Stapleton, "Identifying
   the *twelve runa* in the Old English *Seasons for Fasting*," *N&Q* 59 (2012): 310-14. The word
   run "mystery, secret" is used elsewhere in the poem to describe a scriptural or liturgical texts.

Heaven's high king, honor the proud
Giver of glory with praise and song.

The second fast for the people of Britain   55
is to be observed with equal praise
during Easter-time, and is observed
in the week which comes after
the Sunday that across the wide land
priests call the day of Pentecost,   60
in the month, so it seems to me,
of the year that one calls June.

The third fast is likewise appointed
for the sons of men in all situations
throughout the earth, in the dear hall,   65
to celebrate with bright song,
in the week that is before
the equinox day for the children of men,
in the month, as was said to me,
that one calls September.   70

We ought to observe the fourth fast
in the week that is complete before
our Lord's birth, and in the same time
we ought to confess the King of glory
with hidden words and deeds, with all our hearts,   75
as prince of all earthly things,
as He has always been, and ask the honored
beloved Lord of all people for life.

During these fasts, the fourth day
and sixth, and the seventh following,   80
are for giving glory to the Lord of life,
and observing just as books prescribe;
before the ninth hour[1] there is nobody,

---

1   *before the ninth hour* In popular reckoning the day was reckoned as consisting of two
    twelve-hour periods, one of day and one of night, counted from sunrise and sunset. The
    "first hour" of the day is sunrise, so the "ninth hour" would be around mid-afternoon.

except one afflicted by illness,
who may taste of food or drink before,   85
so the decree of books deems proper.

If Bretons or Franks, come from the south,
should ever come to you and say
that you ought to observe here on earth
any precept which Moses once taught the people,   90
never assent or agree to that,
but observe that same rule that came from the south
from Gregory, the guardian
of the Roman people, pope of men.

For he himself ordained and arranged   95
the services and seasons of fasting
for ministry; we still now willingly
follow these throughout England.
Just as he himself established from the throne
of Saint Peter, priests afterwards   100
have taught the same for a long time,
and you ought not ever to follow another.

We also hold a forty-day fast
before the resurrection of our Lord,
which the nations now call Lent,   105
and that was first begun by the good earl,
the glorious Moses, before he climbed the mountain;
he kept that fast for forty days
and nights together, and he tasted nothing
before he received the Lord's dear law.   110

The Lord himself, surrounded by fire,
gave him the glorious skill of books
inscribed by His own holy hands,
told him to teach and proclaim to the people
the wisdom of the ages as a sign to all   115
that with fasting we may find peace
and the deep mysteries of the dear Lord,

which we proclaim to all people everywhere
if the Lord will bestow on us any of its benefits.

Later Elijah, the glorious earl,   120
received a share of food in the desert
where the Lord's angel arranged for him
feast-bread and fresh water
and by that morsel he was made strong
and able to fast for forty days   125
and nights together; he tasted nothing
before he ascended Mount Horeb, sanctified.

Let us now rightly regard this mystery—
that the glorious thane did not have power
to make the ascent up to the summit   130
before he was given that feast by an angel.
We are in the desert, alone in a wasteland,
away from all joys of the bliss of glory,
now is our hour of need, holy Lord!
How can we climb your glorious mountain?   135

Those who teach the Lord's word with their works
are numbered among the angels on earth.
We eagerly accept that dear food—
our sustenance is the Savior's teaching;
so let us fast for our sinful deeds   140
with abstinence here in our life on earth,
so that we might climb the glorious mountain
as the ancient Elijah did long ago.

We ought to consider how this holy saint
departed this earthly place to seek glory;   145
a fiery chariot with four splendid
proud steeds carried him on his path
to Paradise, where Christ the Savior
has promised us a home with bliss,
if we perform the fast here for our sins   150
and seek out our heavenly homeland.

In the end it was Christ the Savior,
Heaven's holy guardian, who helped and taught us.
He let himself be washed in that precious stream,
the bath of baptism, though set apart from sin,   155
and he refused food for forty days
and nights as well, though by no means guilty,
to teach the people that they, in Lent,
should observe the fast for exactly forty days.

In that vast wilderness Christ's adversary,   160
old and proud, tempted him there;
he saw the glorious Lord in the likeness of a man
and began to scheme, mindful of sin,
how he might shoot his sharp arrows
into that body; there was no sin in that,   165
but the bringer of affliction got behind
and there the angels sought out their lord.

O man of sinful mind, if the master of torment
dares to tempt you, as he did Christ,
the glorious God of Hosts, free from stain,   170
he cannot shoot anything at all inside
if his eyes find no sin-target at which to aim,
but he will skulk away behind you,
and holy angels of mercy will always help you,
if you have walked in the way of the Lord.   175

We have now noted how the great ones
formerly held the fast for forty days,
and we command, through the man of God,
that every one who dwells on the earth
before the resurrection of our Lord   180
hold the fast for forty whole days
until the ninth hour, and he should not enjoy
flesh nor sins, lest he be found guilty.

Priests are supposed to sing the mass
every day, and ask the Lord   185

in their fasting that He be a friend
to people on earth; they in turn ought to tell
every one of their sins to the priest
and amend their darkness with deeds
of words and works, and almsgiving,   190
to make glad the Lord of glory.

Then is much need among many people
that the priests themselves should not sin,
nor lie too firmly fixed in their faults.
Who could intercede for a servant   195
with an honorable lord, if he has earlier
bitterly angered him, and makes no amends,
but angers and offends his master
and repeats it daily with his deeds?

If the priest does not know how to keep himself   200
in upright ways for fear of the Lord,
now you, man of the people,[1] pay no heed
to the sins the ordained man might commit,
but you ought to follow with eager heart
and righteousness the rules he teaches rightly,   205
let him drink muddy water, but let the day-bright
water—the teaching of glory—do you good.

But, heavy with sorrow, I myself can say
how the priests perform new outrages,
every day they anger the Lord   210
and with envy and malice lead astray
any man of the folk who will follow them.
As soon as they've sung mass in the morning
they are consumed with thirst, compelled
to tear off through the streets after a bartender.   215

---

1   *man of the people*   The expression *folces man* used here and elsewhere in the poem seems to
    mean a lay person as opposed to a priest or monk.

Lo! They begin to lie, falsely,
and often lead the bar's server astray;
they say that he, without sin, could give them
oysters to eat and choice wine
in the morning—it seems to me   220
that a dog or wolf keeps the same kind
of way in the world: they don't hesitate
when they fall to their food, lacking self-control.

Sitting there, they start to feel sated,
besotted, they bless the wine as it flows,   225
say "Good life!" again and again,
say that anyone who's tired might take
a measure of wine after he hears mass,
and eat oysters as well as other
fish of the sea....[1]   230

---

1 *fish of the sea....* The ending of the poem is lost.

Two Poems from MS Junius 11

Exodus and *Daniel*

MS Junius 11 in the Bodleian Library at Oxford, written around the year 1000 (or perhaps a generation earlier), contains four poems on biblical subjects called by modern editors *Genesis*, *Exodus*, *Daniel*, and *Christ and Satan*. These were composed by different authors in different places and times, but collected and arranged in one volume by a compiler some time before Junius 11 was made; Junius 11 is a copy of that collection. The manuscript is unique among Old English poetic manuscripts for containing a series of illustrations—about 50 are included in *Genesis*, and blank spaces have been left for almost 90 more in *Exodus* and *Daniel*. It is not known why this elaborate program of illustration was not completed—or for that matter why it was begun, since no other poem in Old English has illustrations. Scholars agree that the poems in Junius 11 were brought together deliberately to be read as a sequence. The manuscript's compilers, like modern editors, followed a design to make meaning by their arrangement of the texts, although the last poem, *Christ and Satan*, may have been an addition or afterthought. Their plan seems to have been to present a poetic outline of salvation history from Satan's fall to the Last Judgment; their model may have been the readings at the liturgy for the Easter Vigil or short works by Augustine and other church fathers.

The subject-matter of these poems is similar to the body of work which Bede ascribes to the poet Cædmon in his *Ecclesiastical History* IV.23; this led early readers of Junius 11 to attribute the whole collection to Cædmon, but it is now generally recognized that the four poems are so different in style that they could not have been written by the same person. The poem *Genesis* begins the manuscript; it is 2936 lines long, and taking into account the leaves now missing from the manuscript, was probably originally as long as *Beowulf*. It retells selected stories from Genesis 1-22, beginning (like Milton's *Paradise Lost*) with the fall of the rebel angels and concluding (presumably, since the ending is lost) with the story of Abraham's sacrifice of his son Isaac. The poem recounts the biblical narrative in the style of traditional heroic verse, with the formulaic language of battles and laments; Cain, for example, is called a "friendless exile" and Abraham a "brave battle-leader." Lines 235-851 of *Genesis* are dramatically unlike the rest of the poem; this section, called *Genesis B* by modern readers, is translated from an Old Saxon poem about the temptation and fall of Adam and Eve and has been inserted into the surrounding poem. *Christ and Satan*, at the end of the manuscript, has little in common with the other poems in Junius 11; it is not from an Old Testament source and no room has been left for illustrations. It tells of the fall of the rebel angels and Satan's lamentations in Hell, the Harrowing of Hell, and Christ's temptation by Satan in the desert.

FURTHER READING

Anlezark, Daniel. *Old Testament Narratives*. Dumbarton Oaks Medieval Library 7. Cambridge, MA: Harvard University Press, 2011.

Hall, J.R. "The Old English Epic of Redemption: The Theological Unity of MS Junius 11." *The Poems of MS Junius 11: Basic Readings*. Ed. R. M. Liuzza. Basic Readings in Anglo-Saxon England 8. New York: Routledge, 2002. 20-68.

Karkov, Catherine E. *Text and Picture in Anglo-Saxon England: Narrative Strategies in the Junius 11 Manuscript*. Cambridge Studies in Anglo-Saxon England 31. Cambridge and New York: Cambridge University Press, 2001.

Remley, Paul G. *Old English Biblical Verse: Studies in "Genesis," "Exodus," and "Daniel."* Cambridge Studies in Anglo-Saxon England 16. Cambridge and New York: Cambridge University Press, 1996.

Exodus

The focus of *Exodus* is on one episode from the biblical story of Moses, the crossing of the Red Sea, but the poet emphasizes the story's typological associations with the Harrowing of Hell and with baptism; its themes and structure have been plausibly connected to the Easter Vigil liturgy. In this way the poem manages to be both more and less than the biblical Book of Exodus. It is also a poem of strenuous energy and sweeping action, very much a representative—some would say the best example in Old English—of the heroic style. Drawing on the traditional language of heroic poetry, the poem depicts the Israelites who fled with Moses from the wrath of Pharaoh as a proud triumphant army ready to march into battle. When Pharaoh's army is drowned in the sea, the sea itself is described as a warrior, fighting a divine battle against the enemies of God. At other times the Israelites in the desert are described as sailors and seafarers—appropriately enough, for they will soon be crossing the sea to a new land. In these ways, perhaps, the Anglo-Saxons found a mirror of their own experience, since they too were seafarers and migrants, conquerors of a new land across the ocean. In this sense the poem's English audience might see it as a kind of self-portrait.

Exodus contains some of the most dazzlingly inventive language of any Old English poem. It is full of metaphoric energy, exuberant wordplay, and sound patterning; in some places its syntax is lively to the point of incoherence. It is a notoriously dense and difficult poem, apparently not well preserved—there are gaps in the text, and some passages may be out of sequence—and the same energy that makes the poem's language so exciting and inventive and its narrative so powerful and surprising occasionally makes it difficult to recognize errors in the text, let alone correct them. The translation is fairly loose in some passages where the text does not make perfect sense; in a few places the translation reflects the obscurity of the original.

SOURCE

Oxford, Bodleian Library MS Junius 11, pp. 143-71.

EDITION

P.J. Lucas, *Exodus* (Exeter: University of Exeter Press, 1977; 2nd ed. 1994).[1]

FURTHER READING

Anlezark, Daniel. "Connecting the Patriarchs: Noah and Abraham in the Old English *Exodus*." *JEGP* 104 (2005): 171-88.

Earl, J.W. "Christian Tradition in the Old English *Exodus*." *The Poems of MS Junius 11: Basic Readings*. Ed. R.M. Liuzza. Basic Readings in Anglo-Saxon England 8. New York: Routledge, 2002. 137-72.

Frank, Roberta. "What Kind of Poetry Is *Exodus*?" *Germania: Comparative Studies in the Old Germanic Languages and Literatures*. Ed. Daniel G. Calder and T. Craig Christy. Woodbridge and Wolfeboro, NH: D.S. Brewer, 1988. 191-205.

Listen! far and wide throughout the world
we have learned how the laws of Moses,
a marvelous code, were proclaimed to men—
a happy reward in heaven above
for every blessed soul's hard struggle,   5
a lasting counsel for all the living,
heavenly life—let him hear who will!

He was exalted in the wilderness, where
the Lord of Hosts, the righteous King,
endowed him with His own power   10
and put mighty deeds into his hands.
Beloved of God, lord of his people,
canny and wise, commander of armies,
a famous leader—but Pharaoh, God's enemy,
he bound with a rod, and all his race.   15

---

1   The translation takes some liberties with Lucas's punctuation, emendations, and proposed readings. For advice and assistance in this translation I am grateful to J.R. Hall, Anne Klinck, and Eileen Joy. They will recognize many of their corrections and suggestions in the lines below; other readers should understand that any errors or inadequacies that remain are the translator's own.

There the God of triumph entrusted and gave
the lives of his kinsmen to that brave leader,
and a habitation in their homeland to Abraham's sons.
Great was the reward, and loyal the Lord,
who gave strength to his arms against the enemies' terror;   20
he conquered many a kingdom on the battlefield
and took dominion over many tribes.[1] In that first time
that the God of Hosts addressed him,[2]
He told him in words many wonderful truths,
how the wise Lord wrought the world,   25
the orb of the earth and the sky above,
established them in glory—and His own name too,
which the sons of men had never known,
wise Patriarchs, though they knew many things.

Afterwards, when he had strengthened and exalted   30
the prince of his people with true powers
for his exodus, enemy of Pharaoh,
then that nation's army was soon drenched
in death, ancient plagues, and the overthrow
of too many of those treasure-hoarders—   35
their lamentation arose, their hall-joys slaughtered,
their wealth plundered.[3] Those wicked oppressors
He annihilated at midnight, many first-born sons,
the city-guards slain. A killer stalked widely,
choked the land with the corpses of the dead,   40
hostile persecutor of the people—and the host went forth.
There was widespread weeping, few worldly joys,
the laughter-smiths' hands were locked shut

---

1   *took dominion over many tribes*   This refers perhaps to a future time when the Hebrews
    settled in the land of Canaan and displaced the inhabitants.
2   *the God of Hosts addressed him*   In the wilderness, in the form of a burning bush, Exodus
    ch. 3.
3   *their wealth plundered*   A complex and multivalent passage; "treasure," "hall-joys," and
    "wealth" all refer to the first-born sons of the Egyptians, but they give the impression that
    the Hebrews somehow conquered them in battle and took possession of their wealth as well,
    as Scyld Scefing conquers his enemies at the beginning of *Beowulf.*

when the people were allowed to depart on their
harsh journey,[1] the fiend and his hellish host 45
were despoiled—Heaven descended,
and their demon idols fell. A most famous day
across the earth it was, when that multitude set out;
so they suffered captivity for many years,
the accursed people of Egypt, 50
because they imagined they could ever hold back
the people of Moses, if the Maker had allowed them,
from their beloved and long-awaited journey.

    The army was eager, and bold their leader,
a brave commander of that nation of kinsmen. 55
He passed with his people through many desert lands,
the habitations of hostile men,
narrow passes, unknown paths,
until they bore their arms among the fierce borderers
whose lands lay shrouded in a cover of clouds,[2] 60
their high mountain dwellings. Moses led
his army past these, through many border-lands.

    Then two nights after they had escaped their enemies,
He commanded that glorious hero[3] to encamp
with all their host around the fortress of Etham, 65
with great clamor and resounding noise,
a mighty force among those borderlands.
Danger pushed their path northward—
to the south, they knew, lay the Sun-dwellers' land,[4]

---

1   *allowed to depart on their harsh journey* The blurring of the Egyptians' death and the
    Israelites' exodus throughout this passage is a complex *double entendre*: the Hebrews are
    reluctantly set free, and the first-born children are sent to their death. The description recalls
    the legends of Christ's Harrowing of Hell (undertaken between the Crucifixion and the
    Resurrection to rescue the souls of the righteous from their imprisonment in Hell), referred
    to in *The Dream of the Rood*.
2   *in a cover of clouds* Though geographically imprecise, this is probably a reference to the
    Nubians, whose name was thought to derive from Lat. *nubes* "clouds."
3   *He commanded that glorious hero* I.e., God commanded Moses.
4   *Sun-dwellers' land* Old English *sigelwara*, usually applied to the Ethiopians, though they
    are not mentioned in the biblical story of the Exodus.

the sunburnt hillsides of a people browned 70
by the hot coals of heaven. There Holy God
shielded the people from the scorching heat:
spread a canopy over the searing sky,
hung a holy veil in the burning air.[1]
A cloud spread broad across the sky 75
evenly divided earth and heaven,
went before that company, and heaven's bright fires
were quenched in its heat. The host, most happy people,
marveled at it. The sheltering day-shield
glided across the heavens; wise God 80
unfurled a sail across the course of the sun
whose halyards none could know
nor could the sailyard be seen
by any earth-dweller, no matter how skilled,
how that greatest of tabernacles was tied, 85
when he had honored with glory
those faithful people. The third encampment
was a comfort to them; the army observed
how those holy sails billowed above,
radiant miracle aloft; the multitude of Israel, 90
that people, saw in that place how the Lord,
the Lord of hosts himself, had come to make camp.
Before them headed the fire and cloud
in the bright sky, twin beams,
each of them equally shared 95
in the high service of the Holy Spirit,
by day and night on the daring journey.

Then, as I've heard, the next morning,
that bold-hearted people raised their brave trumpets,
heralds of glory. The group all arose, 100
a mighty army eager to set out
as Moses, their great leader, commanded them,
the people of God. Going before them they saw

---

1   *a holy veil in the burning air*   This is the pillar of cloud described in Exodus; its purpose
there is to conceal the Hebrews from their pursuers and protect them from the heat.

their life-guide lay out the path of life;
the sky set the course, the sailors followed   105
on the sea-path.[1] The people were joyful,
loud the army's clamor. Each evening arose
a heavenly beacon, second marvelous sign,
wondrously held the setting sun's place
and blazed with light above the people,   110
a gleaming beam. Bright rays
stood blazing above the soldiers,
a shining shield-cover—shadows vanished,
and the deep shades of night could scarcely
stay hidden in their dens. Heaven's candle burned,   115
the new night-watchman had great need
to guard the host, lest the desert horror,
grey heath-stalker, should sever their lives
with the sudden clutch of violent storms.
Their forerunner had fiery locks,   120
bright beams, threatening to burn up
those desert troops with flaming terror,
a blaze of fire on that army, unless
they were brave in heart and obeyed Moses.

The bright troops shone, their shields gleamed,   125
the shield-bearers kept sight of the true path,
the sign above, until the barrier of the sea
at land's end prevented their progress,
their eager advance. Exhausted, they pitched
their camp, refreshed themselves with food   130
served by noble stewards, and restored their strength.
When the trumpets sang, the sailors spread
their field-tents in the hills; this was the fourth camp,
the shield-bearers' rest, by the Red Sea.

---

1   *their life-guide ... on the sea-path*   The "life-guide" is the pillar of cloud; the nautical im-
agery is somewhat disconcerting for the desert passage of the Hebrews from Egypt, but
resonates powerfully in traditional Old English poetry—and will, of course, become more
appropriate when the travelers cross the Red Sea.

Then terrible news arose among the army—   135
inland pursuit. Fear of slaughter
spread among the troops, those exiles awaited
their hostile pursuers, who had long punished
those homeless people with harsh affliction
and woeful oppression. They ignored their pledge,   140
the promise given by the elder Pharaoh ...[1]

＊   ＊   ＊   ＊   ＊

Then he became the custodian of the treasure
of all the Egyptians, and he greatly prospered.
But they forgot all that; the Egyptian nation
grew grim and hostile, did not hesitate at all,   145
carried out crimes against his kinsmen,
stirred up strife and devoured their pledges.
Seething desires surged in their hearts,
mighty passions; they wanted to repay
that good with evil, lies and treachery,   150
so the people of Moses would have paid in blood
for that day's work, if almighty God
had granted success to their mission of destruction.

    The men's spirits began to despair
when they saw surging up from the south   155
the army of Pharaoh advancing forward—
a great forest moving, the cavalry gleaming,
with spears ready, the battle swarming,
shields shining, trumpets sounding,
banners aloft, an army marching across the border.   160
Black birds of prey croaked for carrion, greedy for slaughter
and a feast of corpses, dewy-feathered

---

1 *the elder Pharaoh* There is a gap of perhaps four pages in the manuscript here; the missing
lines apparently recounted how an earlier Pharaoh had given Joseph authority over all Egypt
(Genesis 41), but when a new Pharaoh arose who knew nothing of Joseph, the oppression
of the Israelites began (Exodus 1). The passage, emphasizing the treachery of the Egyptians,
is a dramatic delaying device between the first mention of their pursuit and their visible
approach.

dark Furies.[1] The wolves howled
a grim evening-song, eager for prey,   165
pitiless beasts, bold scavengers, followed
in their tracks, waiting the warriors' fall.
These border-stalkers bayed in the black of night,
doomed souls grew faint as the people despaired.

At times proud thanes from the host   170
measured the miles with their galloping horses;
there the proud king, prince of men,
rode before the border-troop brandishing the standard;
the warriors' warlord fastened his helmet,
strapped on his chin-guard as the standard gleamed,   175
ready for battle, he rattled his war-coat,
commanded his chosen troops to stand fast
and hold their formation. The friends[2] watched
the approach of that land-host with eyes full of hate.

Around him[3] roved fearless warriors,   180
grey sword-wolves who welcomed battle
with a lust for combat, loyal to their leader.
For the host, he himself had chosen
from that nation two thousand most noble,
and all were kings and royal kinsmen   185
in the old order, esteemed for their ancestry:
each of them in turn had led forth
each and every male soldier
he was able to find on that occasion.
All the kings of that country were there   190
together in formation; the well-known trumpet

---

1   *dark Furies*   The meter is defective here but no proposed solution is entirely satisfactory.
    The word translated here as "Furies" is *wælceasega*, "chooser of the slain," a word cognate
    with the "Valkyrie" of Norse mythology but also used in Old English to gloss classical
    figures like the Fates and Furies, and to describe metaphorically the carrion birds that circle
    above the battlefield.
2   *The friends*   The Israelites.
3   *him*   Pharaoh.

announced among the throng where the young men,
a horde of warriors, should bear their weapons.

And so those dark legions surged forward,
foe upon foe, a vast multitude of the nation's might,   195
thousands at a time, eager to advance.
They meant with their mighty troops to attack
the people of Israel at the first light of day,
destroy them with swords to avenge their brothers.
And so there was weeping and wailing in the camps,   200
a grim song at evening, terror spreading;
they put on their war-coats when panic seized them,
and fled the fearful tidings.[1] The enemy was united,
the army war-bright, until the mighty angel
who protected the multitude repelled those proud ones,   205
so that those two enemies were no longer able
to see one another: their ways were separated.

The exiles experienced a night-long reprieve,
though enemies loomed on either side—
the army or the sea, and no other way out.   210
Giving up hope for their homeland,
they sat among the sloping hills in somber clothing,
expecting sorrow. Watchful, they awaited,
all that company of kinsmen together,
the greater forces, until in the first light of dawn   215
Moses bade the heralds with brass trumpets
to assemble the people, and soldiers to arise,
put on their mail coats and consider their courage,
bear the bright armor, and with banners summon
the war-band to the shore. Swiftly the defenders   220
heeded the battle-call, the host was alerted;
they heard the trumpets, and the sailors hurried
over the hills from their tents, a troop in haste.
Then they assigned twelve troops to stand

---

1 *they put on ... the fearful tidings* Or, "their war-coats weighed them down when panic
seized them, / and bold speeches fled" (Lucas).

against the vicious attack of the advancing enemy,   225
brave-spirited men whose courage was stirred.
In each one, fifty companies were chosen
from the most noble families among the nations,
assembled in battalions to bear arms;
and each hand-picked company of that famous host   230
was composed of ten hundred spear-carriers
and fighting men, gloriously favored—
a warlike host! The army's commanders
did not welcome the weak among their ranks,
the young who were not yet able   235
to defend themselves against the treacherous foe
in the shelter of a shield and a mail-shirt,
or those who had not known a sharp wound
over the edge of a shield, or borne battle-scars
from boasting spear-play. Nor could the old,   240
grey-bearded warriors, hold their own in battle
if their might had diminished among the brave men.
Instead, they selected battalions by their stature,
how their courage would endure honorably
among the people, and how powerfully   245
their skilled hands could grasp a spear.
When the stalwart army was assembled,
eager to advance, the ensign[1] rode on high,
brightest of beams; there they abided
until their guide, glittering above their shields,   250
burst through the gates of the air by the sea.

    Then the herald leapt up before that host,
bold battle-crier, raised up his shield
and ordered the commanders to quiet the army
so all could listen to their leader's speech.   255
That kingdom's guardian wanted to counsel
the hand-picked troops. With his holy voice,
the leader of that host spoke with worthy words:
"Do not be afraid, even though Pharaoh

---

1   *the ensign*   I.e., the pillar of cloud and fire.

has brought a vast army of sword-warriors, 260
countless men. The almighty Lord
intends today, through my hand,
to pay them back for their past deeds,
so that they shall no longer survive
to keep the people of Israel in misery. 265
You will not fear those dead foot-soldiers
in their doomed bodies—their brief lease on life
has come to an end. God's counsel
has fled your heart; I have a better way:
that you should always praise the Prince of glory, 270
pray for the grace of the Lord of Life
and the salvation of victory as you set forth.
It is the eternal God of Abraham,
the Lord of Creation, lofty and powerful,
who guards this host with his almighty hand." 275

Then the lord of the living lifted up his voice
and spoke before the army to all the nation:
"Behold! most beloved of people, now you see
with your own eyes a most awesome wonder,
now with this green rod[1] in my right hand 280
I myself have struck the depths of the sea:
the waves ascend, and swiftly the waters
form a sturdy wall. The ways are dry,
a glistening road, the deep has revealed
its ancient foundations, where no man before, 285
as I have heard tell, has ever traveled,
mottled plains which always remain
forever hidden by the foaming waves.
A south wind, breath of the ocean, has unsealed
the sea's depths, the waves are split, 290
the surf churns out sand. Well I know
that almighty God has shown mercy to you,
happy as in days of old. Now hurry,

---

1 *this green rod* The Old English phrase is *grene tacn*, literally "green (*or* living) sign," which
has occasioned much comment. The phrase may simply be an error for *grene tane* "green
rod" (corresponding to Latin *virga* "rod," the staff of Moses mentioned in Exodus 14.16).

that you may escape the embrace of your enemies,
now that the Ruler has raised up   295
red sea-streams as a sheltering rampart.
The retaining walls of this wondrous wave-road
are fairly raised to the roof of the heavens."

    With these words, all the host arose,
a courageous force. The sea lay calm;   300
upon the sand the hand-picked troops raised
their banners and bright shields. The sea-wall
stood upright alongside the Israelites
for an entire day.[1]
That troop of earls was of one mind,   305
kept their covenant in close embrace—
they did not despise their dear lord's
holy teaching, when his sweet words were still
and his voice silent by their path through the sea.[2]

    The fourth tribe was the first to lead them,   310
an army of men marching through the waves
upon the green sea bed.[3] The soldiers of Judah
hastened alone down that unknown path
before all their brothers. And so almighty God
gave them a great reward for that day's work—   315
glorious deeds of victory were granted to them,
so that later they might have lordship
over kingdoms, and rule their kinsmen.
When they entered the sea they raised their ensign,
a battle-standard high above their shields,   320
among the mass of spears those most lordly men
lifted up a golden lion, bravest of beasts.

---

1 *for an entire day* A half-line is apparently missing here (or after the following line?); vari-
   ous suggestions, none compellingly plausible, have been made to fill the gap, and none is
   adopted here.
2 *his voice silent by their path through the sea* The original is obscure here; this is a guess at its
   probable meaning.
3 *upon the green sea bed* The description of the sea floor as "green" has occasioned much
   debate; elsewhere in Old English poetry the road to Paradise is described as "green," and the
   poem may be pointing towards the moment's typological or allegorical significance.

With it, those warriors would not long suffer
insult or injury from any lord living,
as long as they could lift a spear in battle   325
against any nation. Ahead lay the attack,
hard hand-play, young men brave
in the carnage of weapons, fearless warriors,
bloody wounds and the rush of battle,
the grim grinding of helmets, when Judah advanced.   330

After that army the sailor followed boldly,
the son of Reuben; those sea-dwellers[1]
bore their shields over the salty marsh,
a multitude of men, a mighty legion
went forth fearlessly. In sinful deeds   335
he[2] squandered his lordship, and so he marched
in his beloved's footsteps—his brother had taken
his natural rights as first-born of that nation,
his wealth and status—yet still he was no coward.

After them, among the throng of peoples,   340
the sons of Simeon advanced in troops,
the third tribe. Their banners waving,
the battalion pressed on, spear-points flashing
and shafts gleaming. The glimmer of day
came over the crest of the sea, God's bright beacon,   345
the glorious morning. The multitude went forth
there while one family followed after another,
in iron-clad armies—one man led these,
greatest in might, for which he became famous
on their march—beneath the pillar of cloud,   350
kin after kin; each one observed
the rights of each tribe and the rank of earls,
as Moses instructed them. They had one father,

---

1   *sea-dwellers*   Old English *sæwicingas*, literally "sea-vikings." It is by no means certain that
    the word had any of its later negative connotations in this passage, and a more neutral
    translation (reflecting Old English *wic* "dwelling") is given here.
2   *he*   I.e., Reuben.

a beloved prince, dear to his people,
ancient and wise, who held the land-right;   355
that great patriarch begat a line
of brave noblemen, a holy nation,
the race of Israel, righteous before the Lord.
This is how ancient writers in their wisdom
tell it, who know most about these tribes,   360
each one's lineage, origin and ancestry:

   Over new seas Noah sailed,[1]
glorious prince, together with his three sons,
over the deepest of drenching floods
that had ever come over the earth.   365
He had in his heart a holy faith,
and so he steered over the ocean streams
the greatest treasure-chest[2] I have ever heard tell of.
The wise sea-prince, to save the lives
of all who dwell upon on earth,   370
had reckoned up a lasting remnant,
a first generation, father and mother
of all who bear offspring, more diverse
than men can imagine. Likewise the heroes brought
into the bosom of the ship every kind of seed   375
which men make use of beneath the heavens.

   And so the words of wise men tell us
that the ninth in lineage from Noah
was Abraham's father among that folk.
This is the Abraham to whom the God of angels   380

---

1 *Over new seas Noah sailed*   Many readers and editors have felt the transition to be abrupt,
   and assumed that this passage originally belonged somewhere else. But the nautical imagery
   connects it to the action described in the rest of the poem, and the typological connections
   found in the Easter Vigil liturgy make the linkage of Noah, Abraham, and Moses more
   natural to a medieval reader than it might be to a modern one. The kind of unity found
   here might be thought of as "liturgical" rather than "dramatic," and narrative sequence less
   important than theological significance.
2 *the greatest treasure-chest*   I.e., the ark and its contents, usually identified with the Church
   in medieval readings of Genesis.

gave a new name; and near and far
entrusted the holy tribes into his keeping,
and lordship over nations. He lived in exile.
Later, he led the most beloved of creatures
at the Lord's behest; into the highlands   385
climbed the two kinsmen, up to mount Sion.
They found the Covenant there, gazed on God's glory,
the holy pledge, as men have heard tell.

    In that same place the wise son of David,
glorious king, through the counsel of the prophet   390
later built the temple of the Lord,
a holy shrine, highest and holiest—
the wisest among the world's kingdoms
of all earthly rulers, most renowned among men—
the greatest and most glorious that the sons of men   395
in all nations on earth ever made with their hands.

    To the appointed meeting-place he led his son,
Abraham took Isaac; up blazed the pyre,
most deadly slayer—but he was not doomed to die—[1]
he intended to offer his offspring to the flames,   400
his best of children to the blazing pyre,
his sweet son as a sacrifice for victory,
his only heir upon the earth,
his life's consolation, which he had long awaited
his lasting hope, for the nation's legacy.   405
He made it clear, when he took the child
fast in his hands, and the famous man drew
his ancient heirloom (its edge rasping),
that he did not hold his son's life dearer
than his obedience to the king of Heaven.   410

---

1   *most deadly slayer ... doomed to die* Or "the foremost life-slayer (i.e., Satan) was no happier
for that."

Up he rose,[1]
ready to slay his only son,
still a boy, with his bloody blade,
put his child to the sword, if God had not stopped him;
the bright father would not take the boy   415
as a holy sacrifice, but laid his hands upon him.[2]
Then to restrain him came a voice from the heavens,
a sound of glory, and spoke these words:
"Abraham! do not slay your own child,
your son, with a sword. The truth is known,   420
now that the King of all creation has tested you,
that you have kept your covenant with God,
a firm faith, which shall be a protector
for you all the days of your life
forever and ever, unfailing.   425
Why should the Son of Man need a stronger pledge?
Heaven and earth cannot confine
the words of His glory, wider and broader
than all the ends of the earth can enfold,
the orb of the world and the firmament above,   430
the depths of the sea and the yearning sky.[3]
The King of Angels, God of hosts,
Ruler of destinies, righteous in victory,
swears you an oath by his own life,
that men across the earth, in all their wisdom,   435
will never know how to count the number
of all your tribe and offspring,
shield-bearing warriors, nor say it truly
unless someone might grow so wise in spirit
that he alone might reckon the number   440
of stones on the earth, stars in the heavens,

---

1   *Up he rose*   A half-line is usually assumed to be missing here, but (as at line 304) the text
    makes sense as it stands, so nothing has been invented to fill the possible gap.
2   *the bright father ... laid his hands upon him*   "Father" and "his" refer equally to Moses and
    to God.
3   *the yearning sky*   It is not clear why the sky is described as *geomre* "yearning, sad, dreary"
    at this particular moment—the phrase may be traditional in origin, but it does not occur
    elsewhere in Old English poetry.

the sands of the sea-swell's salty waves;
But your people, most noble of nations,
free-born of their father, will occupy
the land of Canaan, between the two seas   445
even unto the borders of Egypt ..."[1]

*   *   *   *   *

All that folk[2] fell into a panic; fear of the flood
filled their wretched hearts, and the sea wreaked death.
The steep sea-slopes were soaked with blood,
churning with gore, chaos was in the waves,   450
the water full of weapons, a death-mist arose.
The Egyptians were thrown into retreat:
they fled terrified, felt sudden fear,
cowards, deserters, they sought out their homes—
their boasts were milder. The wild tossing waves   455
darkened over them again: none of that army
came home again, but fate cut off their retreat
and locked them in the waves. Where a road lay before,
the ocean raged, that host was overwhelmed,
the sea flowed forth. A storm arose   460
up to high heaven, a great outcry of despair,
the enemies shrieked, the sky grew dark
with doomed voices,[3] the flood was blood-muddy.
The shield-walls were shattered, and the greatest of sea-deaths
lashed the sky; those proud kings and their legions   465
were slain. Their screams grew silent,
the waves at an end; war-shields gleamed.
High above those heroes rushed a wall of water,

---

1   *the borders of Egypt*   A page is missing in the manuscript here; it probably would have told
    the story found in Exodus 14.23-26—the people of Israel cross the Red Sea; the Egyptians
    pursue them; when Moses stretches out his hand the sea returns to its former place and the
    army of Pharaoh is destroyed.

2   *that folk*   The Egyptians.

3   *A storm arose ... doomed voices*   Some critics have interpreted these lines differently, but it
    seems best to read the passage as an example (by no means the only one in Old English po-
    etry) of synesthesia—the noise of the drowning army is described as a storm which darkens
    the sky.

a mighty sea-stream. That multitude was caught
fast in death's fetters, deprived of escape,   470
snagged in their armor. The sands awaited
their ordained fate, when the flowing waves,
the ice-cold sea, the salty billows,
bare bringer of doom, driven from its course
might come seeking again its ancient bed,   475
an angry wandering spirit smiting his enemies.
With blood was the blue air defiled,
the flood threatened bloody terror wild
on the seafarers' march, while the true Maker
revealed his fury through the hand of Moses.   480
Ravaging, seething, the surging flood swept them away
in its deadly clutches; doomed men dropped,
the sea fell upon the land, the sky was shaken.
The ramparts gave way, the waves burst,
the sea-columns melted, when the Mighty one,   485
Heavenly guardian, struck with His holy hand
those wretched warriors of a proud nation—[1]
no restraining the course of the saving waters,
the might of the sea-streams; He wrecked the multitudes
in shrieking terror. The raging ocean   490
towered high, glided over them, terror mounted,
murderous waves gushed, and God's handiwork,
foamy-bosomed, fell upon the battle-path
from the heights of heaven; the flood's guardian
struck the unprotected way with an ancient sword,   495
so that at the death-blow the legions slept,
a sinful throng, fast shut in,
lost their lives, an army flood-pale,
when they were buried under the brown water,
the proud and mighty waves.[2] The force all fell,   500

---

1 *The ramparts gave way ... proud nation* These lines are difficult and no single solution
  is entirely satisfactory; the translation is fairly loose. The vivid impressionistic style of the
  passage seems almost to have gone out of control, and the chaos of the scene described has
  shaken the syntax of the description itself.
2 *an army flood-pale ... mighty waves* These lines are difficult and this translation is conjec-
  tural.

the afflicting ones, the legions of Egypt,
Pharaoh and all his army. God's adversary
quickly found as he sank to the sea-floor
that the Guardian of the waves was stronger than he—
angry and enraged, he had intended to settle   505
the battle in a deadly embrace. For that day's work
the Egyptians received an overwhelming reward,
for none of that army, vast beyond number,
ever survived to return home again
to tell of his fate, or proclaim in the cities   510
the worst tidings to the wives of those warriors,
the fall of their treasure's protectors,
but a mighty sea-death swallowed their legions
and their heralds with them. He who has power
drained the boasts of men—they fought against God.   515

    Then Moses, man of noble virtue,
gave a holy speech on the shore of the sea,
spoke eternal wisdom to the Israelites
and deep counsel. Even now the nations speak
of that day's work,[1] discover in Scripture   520
every law which the Lord, in words of truth,
ordained for them on that journey.
If the interpreter of Life will unlock,
the body's Guardian radiant in the breast,
these expansive blessings with the keys of the spirit,   525
the mysteries will be clear and good counsel will emerge,
for it has words of wisdom in its keeping,
and earnestly seeks to instruct our heart
so we will not lack for fellowship with God,
the Maker's mercy. He will enlighten us even more;   530
for now, scholars inform us of the better
and more lasting joys of heaven. Here pleasure fades,
cursed with sin, allotted to exiles,
a wretched time of waiting. Homeless,

---

1 *Even now ... that day's work* Lines 519-48 have struck many critics as a later addition
to the poem; they interrupt the speech of Moses (which resumes at 549) and may well be
misplaced here, but no compelling alternative to the existing text has been proposed.

we anxiously inhabit this guest-house, 535
mourning in spirit, mindful of the house of pain
fast under the earth, a place of fire and worms,
the den of every kind of evil ever open,
while here those arch-thieves divide up their domain,
old age and early death. The day of reckoning draws near, 540
greatest of all glories, upon the earth,
a day marked by deeds: in the meeting-place
the Lord himself will judge the multitude,
when he will lead into heaven above
the souls of the righteous, blessed spirits, 545
where there is light and life and the joy of bliss.
In delight that troop will praise the Lord,
King of Glory, God of hosts, for all eternity.

And so he spoke, mindful of wise counsel,
mildest of men made strong in might, 550
in a loud voice—awaiting their leader's will
the army stood silent, perceived that wonder,
his brave words of salvation. He said to the multitude:
"Mighty is this multitude, great our Commander,
the strongest of supports who guides our journey. 555
He has given over to us the tribes of Canaan,
their cities and treasures and spacious kingdoms;
he will now fulfill what he long ago promised
with sworn oaths, the Lord of Angels,
to our fathers' generations in ancient days, 560
if you will only hold His holy precepts,
that you will overcome each of your enemies
and hold, rich in victory, the feast-halls of heroes
between the two seas: great will be your glory."

At these words the whole host was glad, 565
trumpets of victory sounded, standards were raised
to the lovely sound. The folk had reached land;
the pillar of glory had guided the host,
the holy troop, under God's protection.
The shield-warriors exulted that they had escaped alive 570

from the power of their enemies, though they had passed
    boldly
under the roof of the waves, and seen the walls standing;
the sea through which they had borne their armor seemed
    brimming blood.
They rejoiced with war-songs when they escaped that army;
the battalions and legions lifted up a loud voice,   575
gave praise to God, raised a song of glory
for that day's work. The women opposite them,
greatest of gatherings, chanted a battle anthem
with voiced raised, sang of all these many wonders.
Then it was easy to see the African woman,[1]   580
adorned with gold at the edge of the sea,
her hands grasping neck-adornments;
they rejoiced, seeing their reward,
received the spoils of war[2]—their bondage was released.
They divided up the sea's leavings, ancient treasures,   585
along the shore by each tribe's ensign,
robes and shields; they divided rightly
gold and good cloth, the treasures of Joseph,
glorious possessions of men, whose guardians lay,
greatest of armies, fast in the arms of death.   590

---

1   *the African woman* Perhaps Zipporah, Moses' Ethiopian wife (Numbers 12.1), who fig-
ures in medieval exegesis as an image of the Christian church.

2   *the spoils of war* I.e., the armor and jewels of the drowned Egyptian army, washed up on
the shores of the Red Sea.

Daniel

Daniel follows *Exodus* in MS Junius 11 Book. The poem covers only the first part of the biblical book of Daniel—a sprawling work of mystical prophecy and apocalyptic history—and focuses instead on a series of illustrations of the consequences of pride. It tells how the Israelites turned to sin and were conquered by the Babylonians, how some held fast to their faith in exile, and how the proud Babylonian kings Nebuchadnezzar and his son Belshazzar (OE *Nabochodonossor* and *Baldazar*) fared in their reigns. The poem omits much biblical material to make the story a straightforward morality tale of sin and swift punishment, along with some deeply-felt expressions of loss and grief.

The title character Daniel has a fairly marginal role in the main action of the poem; the central interest of the poem is in the pride and humiliation of the great Babylonian king Nebuchadnezzar, and in the ordeal of the three youths Annanias, Azarias, and Mishael in the fiery furnace. So central is this story to the poem that it is, basically, told twice—though in this respect the poem mirrors the Latin Vulgate book of Daniel, which also explains the rescue of the three youths twice, first by divine grace and then by an angel. The long praise-songs of Azarias (279-332) and of the three youths in the furnace (362-408) were also used in the liturgy, and much of this section of the poem is found in a different version, somewhat expanded, in a poem in the Exeter Book known as *Azarias*.

The poem is divided into sections in the manuscript, numbered from L to LV (some numbers are omitted). These are probably scribal rather than authorial, and indicate that the poems *Genesis*, *Exodus*, and *Daniel* were in some respects meant to be read as one long sequence. The sections are numbered I-VI here. As elsewhere in the Junius 11 manuscript, spaces have been left for illustrations, but none have been added. Because pages are missing here and there in the Junius manuscript, the poem has some gaps, and the ending may be lost—the Babylonian king Belshazzar has seen the writing on the wall, and Daniel is called in to interpret it; he does not say what the writing means, but condemns the king and his court for their drunken abuse of the sacred vessels pillaged from the Jerusalem temple. The suggestion is that Belshazzar—another example of pride and punishment—will be brought low like his father Nebuchadnezzar before him, but the poem ends abruptly before his fall, and perhaps his repentance, are depicted. The poem's editor considered that "it is reasonable to assume that *Daniel* ends as its author intended it to end" (Farrell, *Daniel and Azarias*, p. 6), but it is hard to imagine that the author would have passed up another chance to depict a proud king humbled by God, as Belshazzar is in the Bible (Daniel 5.29-31).

SOURCE

Oxford, Bodleian Library MS Junius 11, pp. 173-212.

EDITION

R.T. Farrell, ed. *Daniel and Azarias*. Methuen's Old English Library. London: Methuen; New York: Harper and Row, 1974.

FURTHER READING

Anderson, Earl. "Style and Theme in the Old English *Daniel*." *The Poems of MS Junius 11: Basic Readings*. Ed. R.M. Liuzza. Basic Readings in Anglo-Saxon England 8. New York: Routledge, 2002. 229-60.

Finnegan, Robert Emmett. "The Old English *Daniel*: The King and His City." *NM* 85 (1984): 194-211.

Harbus, Antonina. "Nebuchadnezzar's Dreams in the Old English *Daniel*." *ES* 75 (1994): 489-508.

Portnoy, Phyllis. "'Remnant' and Ritual: The Place of *Daniel* and *Christ and Satan* in the Junius Epic." *ES* 75 (1994): 408-22.

I

The Hebrews, I've heard, lived a blessed life
in Jerusalem, shared their gold-hoard,
held that kingdom; it was their inheritance,
for by the Maker's might into Moses' hand
an army was given, a great many warriors,   5
and they fared forth from Egypt,
a mighty multitude. That was a bold people!

While they were allowed to rule that land,
they held their cities and had shining wealth;
while they kept their father's covenant   10
among themselves, their shepherd was God,
Heaven's guardian, the holy Lord,
Ruler of glory. He gave to that host
courage and strength, the Creator of all,
so that they always conquered other peoples,   15
took the lives of leaders who were disloyal to them,
until pride took possession of them at their feasting,
with devilish deeds and drunken thoughts.
Then at once they left the law's teaching,
the lordship of the Maker—no man should   20
sunder the love in his soul from God.

   Then I saw that nation stray into error,
the people of Israel doing evil
and committing sins—that saddened God!
Often he sent holy souls to that people   25
to teach them, Heaven's protector;
they offered wisdom to that host.
They trusted the truth of that wisdom
for a little while, until a longing
for earthly pleasures cheated them of eternal counsel,   30
so that in the end they all abandoned
the decrees of God, and chose the devil's craftiness.

   Then the Prince of that people grew fierce,
unfaithful to the folk he had prospered.
In the beginning He had guided them, those who   35
had at first been dearest of mankind to their maker,
most favored people, most loved by the Lord;
he had shown them a path to their lofty city,[1]
led those wandering exiles to their native land
where Salem stood, sealed with battlements   40

---

1   *had shown them ... lofty city*   This is a single half-line without a partner; it is also hypermet-
    ric, having more than the usual two stresses.

and ringed with walls. There wizards ventured
towards the city, the Chaldean people,[1]
where the wealth of Israel was kept,
hidden by fortifications—a host rose up against them,
a mighty war-troop, thirsty for murder.   45

The prince of Babylon, Nebuchadnezzar,
lord of men, in deadly malice
stirred up this slaughter from his stronghold;
he began to search the thoughts of his heart
how he most easily might press against   50
the Israelites with a fierce attack.
He summoned then from south and north
savage legions, and surged westward
with an army of heathen kings to that high city.
Those who looked after Israel's homeland   55
had love and prosperity while the Lord allowed it!

Then that race of ancient enemies, as I've heard,
sacked the city—those soldiers, unbelievers,
plundered that glorious hall of its red gold,
stole treasure and silver from Solomon's temple.   60
They robbed the riches from the ruined buildings,
all that those noble earls should have possessed,
until they had destroyed every one of the cities
which had stood as sanctuaries for that people.
They took as spoils the hoarded treasure,   65
whatever they could find of cash and cattle,[2]
and then returned with these possessions;
they led as well on the long journey
the people of Israel, on the eastward road
to Babylon, a host beyond number,   70
these heroes into the hands of heathen judgment.
Nebuchadnezzar showed no mercy

---

1   *the Chaldean people*   The Chaldeans had a widespread reputation in the ancient and medieval world as magicians.

2   *cash and cattle*   The manuscript reading *fea and freos* has been interpreted to mean "cattle and princes." Here the reading *fea and feos*, "property and cattle" is preferred.

to the children of Israel who survived his sword,
but instead forced them to be his slaves.
He sent then a great host of his thanes,   75
told his troops to travel westward
so that they might hold that land for him,
that desolate home, in place of the Hebrews.

    Then he ordered his officials to seek out
throughout the wretched remnant of the Israelites   80
which of those youths were wisest
in books of the law, of those he had brought there.
He wanted those young men to master that skill
that they might tell them the thoughts of their mind,
but not by any means so that he would remember   85
to be thankful to God for all the gifts
which the Lord had lavished upon him.
There they found three godly-wise
and lordly youths, firm in the law,
young and devout from a virtuous line: 90
one was Annanias, another Azarias,
the third Mishael, chosen by the Maker.
Hardy and thoughtful, these three
came to their prince, where the heathen king
sat lusting for pomp in his Chaldean stronghold.   95
When the men of the Hebrews had to show wisdom
to the proud one, they made known with words
their high learning with a holy heart;
then the prince ordered his officers,
ruler of Babylon, bold-minded king,   100
that his leaders should, on pain of their lives,
see that there be for the three young men
no lack of food or clothing as long as they lived.

II

    At that time the proud prince of Babylon
was mighty in renown across this middle-earth,   105
a terror to the sons of men; he scorned the law,

and lived arrogantly in every way.
And then to the sovereign in his first slumber,
when the prince of the land had lain down to rest,
there came hurtling into his heart a half-seen dream,   110
how the world was to be wondrously formed
into a new creation, not like the former age.
The truth was shown to him in his sleep
that cruelly an end should come about
for every empire, and all earthly joy.[1]   115
Then the wolf-hearted ruler of Babylon awoke
from his wine-drunk sleep with no blithe spirit,
but dread crept upon him from his haunting dream,
though he could not recall what his vision had been.

He ordered that those from among his people   120
most skilled in magic be summoned together,
and asked that assembly what his dream had been,
while speech-bearing men lay sleeping.
He was stricken with strange terror,
for he knew neither the words nor the purpose   125
of his dream; yet he ordered them to declare it to him.
Then uneasily they answered him,
those sorcerers—their skill was not sufficient
to explain the dream to the king:
"How can we comprehend, lord, such a hidden thing   130
in your heart, as how you dreamed,
or how wisdom revealed the workings of fate,

---

1   *and all earthly joy*   The dream is described in Daniel 2.31-35: "You were looking, O king, and lo! there was a great statue. This statue was huge, its brilliance extraordinary; it was standing before you, and its appearance was frightening. The head of that statue was of fine gold, its chest and arms of silver, its middle and thighs of bronze, its legs of iron, its feet partly of iron and partly of clay. As you looked on, a stone was cut out, not by human hands, and it struck the statue on its feet of iron and clay and broke them in pieces. Then the iron, the clay, the bronze, the silver, and the gold, were all broken in pieces and became like the chaff of the summer threshing floors; and the wind carried them away, so that not a trace of them could be found. But the stone that struck the statue became a great mountain and filled the whole earth" (New Revised Standard Version translation). It is unclear why the poet does not elaborate on the details of this dream, except that the poem in general downplays the prophetic elements of the biblical book of Daniel in favor of the narrative and moral elements.

if you cannot first recount how it began?"
Then unhappily the wolf-hearted king
answered his wise advisors: 135
"You were not so exalted over all other men
in your intelligence as you had said,
when you told me that you knew
my fate, and how it should befall me hereafter,
or what I should find in the future.   140
You do not understand my dream,
you who offer me wisdom before the host;
you shall suffer death, unless I know the truth
of the meaning of this dream which my heart remembers."
But the company assembled in that council room   145
could not consider or conceive anything
by divination, for it was denied to them
to reveal to the king his dream-vision
or the secrets of fate, until a prophet came,
Daniel to judgment,[1] wise and righteous,   150
chosen by the Lord, into that chamber.
He was the leader of that wretched remnant
who had to serve the heathen king;
God had given him grace from Heaven,
through the sweet speech of the Holy Spirit,   155
so that an angel of God told him everything
just as his master had met it in his dream.

      Then Daniel came at break of day
to explain the dream to his prince,
wisely discoursed on the destinies of nations   160
so that soon the haughty king understood
what was shown to him, from start to finish.
Then Daniel had great renown,
success among the scholars of Babylon,
after he had interpreted the dream that the king,   165
for his sinfulness, could not understand

---

1   *Daniel to judgment* Old English *Daniel to dome.* More than once the Old English poet
links the name *Daniel* with the noun *dom* "judgment," a play upon the symbolic meaning
of the name *Daniel* in Hebrew (*Dan-el,* "God has judged").

in his heart, that high prince of Babylon.
Yet Daniel could not bring it about
that he[1] might believe in the Lord's might,
but he began to build an idol[2] on the plain   170
that bold-minded men have named Dura,
among the nation that is known as
Babylon the great. The guardian of the city
raised up for men, against the Maker's grace,
a human image, a golden idol,   175
for he was not wise, that kingdom's guardian,
rash and reckless, right ...[3]

＊　　＊　　＊　　＊　　＊

When the call came over the citizens,
the loud voice of the trumpet, the people listened;
they fell to their knees before that image,   180
that heathen nation honored an idol,
bowed down to that altar and knew no better,
acted unrighteously just as their ruler did,
tainted with sin and twisted in mind.
That foreign race, like their lord before them,   185
acted on ill counsel—later they received
a grim reward for that—and did great wrong.

There were three noble men of Israel
in that prince's city, who would never
comply with their lord's command   190
that they should offer prayers to that shrine,
though the trumpets rang throughout the host.
They were of the ancient noble line of Abraham,
keepers of the covenant, who knew the Lord,
the everlasting God eternally on high.   195

---

1   *he* Nebuchadnezzar.
2   *an idol* The manuscript reads *woh* "evil"; many editors emend to *weoh* "idol."
3   *rash and reckless, right* A page is missing from the manuscript here; the action presumably
    corresponds to Daniel 3.2-6: the king summons all officials and leaders of his nation to the
    dedication of the statue; they are told that when they hear the trumpet, they must fall down
    and worship the idol on pain of death by burning.

These noble youths made it known
that they would not have this gold as a god
or honor it, but rather the high King,
shepherd of souls, who gave them grace.
Moreover, they often boldly declared   200
that they cared not at all for the idol,
nor could the heathen leader of the host
compel them to pray or constrain them to bow
before the golden idol which he had raised up as a god.
The king's retainers told him of the resolution   205
of these nobler slaves in that noble city,
that they would not bow,[1]
nor worship this idol that you have wondrously ordained for
     yourself.[2]

Then the enraged ruler of Babylon
gave a harsh and angry answer   210
to the young men, fiercely said
that they must offer homage at once
or else suffer terrible torment,
hot surges of fire, unless the Hebrew men
would ask for peace from that most evil thing,   215
the gold which he had set up as a god.
But these youths would not yield in their hearts
to that heathen counsel. They keenly resolved
that they should keep all the law of God
and not forsake the Lord of Hosts,   220
nor fall away into heathen folly,
nor seek peace from that perverse thing,
though a painful death were appointed for them.

III

Then the fierce king was angry, bid a furnace be kindled
to destroy the youths' lives for opposing his schemes.   225

---

1   *that they would not bow*   This is a single half-line.
2   *ordained for yourself*   The shift to direct discourse is unusual.

When it was as fiery and fierce as could be,
terrible flames, he gathered the people together,
and Babylon's guardian, grim and murderous,
ordered God's messengers to be bound;
he commanded his servants to shove the youths,   230
those young boys, into the blaze.
But He who offered them help was at hand; though he had
    harshly forced them
into the arms of the fire, yet the Almighty's protection
saved their lives, as many have learned.
Holy god, guardian of men, helped them there,   235
sent from the high heavens a holy spirit;
an angel appeared in the oven where they suffered torment,[1]
enfolded the noble youths in his arms under that fiery roof.
The surging flickering flames could not even scar
their fair appearance, while the Lord protected them.   240

    The pagan prince was enraged, and ordered them burned
    at once.
The fire was huge, enormous, the oven heated,
the iron all aglow; a great many slaves
threw wood into it, as they were commanded,
carried blazing brands into the glaring fire—   245
the savage king wanted to build an iron wall
around the righteous men—until up rose the flame
over the favored ones and furiously slew
many more beyond measure,
when the flame wrapped round the hateful   250
heathens, away from the holy ones.
The young men rejoiced, the slaves were charred
around the furnace, the fire flew
and turned on the persecutors while the prince
of Babylon beheld it. The Hebrew men   255
were joyful, with zeal they praised the Lord

---

1   *an angel appeared ... suffered torment*   This is taken as two lines (one of them an incomplete
    half-line) in Farrell's edition; the line count is adjusted accordingly.

with gladness, as best they could
in that furnace, for their lives were spared.
Glad of heart, they worshipped God,
in the embrace of the one by whom the heat   260
of the fire had been put to flight. These noble youths
were sheltered from the fire, and no harm befell them.
The searing fire was no worse to them than sunshine,
nor was the blaze a threat to those threatened men,
but the fire wrung fire onto those who did that wrong,   265
flew away from the holy men onto the heathen slaves,
marred the faces of those men rejoicing in their work.

When that haughty king could trust his own eyes,
he saw a miracle in the midst of the torment.
The three righteous youths were walking about   270
safe in the oven; there was seen with them
another, the angel of the Almighty.
They were not harmed at all in the heat of that oven,
but rather inside it was just as if
the sun were shining on a summer's morning,   275
when the dew dries as dawn becomes day,
wind-strewn—it was the God of wonders
who saved them from that savage heat.

Then holy Azarias opened his heart
in song in the midst of the searing flames,   280
a man filled with zeal, free from sin,
he praised the Lord and uttered these words:[1]
"Maker of all, listen! Your might is strong
to save mankind. Sublime and glorious,
your name is exalted over all the nations,   285
your judgments true in every generation,
strong and secured with victory,
just as you yourself.[2]

---

1   *uttered these words*   The "Song of Azarias" (lines 279-429) is found in a somewhat different
    form in the Exeter Book *Azarias*.
2   *just as you yourself*   This is a single half-line.

Your acts of will in earthly affairs
are just and generous, Lord of the heavens. 290
Grant us now your aid, God of spirits,
and your help and protection, holy Lord,
as now in our affliction and oppression
and humility, hemmed in by fire,
we ask for your mercy. Just as our ancestors 295
committed sin, so we have done
in our own lives; in their arrogance
those city-dwellers scorned the commandments
and despised the summons to a holy life.
We are exiled across the earth, 300
tossed about, lacking protection.
Our life is a scandal, scorned and despised
in many lands among many peoples
who have betrayed us into the hands
of the worst of worldly tyrants, 305
captivity to savages, and now we suffer
oppression among heathens. Praise and thanks to you,
Lord of hosts, who has laid this punishment upon us.

"Do not leave us all alone, eternal Lord,
for those mercies which men ascribe to you, 310
and for the covenant which you, steadfast in glory,
savior of men, creator of souls,
once made with Abraham
and with Isaac and with Jacob.
By the word of your mouth you made a promise 315
that you would multiply in years to come
their offspring, so that after them
generations would be brought forth,
and that multitude would be mighty,
raise up a race as the stars in heaven 320
encircle the broad sky, or the ocean sand
supports the sea, the salty waves,
brimming waters, that they should be

beyond number in years to come.[1]
Fulfill now your promise, though few survive: 325
show forth the splendor of your word in us,
declare your strength and power—the Chaldeans
and many other nations living as heathens
under the heavens have heard tell of it—
and that you alone are the eternal Lord,   330
ruler of hosts and of all worldly creation,
judge of victories and righteous God!"

    As this holy man kept up his praise
of the Maker's mercy and mighty power,
told forth in speech, a shining angel   335
was sent down from the heavens above,
glittering, beautiful, robed in glory,
who came to comfort and protect them
with loving favor. He pushed back the fire,
holy and heaven-bright, the hot flames,   340
swept back and brushed aside by his great might
the glaring blaze, so that their bodies were not
harmed at all—rather he angrily struck
their enemies with fire for their evil deeds.

    When the angel came into the oven   345
it was breezy and beautiful, most like the weather
in summertime when a sprinkle of rain
is sent during the day, warm showers
from the clouds. As in the choicest weather,
so it was in the fire, by the Lord's power,   350
as a help to those holy men. The hot flame
was driven back and quenched wherever those bold men
walked in the oven, the angel with them,
preserving their lives, the fourth alongside them,
with Annanias and Azarias   355

---

1   *beyond number in years to come* The manuscript is confused here and the translation is conjectural.

and Mishael, those stalwart men,
all three offered praise and thanks to the Prince,
asked the children of Israel to bless
the eternal Lord, and all earthly creatures,
the Ruler of nations. With knowing hearts 360
the three spoke wisely with one accord:[1]

IV

"Let the beauty of the world and all its works
give you blessing, most gracious Father!
The heavens above, the angels, the bright waters
that dwell gloriously by your great decree 365
above the heavens, all these praise you!
Let all creation, Almighty God,
praise you—the shining planets in their courses,
the sun and moon, let each separately
praise you in its own way. Let heaven's stars, 370
dew and rainstorm, give you glory.
Let the souls of men praise you, mighty God.
Burning fire and bright summer
praise the Savior! Both night and day,
and every land, light and darkness, 375
heat and cold, praise you in its own degree.
And frost and snow, winter fierce
and scurrying clouds, praise you from the skies,
Lord almighty. The flash of lightning,
bright glittering instant, gives you blessing. 380
All the surface of earth, eternal Lord,
hills and plains and high mountains,
the salty sea-waves and ocean streams,
righteous Creator, and the rising up
of springs of water, all these praise you. 385
Whales bless you, and birds of the heavens
that soar aloft, and those that stir the ocean streams,

---

1 *spoke wisely with one accord*   This long speech of praise, the "Song of the Three Children"
(lines 362-408) paraphrases the Canticle *Benedicite*, based on Daniel 3.26-90 (in the Latin
Vulgate) and sung at Sunday Lauds in the monastic Divine Office.

the wide sea, and let wild creatures
and every beast bless your name!
And let the sons of men love you in their hearts,   390
and let Israel praise you, Lord of all possessions,
your servants, in their own degree.
And let the heartfelt intentions of holy men,
the spirits and souls of the just,
give praise to the Lord of life, who grants reward   395
to all, the eternal Lord.[1]
Let Annanias, and Azarias,
and Mishael praise the Maker
in the thoughts of their breast! We bless you,
Master of every nation, Father almighty,   400
and true Son of the creator, Savior of souls,
helper of mankind, and you, Holy spirit,
we worship and glorify, wise Lord!
We give you praise, and extol you in prayer,
O Holy Lord. Truly you are blessed,   405
worshipped forever above the world's roof,
high king of Heaven, in your holy might,
author of light and life, in every land!"

Then Nebuchadnezzar, lord of the nation,
spoke to those who stood by him   410
among the people: "Many of you saw,
my lords, that we cast three men
sentenced to suffer in the burning
flames of the fire. Now I see four men
certainly—my senses do not deceive me."   415
Then one who was a counselor of the king spoke,
wise and prudent: "It is a great wonder
which we behold with our own eyes.
Consider, my prince, what is proper!
Know clearly who has given this grace   420
to these young men! They praise God,
the one, eternal, and wholly upon him

---

1   *to all, the eternal Lord*   This is a single half-line.

they call by every name in their need,
give thanks for his glory with bold words,
say that He alone is Lord almighty,   425
wise King of glory, the world and the heavens.
Call forth these men from the furnace,
O prince of Chaldea! It is not at all good
that they linger in that torment any longer than necessary."

    Then the king commanded the youths be brought to him.   430
The hardy youths obeyed his behest,
went, well-born, as they had been instructed,
the young heroes came before the heathen king.
The fetters were burnt which had lain on their limbs,
the evil bonds of the king, and their bodies spared.   435
Their fair faces were unmarred, their clothes unharmed,
their hair unsinged by fire, but with God's favor
they walked rejoicing out of that grim torment
with discerning hearts, and protected by the spirit.

    Then the angel ascended to find eternal joy   440
above the high roof of the heavenly realm,
a lofty and loyal servant of the holy Lord;
his marvel had honored those who had merited it.
The youths praised the lord before the heathen people,
taught them with true words and told many   445
truthful signs, until he himself believed
that He who rescued them from darkness was a Ruler of
    mighty power.
Then the bold and stern lord of the Babylonians
ordered his people that anyone would forfeit his life
who tried to deny that it truly was   450
the great Ruler of might who delivered them from that death.
He gave back to God the remnant of His people,
led captive to ancient enemies, so that they should have mercy.
Their fame was great in Babylon after they had passed through
    the fire,
their name renowned among the nations, after they had obeyed
    the Lord;   455

their counsels were heeded after the Lord of the heavens,
holy guardian of heaven's kingdom, shielded them from harm.

    Then, as I've heard, the Lord of Babylon,
when he had seen the miracle[1]
sought to understand the searing heat   460
in truthful words, how those three young men
had passed through the fiery terror of the furnace.
They went through the surging flame as if its fierce violence
did not harm the Lord's messengers at all,
the grim fire, but God's protection   465
shielded their lives from the awful terror.
Then the prince commanded a council at once,
summoned his people to assemble,
and there declared before that multitude
what had occurred, a wonder of God   470
that had been made known in those young men:
"Consider now the holy strength
and wondrous work of God! We have seen
how he saved from death those who sang his praise,
the young men in the furnace, the leaping fire;   475
therefore He alone is eternal Lord,
almighty Judge, who has given them glory;
abundant triumph to those who bear his word.
Thus by many miracles he reveals himself
to holy souls who have sought his favor.   480
It is well known that Daniel declared the truth
of my hidden dream, which had baffled
the minds of many men among my people,
because the Almighty has sent to his heart
an ample spirit, and strength in wisdom."   485

    So spoke the leader of that host,
protector of Babylon, when he perceived the token,
clear sign from God. Yet it did him no good,
but pride overruled that prince—
his mind grew haughtier, the thoughts of his heart   490

---

1   *when he had seen the miracle*   This is another single half-line.

grew great beyond measure in his breast,
until the almighty Lord lowered him
by force, as He has done to many
who in their arrogance raise themselves up.

V

Then a dream was shown to him in his sleep   495
which concerned Nebuchadnezzar closely.[1]
It seemed to him that there stood a lovely tree
firm in its roots, wondrously fair,
bright with fruit. It was not like other boughs,
but it soared high to the stars in heaven,   500
so that it overshadowed the surface of the earth,
all this middle-earth to the ocean streams
with its branches and boughs. As he beheld it
it seemed to him that the tree sheltered wild beasts,
and it alone held food for them all,   505
likewise songbirds took their sustenance
from the fruits they found on that tree.
It seemed to him that an angel came descending
from the heavens above, and with a bright voice
commanded that the tree be cut down,   510
and the wild beasts driven away,
and the birds also, when its fall should come.
He commanded that its fruit be cut off,
its twigs and branches, and yet a token should stay,
the root-stump of the tree should remain   515
fixed in the ground, until green shoots
should come again, as God ordains.
And he bade that the great tree be bound
in fetters of brass and bands of iron,
and turned over to its torment,   520
so he might know in his mind that a being mightier
than he can resist wields the power of punishment.

---

1   *which concerned Nebuchadnezzar closely*   This dream is detailed in Daniel 4.10-17. The
beginning of the poetic description is very much like the beginning of the Old English
Dream of the Rood.

The earthly prince, his dream ended,
awoke from sleep, but the horror stayed with him,
terror from the spirit which God had sent.   525
He commanded his people to come together,
summoned his leaders; the stern king
asked them all what this dream meant—
not because he thought they would know,
but he was testing what they would say.   530

Then Daniel was called to the debate,
God's prophet. A holy spirit was given to him
from heaven, which strengthened his heart.
In him the lord of men saw deep learning,
an ample spirit, skillful mind,   535
and wise speech. Once again he showed forth
many wonders, the Maker's power.
Then the haughty heathen leader of armies
began to explain the puzzling dream,
all the horror that was revealed to him.   540
He ordered him to explain what this mystery meant,
summon holy words and find in his heart
how to say in true speech
what the tree signified which he had seen shining,
and interpret the appointed course of events.   545

Then Daniel at the debate fell silent,
but he saw the truth, that his lord,
master of men, was guilty before God.
He waited and paused, then spoke these words,
skilled in the law, said to his lord: 550
"It is no little wonder, O lord of hosts,
what you have seen in your dream—
a tree high as heaven and the holy words,
angry and terrible, that the angel spoke,
that the tree, stripped of its branches, should   555
fall where formerly it had stood fast,
and then be joyless among the beasts,
dwell in the desert, and its root-stump

stay fast in the earth, still in its place
for a long time, as the voice told, 560
and after seven seasons regain its seed.
So shall your glory lie fallen—as the tree grew
lofty into the heavens, so you alone
among all men dwelling on earth
are sole ruler and guide. You have no rival 565
among men on earth, but only the Maker.
He will cut you off from your kingdom
and send you friendless into exile,
and then He will change your heart so that
you will not remember the pleasures of men, 570
nor have any wits but those of a wild beast,
and you will live for a long time
in the depth of the wood in the tracks of the deer.
You will have no food but the grass of the field,
and no resting place, but rain showers 575
will wake you and break you like a wild beast,
until after seven winters you will see the truth,
that there is one Maker of all mankind,
holding rule and power, who is in Heaven.
Yet it is my will[1] that the roots remain 580
fixed in their foundation, as the voice foretold,
and bring forth seed after seven years.
So your kingdom will stand untouched,
unharmed before men, until your return.

"My lord, consider this firm counsel: 585
give alms, be a refuge for the wretched,
atone before the Prince before the time comes
when He topples you from your earthly throne.
Often the Lord has allowed many nations
to do penance, when they would do so, 590
though fixed in their sin, before God's sudden stroke
crushes their life with a terrible violence."
But Daniel did not speak enough true words

---

1   *my will*   I.e., God's will.

to his prince, through the power of his wisdom,
that this mighty lord of the earth would ever   595
pay heed to them, but his pride rose up
haughty in his heart; he paid dearly for it.
He continued to brag with much boasting,
this king of Chaldeans, when he ruled his fortress;
he saw in its glory the city of Babylon,   600
surrounding the spacious plain of Shinar,[1]
towering aloft, that he, lord of warriors,
had built for the multitudes with great marvels.
He became headstrong above all men,
arrogant of spirit for the special gifts   605
which God had given him, rule over men
and a world to control during the course of his life:
"You are the great and glorious city of mine,
which I have made for my remembrance,
a vast realm. I will take my rest in you,   610
in you I will have a dwelling and home."

   Then for his loud boasting the lord of men
was stricken, seized, and fled into exile,
alone in his pride above all men.
So he departed from men into days of strife,   615
trod the bitterest path of God's punishment
of any who ever lived to see his people again,
Nebuchadnezzar, after God's vengeance
swift from heaven had suddenly struck him.
For seven winters he suffered torment,   620
a wilderness of wild beasts, this king of the joyful city.
When this wretched man looked upward,
companion of wild beasts, through the drifting clouds,
he remembered in his mind that there was a Creator,
heaven's high king, one eternal spirit   625
for all the children of men. Then he recovered
his mad wits, where he had widely borne

---

1   *the spacious plain of Shinar*   The city of Babylon was associated with the Tower of Babel
    (Genesis 11), built on the plains of Shinar.

a violent spirit very close to his heart;
then his mind and soul, remembering God,
returned to men, when he accepted the Maker.   630
The wretched man made his way back,
a naked beggar submissive to sinfulness,
a wandering wonder with no clothes on his back,
humbler in his heart than he had been
as lord of men, in all his loud boasting.   635
The earth had stood for seven years,
home and native land, behind its lord
and master, so that it had not diminished
under the heavens, until the ruler returned.

    When he was restored to his royal throne,   640
the lord of Babylon had a better habit of mind,
a more enlightened faith in the Lord of Life—
that God gave to every man
wealth or woe, as He himself wished.
Nor did the lord of men linger longer   645
over the words of the prophets, but preached abroad
the might of the Maker, when he made a proclamation,
spoke to his people of his experience,
his wide wandering with the wild beasts,
until steadfast reason returned to his soul   650
from the Lord God, when he looked to the heavens.
Fate was fulfilled, the wonder made known,
his dream come to pass, his torment endured,
his judgment judged just as Daniel had said,
that the king of the people would discover   655
times of hardship for his arrogance.
So he preached the power of the Maker
most zealously before all mankind.

    Afterwards Daniel brought wisdom to Babylon,
taught the law for a long while   660
to its citizens, after the companion of animals,
neighbor of wild beasts, Nebuchadnezzar,
came back from his wandering in exile;

later he reigned over a broad kingdom,
held the treasury and the high city,   665
old, wise, and mighty leader of men,
king of the Chaldeans, until death destroyed him,
for over the earth he had no rival
among men, until God wished
to take away his lofty empire through his death.   670
Afterward his heirs enjoyed prosperity
wealth and wound gold, in that vast palace,
city of warriors, no small amount,
a great treasury, when their lord lay dead.

VI

   Then a third generation arose in that nation;   675
Belshazzar was lord of that city
and held sway over men, until pride destroyed him,
hateful arrogance. That was the end
of the days of Chaldean domination,
when the Lord for a little while   680
gave power to the Medes and Persians,
let the glory of the Babylonians grow less,
which they should have guarded closely.
He knew that the elders were unrighteous
who should have given guidance to the empire.   685
Then the lord of the Medes, in his own land,
resolved to do what had never been done—
he determined to destroy Babylon,
city of warriors, whose noblemen
enjoyed their wealth in the shelter of its walls.   690
That was the most famous of fortresses
ever built by men, greatest and best-known,
the city of Babylon, until Belshazzar
in his terrible boasting tempted God.

   They sat at their wine, protected by walls,   695
never fearing the anger of any enemies—
though a hostile foe in full battle-dress

should come for them in that lofty city—
that anyone could determine to destroy Babylon.
So when the king of the Chaldeans with his kinsmen   700
sat down to his feast on his final day,
the leader of that multitude grew drunk with mead.
He bade them bring the treasure of Israel,
put the holy vessels into his hands
which the Chaldeans with their kingly host,   705
soldiers in that city, had completely seized,
the gold of Jerusalem, when they routed the Jews,
shattered their glory with the sword's blade,
and with a trumpet cry of battle the troops
pillaged the bright treasure—when they plundered   710
Solomon's temple, they boasted greatly.

    Then the lord of cities grew light-hearted,
boasted fiercely, defying God,
saying that his own idols were higher
and more mighty to save mankind   715
than the eternal God of the people of Israel.
But as he gazed there appeared an awesome sign
in the presence of all the men in the palace,
that he had spoken lies before his people,
when there awesomely an angel of the Lord   720
caused his hand to appear in the high hall,
wrote secret words upon the wall,
scarlet letters before all the citizens.

    Then the leader of armies was afraid at heart,
struck with awe. He saw the angel's hand   725
inscribe the doom of the Shinarites in the hall.
A multitude of men debated there,
heroes in the hall, what that hand had written
as a warning sign to the citizens there.
Multitudes came to gaze on that marvel,   730
and wondered mightily in their mind's thoughts
what the hand of the Holy Spirit had written.

Neither men skilled in secrets,[1] nor noblemen's sons,
could explain the angel's message,
until Daniel came, God's chosen one,   735
wise and righteous, walking into the hall.
In his spirit was God's great skill,
so that the guardians of the city, it is said,
eagerly offered him gifts if he would only
read and decipher what the mystery meant.   740

    God's messenger, learned in the law,
wise in his thoughts, answered them all:
"I will not pronounce the Lord's judgments
to the people for riches, nor to you for profit,
but freely I will tell you your fate,   745
the secret message which you cannot escape.
You took into your possession the treasure of Israel,
put the holy vessels into human hands;
you have drunk to devils out of those vessels,
which the Israelites once kept according to the law   750
before the ark of God, until boasting betrayed them,
wits soaked in wine—which shall happen to you.
Your father would never have done this,
borne God's sacred golden vessels in boast,
nor did he so readily brag, though battle brought   755
the treasures of Israel into his possession,
but the nation's leader more often announced
in true words to all his troops,
after the Guardian of Glory revealed Himself with wonder,
that He alone was Lord and Ruler   760
of all creation, Who granted him glory,
blameless happiness in his earthly kingdom,
and now you deny that He exists,
Who rules in majesty above all devils."[2]

---

1   *men skilled in secrets* Old English *runcræftige men* might also mean "men skilled in runes."
2   *above all devils* The manuscript may be missing a leaf or more here, and the ending of the
    poem may be lost, but the sense is not obviously incomplete.

Poems from the Vercelli Book

The Dream of the Rood, Andreas, The Fates of the Apostles

The Vercelli Book (Vercelli, Biblioteca Capitolare, CXVII) was written in the southeast of England in the later tenth century but taken to the northern Italian town of Vercelli, an important stop on the pilgrimage route from England to Rome, some time before the end of the eleventh century. As with most Old English literature, the manuscript's origins, authorship, audience, and early history are all unknown. The Vercelli Book contains twenty-three anonymous prose homilies and six poems—in addition to the poems presented here, there are two short fragmentary poems called *Soul and Body I* and *Homiletic Fragment I* and a long poem called *Elene* which tells the legendary story of the finding of the True Cross by St. Helen, mother of the emperor Constantine. Poetry and prose homilies are mixed together, and the poems are not distinguished from the prose—if anything, they are less distinct, lacking the titles and elaborate capitals found at the beginning of most of the prose homilies.

The prose homilies in the Vercelli Book are edited by D.G. Scragg, *The Vercelli Homilies and Related Texts*. Early English Text Society o.s. 300. Oxford and New York: Oxford University Press, 1992.

FURTHER READING

Orchard, Andy, and Samantha Zacher, eds. *New Readings in the Vercelli Book*. Toronto: University of Toronto Press, 2009.

Treharne, Elaine. "The Form and Function of the Vercelli Book." *Text, Image, Interpretation: Studies in Anglo-Saxon Literature and Its Insular Context in Honour of Éamonn Ó Carragáin*. Ed. Alastair Minnis and Jane Roberts. Studies in the Early Middle Ages 18. Turnhout: Brepols, 2006. 253-66.

The Dream of the Rood

Although the Vercelli book itself was copied in the tenth century, *The Dream of the Rood* may be considerably older. Several lines from the poem are carved in runic characters on a large stone monument known as the Ruthwell Cross, found in a small church in Dumfriesshire on the western border of England and Scotland. The Cross, which has been dated to the early eighth century, is elaborately carved with scenes from the Gospels and lives of the saints, antiphons in Latin, and decorative scroll-work; if the runic inscriptions were part of the original monument (and not a later addition), then *The Dream of the Rood*—or at least those portions carved on the Ruthwell Cross—would be among the earliest written Old English poems.

The Dream of the Rood tells the story of the Crucifixion of Christ from the point of view of the Cross, which appears to the narrator in a dream and recounts its experiences. Christ is presented as a heroic warrior, eagerly leaping on the Cross to do battle with Death; the Cross is a loyal retainer who is painfully and paradoxically forced to participate in his lord's execution. The narrator who witnesses this then shares his vision, describes the virtues of devotion to the Cross, and looks forward to the time when righteous Christians, protected by the Cross, are taken up into the banquet-halls of heaven. The blending of Christian themes and heroic conventions is a striking example of how the Anglo-Saxons vigorously re-imagined Christianity even as they embraced it. *The Dream of the Rood* interweaves biblical, liturgical, and devotional material with the language of heroic poetry and elegy, and something of the ambiguity and wordplay of the Riddles; its complex structure of echoes, allusions, repetitions, and verbal parallels makes it one of the most carefully constructed poems in Old English.

SOURCE

Vercelli, Biblioteca Capitolare, CXVII, fols. 104v-106r.

EDITION

G.P. Krapp. *The Vercelli Book*. Anglo-Saxon Poetic Records II. New York: Columbia University Press, 1932.

Johnson, David F. "Old English Religious Poetry: *Christ and Satan* and *The Dream of the Rood*." *Companion to Old English Poetry.* Ed. Henk Aertsen and Rolf H. Bremmer, Jr. Amsterdam: VU University Press, 1994. 159-87.

Kendall, Calvin B. "From Sign to Vision: The Ruthwell Cross and *The Dream of the Rood*." *The Place of the Cross in Anglo-Saxon England.* Ed. Catherine E. Karkov, Sarah Larratt Keefer, and Karen Louise Jolly. Publications of the Manchester Centre for Anglo-Saxon Studies 4. Woodbridge: Boydell, 2006. 129-44.

McEntire, Sandra. "The Devotional Context of the Cross before A. D. 1000." *Sources of Anglo-Saxon Culture.* Ed. Paul E. Szarmach with the assistance of Virginia Darrow Oggins. Studies in Medieval Culture 20. Kalamazoo, MI: Medieval Institute Publications, Western Michigan University, 1986. 345-56.

Ó Carragáin, Éamonn. *Ritual and the Rood: Liturgical Images and the Old English Poems of the "Dream of the Rood" Tradition.* British Library Studies in Medieval Culture. London: British Library and University of Toronto Press, 2005.

Listen! I will speak of the sweetest dream,
what came to me in the middle of the night,
when speech-bearers slept in their rest.
It seemed that I saw a most wondrous tree
raised on high, wound round with light,   5
the brightest of beams. All that beacon was
covered in gold; gems stood
fair at the earth's corners, and there were five
up on the cross-beam. All the angels of the Lord looked on,
fair through all eternity;[1] that was no felon's gallows,   10
but holy spirits beheld him there,
men over the earth and all this glorious creation.

---

1   *All the angels ... through all eternity*   These lines are difficult and much debated; another possible translation is "All creation, eternally fair / beheld the Lord's angel there," the Lord's angel presumably being the Cross itself, God's messenger to earth (the Greek word *angelos* meaning "messenger").

Wondrous was the victory-tree, and I was stained by sins,
wounded with guilt; I saw the tree of glory
honored in garments, shining with joys,   15
bedecked with gold; gems had
covered worthily the Creator's tree.
And yet beneath that gold I began to see
an ancient wretched struggle, when it first began
to bleed on the right side. I was all beset with sorrows,   20
fearful for that fair vision; I saw that eager beacon
change garments and colors—now it was drenched,
stained with blood, now bedecked with treasure.
And yet, lying there a long while,
I beheld in sorrow the Savior's tree,   25
until I heard it utter a sound;
that best of woods began to speak words:

"It was so long ago—I remember it still—
that I was felled from the forest's edge,
ripped up from my roots. Strong enemies seized me there,   30
made me their spectacle, made me bear their criminals;
they bore me on their shoulders and set me on a hill,
enemies enough fixed me fast. Then I saw the Lord of mankind
hasten eagerly when he wanted to ascend upon me.
I did not dare to break or bow down   35
against the Lord's word, when I saw
the ends of the earth tremble. Easily I might
have felled all those enemies, yet fast I stood.
Then the young hero made ready—that was God almighty—
strong and resolute; he ascended on the high gallows,   40
brave in the sight of many, when he wanted to ransom mankind.
I trembled when he embraced me, but I dared not bow to the
        ground,
or fall to the earth's corners—I had to stand fast.
I was reared as a cross: I raised up the mighty King,
the Lord of heaven; I dared not lie down.   45
They drove dark nails through me; the scars are still visible,
open wounds of hate; I dared not harm any of them.

They mocked us both together; I was all drenched with blood
flowing from that man's side after he had sent forth his spirit.

    "Much have I endured on that hill   50
of hostile fates: I saw the God of hosts
cruelly stretched out. Darkness had covered
with its clouds the Ruler's corpse,
that shining radiance. Shadows spread
grey under the clouds; all creation wept,   55
mourned the King's fall: Christ was on the cross.
And yet from afar men came hastening
to that noble one; I watched it all.
I was all beset with sorrow, yet I sank into their hands,
humbly, eagerly. There they took almighty God,   60
lifted him from his heavy torment; the warriors then left me
standing drenched in blood, all shot through with arrows.
They laid him down, bone-weary, and stood by his body's head;
they watched the Lord of heaven there, who rested a while,
weary from his mighty battle. They began to build a tomb
      for him   65
in the sight of his slayer; they carved it from bright stone,
and set within the Lord of victories. They began to sing a dirge for
      him,
wretched at evening, when they wished to travel hence,
weary, from the glorious Lord—he rested there with little
      company.[1]
And as we stood there, weeping, a long while   70
fixed in our station, the song ascended
from those warriors. The corpse grew cold,
the fair life-house. Then they began to fell us
all to the earth—a terrible fate!
They dug for us a deep pit, yet the Lord's thanes,   75
friends found me there …
      adorned me with gold and silver.[2]

---

1   *with little company*   I.e., utterly alone.
2   *adorned me with gold and silver*   There is no gap in the manuscript here, but something is
     obviously missing—the story of the Finding of the True Cross, told (among other places) in
     the Old English poem *Elene* later in the Vercelli Book. The Cross is buried, hidden, forgotten,

"Now you can hear, my dear hero,
that I have endured the work of evil-doers,
harsh sorrows. Now the time has come   80
that far and wide they honor me,
men over the earth and all this glorious creation,
and pray to this sign. On me the Son of God
suffered for a time; and so, glorious now
I rise up under the heavens, and am able to heal   85
each of those who is in awe of me.
Once I was made into the worst of torments,
most hateful to all people, before I opened
the true way of life for speech-bearers.
Lo! the King of glory, Guardian of heaven's kingdom   90
honored me over all the trees of the forest,
just as he has also, almighty God, honored
his mother, Mary herself,
above all womankind for the sake of all men.

"Now I bid you, my beloved hero,   95
that you reveal this vision to men,
tell them in words that it is the tree of glory
on which almighty God suffered
for mankind's many sins
and Adam's ancient deeds.   100
Death He tasted there, yet the Lord rose again
with his great might to help mankind.
He ascended into heaven. He will come again
to this middle-earth to seek mankind
on doomsday, almighty God,   105
the Lord himself and his angels with him,
and He will judge—He has the power of judgment—
each one of them as they have earned
beforehand here in this loaned life.
No one there may be unafraid   110
at the words which the Ruler will speak:

---

then recovered by Helen, mother of the emperor Constantine; its authenticity is established
and it becomes an object of veneration and sign of victory.

He will ask before the multitude where the man might be
who for the Lord's name would taste
bitter death, as He did earlier on that tree.
But they will tremble then, and little think   115
what they might even begin to say to Christ.
But no one there need be very afraid
who has borne in his breast the best of beacons;
but through the cross shall seek the kingdom
every soul from this earthly way,   120
whoever thinks to rest with the Ruler."

    Then I prayed to the tree with a happy heart,
eagerly, there where I was alone
with little company. My spirit longed to start
on the journey forth; it has felt   125
so much of longing. It is now my life's hope
that I may seek the tree of victory
alone, more often than all men,
and honor it well. I wish for that
with all my heart, and my hope of protection is   130
fixed on the cross. I have few wealthy friends
on earth; they all have gone forth,
fled from worldly joys and sought the King of glory;
they live now in heaven with the High Father,
and dwell in glory, and each day I look forward   135
to the time when the cross of the Lord,
on which I have looked while here on this earth,
will fetch me from this loaned life,
and bring me where there is great bliss,
joy in heaven, where the Lord's host   140
is seated at the feast, with ceaseless bliss;
and then set me where I may afterwards
dwell in glory, have a share of joy
fully with the saints. May the Lord be my friend,
He who here on earth once suffered   145
on the hanging-tree for human sin;
He ransomed us and gave us life,
a heavenly home. Hope was renewed

with cheer and bliss for those who were burning there.[1]
The Son was successful in that journey,   150
mighty and victorious, when he came with a multitude,
a great host of souls, into God's kingdom,
the one Ruler almighty, the angels rejoicing
and all the saints already in heaven
dwelling in glory, when almighty God,   155
their Ruler, returned to his rightful home.

---

1   *Hope was renewed … burning there*   A well-known Christian tradition known as the "Har-
   rowing of Hell" tells how Jesus, after his death on the Cross, descended into Hell and broke
   open its gates, releasing the souls of those unjustly imprisoned by Satan since the Creation
   of human beings. He conveyed them to Heaven, then returned to earth in time for his
   resurrection.

Andreas

Andreas is based on a now-lost Latin version of the apocryphal *Acts of Andrew and Matthew in the City of the Cannibals*, which is itself probably a version of a Greek original. An English prose life of St. Andrew which survives in two manuscripts (the Blickling Homilies and Cambridge, Corpus Christi College 198) is apparently derived from the same source; Ælfric's *Life of St Andrew* (*Catholic Homilies* I.38)[1] tells the story of Andrew's martyrdom in Achaia.

The poem tells of Andrew's rescue of his fellow-apostle Matthew from a cannibalistic race called the Mermedonians. Matthew has been blinded and thrown in prison, where he is to be held, fattening on grass, until the day appointed for the Mermedonians to have their cannibal feast. God commands Andrew to rescue Matthew; the saint initially refuses, but finally agrees. With Jesus himself at the helm in disguise, Andrew sails across the stormy sea, catechizing all the way. Prompted by his helmsman, he recounts some of the miracles of Jesus, both biblical and non-biblical (including the raising of Abraham from the dead); along the way he does not miss a chance to condemn the Jews, a depressingly common theme in medieval Christian writing. He recognizes Jesus when he and his companions are miraculously rescued from a storm and transported to Mermedonia by air. Andrew frees Matthew and other prisoners from their cells but is captured by the hungry and now angry Mermedonians. He is tortured for three days, but God spares and heals him, and punishes the Mermedonians with a flood which bursts from a stone pillar. When the citizens repent in panic, God spares them too, and Andrew converts them all and builds a church. After appointing a bishop, Andrew sails off to meet his death elsewhere.

The poem retains much of the narrative force of the original story; its combination of piety and adventure is characteristic of Hellenistic romance, with shipwrecks, prison cells, devilish tormenters, magical wonders, reunions of long-lost companions, and convulsive outpourings of emotion. But it is more than just a translation. *Andreas* transforms the saintly Andrew into a

---

1   Ed. Peter Clemoes, *Ælfric's Catholic Homilies: The First Series, Text*, Early English Text Society s.s. 17 (Oxford: Oxford University Press, 1997), 507-19.

Germanic hero, a great war-leader, and invests the poem with all the trappings of a heroic narrative like *Beowulf*—loyal thanes, rattling armor, storms at sea, and so on. The twelve apostles are called *tireadige hæleð* "glorious heroes," *frome folctogan* "bold folk-leaders" (8), and *rofe rincas* "strong soldiers" (line 9), all in just the first few lines, clearly setting the poem in the Germanic world of heroic action. In fact the poem seems to have borrowed much of its language directly from *Beowulf,* beginning with its opening lines:

> *Hwæt! We gefrunon   on fyrndagum*
> *twelfe under tunglum   tireadige hæleð*
> *þeodnes þegnas. No hira þrym alæg....*

> Listen! We have heard of twelve heroes in distant days,
> blessed in honor under the heavens,
> thanes of God—their glory never failed....

—which distinctly echo the opening of *Beowulf:*

> *Hwæt! We gardena   in geardagum*
> *þeodcyninga   þrym gefrunon*
> *hu ða æpelingas   ellen fremedon.*

> Listen! We have heard of the glory in bygone days
> of the folk-kings of the spear-Danes,
> how those noble lords did lofty deeds.   (*Beowulf* 1-3)

Examples like this could be multiplied through almost every episode of the poem. Some scholars have argued that rather than one poem borrowing from another, both poets borrowed from a common stock of heroic epithets and formulae, and this is undoubtedly true in many instances, but the parallels between these two poems are so close, so numerous, and so striking that a dependence of *Andreas* on *Beowulf* itself seems the only satisfying explanation (the pattern of borrowing makes the opposite possibility, that *Beowulf* borrowed from *Andreas,* far less likely). And so the poem can be thought of as a kind of Christianized version of *Beowulf* with an apostle for its hero and pagan cannibals for its monsters. *Andreas* is, among other things, a fascinating record of what one reader of *Beowulf* thought most memorable or most worthy of imitation in that poem. And like *Beowulf*, it has gripping action, lively descriptions of the natural world, moments of grim humor, and some surprising psychological depth.

Andreas is followed by *The Fates of the Apostles*, one of four poems containing the runic signature of the poet Cynewulf (the others are *Elene* in the Vercelli Book, and *Christ II* and *Juliana* in the Exeter Book). Because it follows *Andreas*, it has sometimes been treated as a conclusion to or continuation of that poem, but despite some verbal parallels, the two are apparently not related, and the overall style of *Andreas* has little in common with the style of Cynewulf's signed poems. Still, the placement is skillfully done—it makes a fitting coda to the long heroic saga of the adventures of Andreas, bringing the reader from the far-flung corners of the world back to the author's study, and from the strenuous work of converting violent heathens to the more personal business of praying for God's mercy.

SOURCE

Vercelli, Biblioteca Capitolare, CXVII, fols. 29v-54r.

EDITION

The poem was edited by G.P. Krapp, *The Vercelli Book*. Anglo-Saxon Poetic Records II (New York: Columbia University Press, 1932); a better and more recent edition is that of Kenneth R. Brooks, *Andreas and the Fates of the Apostles* (Oxford: Oxford University Press, 1961). *Andreas* is divided into sections in the Vercelli book; these are not numbered, but are given roman numerals in this translation.

FURTHER READING

Boenig, Robert. *Saint and Hero: "Andreas" and Medieval Doctrine.* Lewisburg, PA: Bucknell University Press; London and Toronto: Associated University Presses, 1991.

Garner, Lori Ann. "The Old English *Andreas* and the Mermedonian Cityscape." *Essays in Medieval Studies* 24 (2007): 53-63.

Herbison, Ivan. "Generic Adaptation in *Andreas*." *Essays on Anglo-Saxon and Related Themes in Memory of Lynne Grundy.* Ed. Jane Roberts and Janet Nelson. King's College London Medieval Studies 17. London: Centre for Late Antique and Medieval Studies, King's College, University of London, 2000. 181-211.

Irving, Edward B., Jr. "A Reading of *Andreas*: The Poem as Poem."
  Anglo-Saxon England 12 (1983): 215-37.

Riedinger, Anita R. "The Formulaic Relationship between *Beowulf*
  and *Andreas*." *Heroic Poetry in the Anglo-Saxon Period: Studies
  in Honor of Jess B. Bessinger.* Ed. Helen Damico and John Ley-
  erle. Studies in Medieval Culture 32. Kalamazoo, MI: Medieval
  Institute Publications, Western Michigan University, 1993.
  283-312.

Wilcox, Jonathan. "Eating People Is Wrong: Funny Style in *Andreas*
  and Its Analogues." *Anglo-Saxon Styles.* Ed. Catherine E. Karkov
  and George Hardin Brown. SUNY Series in Medieval Studies.
  Albany: State University of New York Press, 2003. 201-22.

I

Listen! We have heard of twelve heroes in distant days,
blessed in honor under the heavens,
thanes of God—their glory never failed
in the field of battle when banners clashed.
Later they were scattered, as the Lord himself,   5
high king of Heaven, assigned their lots.[1]
These were mighty men over the earth,
bold folk-leaders, brave in the fight,
strong soldiers when shield and hand
protected the helmet on the plain of battle,   10
the fatal field. Among them was Matthew,
who first began, among the Jews, to write
the words of the Gospel with wondrous skill.
Holy God decreed that his lot should be
out on an island where no foreigner   15
was ever yet allowed to enjoy the fruits
of that homeland. Many murderous hands
fought hard against him on that field of battle.
That whole borderland, stronghold of men
and homeland of warriors, was wrapped in death,   20

---

1   *assigned their lots*   The twelve apostles were said to have cast lots to determine where each
    of them would go to spread the gospel; see *Fates of the Apostles* 9-11.

malice and hostility. No morsel of bread
was found in that field, nor sip of water
for men to savor there, but skin and blood,
the flesh flayed from men come from afar,
that people consumed. This was their custom—   25
they took any traveler from foreign lands,
any alien who sought their island from outside,
and made him into food for meatless men.
Such was the savage mark of this people,
the strength of cruel warriors, fierce, sword-grim,   30
that they destroyed the sight of the eyes,
precious jewels of the head, with the point of a spear.
Afterwards, with skills of sorcery, wizards
bitterly blended for them a gruesome drink
that twisted their wits, their inward thoughts,   35
turned the heart in their chest, changed their minds
so that they no longer yearned for the joys of men,
but bloodthirsty warriors, weary with hunger,
exhausted, craved only hay and grass instead.

      When Matthew had come to the mighty citadel   40
inside the city, there was a great outcry
throughout Mermedonia, mobs of wicked men,
crowds of the damned, when those devil's thanes
first found out about the noble one's arrival.
Swiftly they went out to him armed with shields   45
—none was slow—and bristling with spears,
angry ash-bearers eager for battle.
There they bound the hands of the holy one,
held him fast with fiendish craft,
hell-bent warriors, and burst the eyes in his head   50
with the point of a sword. But still in his soul
and heart he honored the heavenly kingdom's guardian,
even when he took that terrible poisoned drink.
Blessed, steadfast, filled with bold courage,
he sang forth the praise of the Prince of glory,   55
the heavenly kingdom's guardian, with a holy voice

from his prison cell. The praise of Christ
was wrapped fast around his heart.
Then he, weeping, with weary tears,
called with sad voice on the Lord of Victories,   60
Prince of peoples, Provider of all good to men,
with sorrowful speech, and said these words:
"What a treacherous web these aliens weave,
what cunning bonds! Forever I have been
in every way eagerly mindful of your will   65
in my soul; now in my sorrow
I must do my deeds like the dumb beasts.
You alone know the minds of all men,
O Maker of mankind, our most inner thoughts.
If it be your will, O Prince of glory,   70
that these faithless men slay me with swords,
the weapon's edge, I am ready at once
to endure whatever you wish to decree
for me, O my Lord, in my homeless exile,
Ruler of all men, the angels' joy-giver.   75
Grant me in your mercy, almighty God,
light in this life, lest I must,
blinded in this citadel by sword-hate
through the hateful words of hostile enemies,
bloodthirsty destroyers, longer suffer   80
their scornful speech. On you alone
have I set my heart and steadfast love,
middle-earth's Guardian, bright giver of bliss,
and I wish to ask you, father of angels,
that you not cut me off among my enemies,   85
wretched workers of sin, to the worst of deaths
upon the earth, O judge of all men."

   After these words came a wondrous holy sign
of glory from the heavens, like a gleaming banner
in the prison cell. Then it was made plain   90
that Holy God had wrought help for him,
when the voice of Heaven's King was heard

wondrous under the sky, the sound of the words
of the mighty Prince. In that woeful prison
He offered cure and comfort to his retainer,   95
bold in battle, with a bright voice:
"To you, Matthew, I give My peace
beneath the heavens. Be not afraid in spirit,
nor mournful in mind—I will remain with you,
and free your limbs from these fetters,   100
and all the multitude that remain with you
in painful confinement. The plain of Paradise,
brightest of blessings, fairest of buildings,
sweetest of homes, lies shining and open for you
with holy might, where you may enjoy   105
the bliss of glory forever and ever.
Suffer this tribulation! The time is not long
that these faithless men will be allowed to afflict you,
sinning through cunning craft, with heavy bonds.
I will straightaway send Andreas to you   110
to solace and shelter you in this heathen city;
he will release you from the hate of this people.
Until that time, to reckon it truly,
it is but a short while—seven and twenty
nights, all told—until you may,   115
spent with sorrow but certain of victory,
go forth from affliction into God's keeping."
Then the holy Protector of all beings departed,
Creator of angels, up to the heavenly
home, his native land. He is rightfully King,   120
steadfast Steersman, Ruler in every place.

II

Then Matthew was mightily heartened
by this new voice. Night's helm slipped by,
passed quickly, and light came after,
the first stirring of dawn. The army assembled,   125
heathen warriors thronged in heaps—

armor creaking, spears clattering—
hearts swollen with rage under their shields.
They wanted to learn whether any still lived
who had been held, fettered fast,   130
in that prison, place without comfort,
and which one they might first take for meat,
deprive him of life at their appointed time.
They had written in runes, reckoned by number
these men's final days, craving his flesh,   135
marking when they might be made into food
for the meat-starved men among that people.
The wild counselors clamored, cold-hearted,
one band crowding another; they cared nothing for right
or the Maker's mercy—their minds were seized   140
in the dim shadows by the devil's teaching,
when they set their hearts on that savage strength.
There they met that holy man,
his mind lucid, locked in his dark cell,
waiting with courage for what the bright King,   145
Commander of angels, wished to grant him.

And when all the term of that appointed time
had nearly passed, except three nights,
as the slaughter-wolves had written it,
then they planned to break their backbones,   150
straightaway sever the soul from the body,
and then divide the flesh of the doomed
among old and young, a morsel for men
and a welcome feast. These greedy warriors
shed no tears for that life, how the soul's travel   155
was decreed after its death and torment—
thus they always ordained, every thirty days,
their awful feast. They felt a great craving
to pull to pieces in their bloody jaws
the flesh flayed from men for their fodder.   160
Then He was mindful, whose mighty strength
established all this middle-earth,

how he languished in misery in a foreign land,
his limbs locked in shackles, who for His love
had suffered among the Hebrews and the men of Israel;   165
and mightily withstood the magic arts
of the Jews.[1]

       Just then a voice
was heard from heaven in the land of Achaia,
where the holy man Andreas was,
teaching that people the true way of life.   170
Then the glorious King, mankind's Ruler,
Lord of hosts, unlocked his secret thoughts
to that stalwart man, and said these words:
"You must travel, undertake a journey,
bring peace to a place where cannibals[2]   175
stalk the land, and with murderous skill
defend home and country. It is their custom
that they will not let the life of any stranger
be spared in that people's stronghold,
once the wicked men of Mermedonia   180
discover a castaway—the only outcome
is a life cut short by miserable slaughter.
There your brother in victory, bound in chains,
lies languishing among those citizens.
It is only three nights now until the time   185
he must send forth his soul, restless and eager,
in close hand-combat among that heathen people,
struck by a spear, unless you come sooner."

At once Andreas gave him an answer:
"How may I, O my Lord, make such a journey   190

---

1   *the magic arts of the Jews* Some early church fathers reported that Matthew preached the
gospel to the Jewish community in Judea before heading off to other assignments (in the
Fates of the Apostles 63-69, he is said to have been martyred among the Ethiopians). The pre-
cise nature of the "magic arts" (Old English *galdorcræftum*) of the Jews is not clear; Brooks
prefers to translate it more generally as "evil machinations."
2   *cannibals* Old English *sylfætan* literally means "self-eaters."

so far and distant over deep seas,
and so quickly, Creator of Heaven,
King of glories, as your word commands?
A holy angel from heaven can easily
accomplish that—he knows the course of the waves,   195
the salt sea-streams and the swan's riding,
the turbulent surf and the water's terrors,
the ways over the wide land. I have no friends
among those alien earls, nor do I know
the mind of any man there; the battle-roads   200
across the cold water are unknown to me."
The eternal Lord answered him there:
"Alas, Andreas, that you should ever
be so slow to set out on this journey!
Nothing is impossible for the all-powerful God   205
to perform anywhere over the paths of earth—
even that the city should be set down here
under the sky's expanse among this people,
its noble high throne and all its inhabitants,
if the God of glory were to give the command.   210
You might not be so slow to set out on this journey,
nor so weak in your wits, if you well considered
how to hold covenant with your Ruler,
and keep true faith. Be ready on time:
let there be no delaying in this errand.   215
You shall venture forth and lay your life
in the clutches of cruel men, where you will be met
with hard struggle, heathen war-cries,
and the battle-skills of seasoned warriors.
You must at once, in the early dawn,   220
this very morning, mount your ship
at the sea's shore, and on the chill water
burst over the ocean ways. Have my blessing
wherever you may go throughout middle-earth."
Then the holy Holder and Ruler, Lord of high angels,   225
departed from him to seek his homeland,
middle-earth's Guardian, the glorious home

where the souls of the righteous, after the ruin
of their bodies, might enjoy eternal life.

III

    Once that message was delivered to the warrior   230
noble in the cities, his soul was not craven,
but he was single-minded, set on brave deeds,
firm, stout-hearted, not slow to the fight,
ready and bold in battle for God.
He went at dawn, in the first light of day,   235
across the sandy dunes to the sea's shore,
bold in thoughts, his thanes beside him
walking across the sand. The deep seas resounded,
the waves pounded; the warrior was hopeful
when, full of courage, he came upon that   240
broad-beamed ship on the shore. Bright morning,
radiant beacon, came racing over the sea,
heaven's holy candle shining in the darkness
over the sea-flood. There he found
three noble thanes guarding the ship,   245
brave men, bold voyagers, sitting in the vessel
as if they had come from across the sea.
That was the Lord himself, Ruler of hosts,
eternal, almighty, with two of his angels.
They were clad in the clothing of sailing men,   250
noble earls in the appearance of seafarers
who toss in a ship in the sea's embrace
on a distant course across the chill water.
He who stood on the sand gave them greeting,
and asked them, eager for his journey: 255
"From whence have you come guiding your keel,
sea-crafty men, in your sea-courser,
solitary deep-floater? Whence has the sea-stream
brought you over the bounding waves?"
Almighty God answered him there,   260
but in such a way that he who awaited his word
did not know what man of counsel he might be

who stood conversing with him on the shore:
"From the distant land of the Mermedonians
we have traveled far. A tall-prowed ship   265
carried us on the flood across the whale's riding,
a swift sea-stallion endowed with speed,
until we sought out the land of this people,
carried onward by the waves as the wind compelled us."
Andreas then answered with humble voice: 270
"I would ask you, though I can offer
but little treasure and few precious things,
that you would take us aboard your tall vessel,
high horned ship, over the whale's home
to that nation. Your reward will be from God,   275
when you have been gracious to us in this journey."
Again the Protector of princes, Maker of angels,
said to him in answer from his sea-vessel:
"Far-wandering men are not welcome there,
nor can aliens enjoy that land,   280
but in that city they all suffer death
who risk their lives from distant lands,
and do you now wish to waste your life
in that conflict across the wide ocean?"
Then Andreas gave him an answer: 285
"Our desire drives us, O dearest of princes,
to that nation's borders and the notorious city,
and great hopes in our heart, if only you will
show your mercy to us on the ocean waves."
The Prince of angels answered him,   290
Savior of men, from the ship's prow:
"We will ferry you gladly, with good will,
freely in our journey over the fishes' bath,
to the very place which your desire compels you
to seek out—once you have   295
given over the agreed-upon fare,
the appointed sum, as the ship's guardians
and sailors on board would wish you to pay."
Then quickly Andreas answered him,
replied in these words to this friendly request: 300

"I have no twisted gold nor store of treasure,
no wealth, no wherewithal, no woven wires,
no land or locked rings, that I might fulfill
your wishes in the world as you have asked."
The Prince of men replied to him,   305
seated on the gangway over the surging waves:
"Then how has it happened, O dearest friend,
that you want to set out on the mountainous sea
and the ocean's expanse empty of wealth,
seek out a ship over the cold sea-cliffs?   310
Have you nothing to sustain you on the sea-ways,
no provision of bread or pure water
for drink to benefit you? Life is brutal
for those who venture on long sea voyages."
Then Andreas gave him an answer,   315
wise in his wits, unlocked his word-hoard:
"It is hardly fitting for you, whom the Lord has given
wealth and food and worldly success,
that you should seek to answer us with arrogance
and bitter words. It is better for every man   320
that he humbly receive the wandering wayfarer
with a kind heart, as Christ commanded,
the Prince of all glory. We are his thanes
chosen as his champions; He is rightfully King,
Ruler and Maker of glory and majesty,   325
one God, eternal over all creation,
encircling all things through his own strength,
heaven and earth in his holy might,
supreme and triumphant. He himself has spoken,
Father of every folk, and bid us set out   330
across the wide world to win souls:
'Go forth now to the four corners of the earth,
even as wide as the waters surround it,
or the plains lie flat along the path.
Proclaim the shining faith in the cities   335
across the earth's bosom. I will keep you in peace.
You need bring no treasure on your travels,
no gold or silver. Every good thing I will supply,

each according to your own wishes.'[1]
Now that you yourself know of our journey,   340
thoughtful in heart, I would quickly hear
what you intend to do to assist us."
The eternal Lord then answered him:
"If you are, as you say, the thanes of the One
who raised up glory over middle-earth,   345
and you hold what the Holy one has commanded,
then with joy I will take you on your journey
over the ocean streams, as you have asked."
Then stouthearted, the brave-spirited men
went up to the ship; the soul of each   350
was filled with joy on the ocean flood.

IV

Then over the surging waves Andreas began
to pray to the Prince of glory for mercy
for the seafarers, and said these words:
"May the Lord, the Maker of mankind,   355
grant you honor and favor, happiness in this world
and the joy of glory, since you have shown
your friendship to me on this far journey."
The holy man sat down near the helmsman,
one noble by another; I have never heard   360
of a fairer vessel so fully laden
with such high treasures. Heroes sat within,
princes filled with glory, fair thanes.
Then the powerful prince spoke,
eternal and almighty, ordered his angel,   365
famous servant, to go and bring food

---

1   *Go forth now ... your own wishes*   These words are similar to the so-called "Great Commis-
    sion" in the Gospels, e.g. Mark 16.15 "Go into the whole world, and preach the gospel to
    every creature" (similar words are found in Matthew 28.16-20, Luke 24.44-49, and John
    20.19-23), mixed with Matthew 10.9-10 "Do not possess gold, nor silver, nor money in
    your purses; nor scrip for your journey; nor two coats, nor shoes, nor a staff; for the work-
    man is worthy of his meat" (Douay-Rheims translation). The passage is also very similar to
    Christ II, 481-90.

to comfort the wretched over the crashing flood,
that on the welling waves they might more easily
endure their undertaking.

                          Then they were tossed,
the high sea was stirred up. Horn-fish[1] played,   370
glided across the deep, and the gray gull
wheeled, greedy for prey. The sky's candle grew dim,
winds swelled, waves ground together,
streams were stirred, the rigging groaned,
billows swept the ship. The strong grip   375
of sea-terror grew tighter; the thanes were
numb with fear. None of them expected
that he might ever reach land alive,
those who sought a ship on the ocean stream
with Andreas. They were not yet aware   380
who guided their vessel on its sea-voyage.
And yet even there the holy Andreas,
on the ocean-ways over the oar-stirred sea,
a thane loyal to his lord, said thanks
to their powerful Guide when he was given food: 385
"For this repast may the righteous Creator,
radiant Prince of life, grant you recompense,
the Ruler of hosts, and may He give you food,
heavenly bread, since you have shown
your favor to me over the deep sea-flood.   390
Now these thanes of mine are troubled,
these young warriors; the sharp-edged waves roar,
the depths of the rushing ocean are roused,
deeply stirred; my troop of men is shaken,
the might of proud men is greatly oppressed."   395
The Lord of heroes answered him from the helm:
"Now let our floating ship ferry you
to dry land across the depths of the sea,
and then let your men, your servants,

---

1   *Horn-fish*   Old English *hornfisc*, probably not "swordfish" but a metathesis (transposition
of letters, either visual or phonological) for *hron-fisc* "whale."

wait there on the shore until your return." 400
At once those men gave him an answer,
those thanes toughened by hardship would not agree
that they should abandon their beloved teacher
in the stern of a ship and choose the land:
"Where would we turn without a lord, 405
sorrowing, sad-minded, starved for good,
wounded by sin, if we should betray you?
We would be hated across the world,
despised by all peoples, wherever the sons of men,
bold in courage, hold counsel to say 410
which of them has always best upheld
their lord in the fight, on the field of battle,
when hand and shield, ground down by swords,
suffered heavy hardship at the sport of war."
Then the powerful Prince replied, 415
the King of true covenants lifted up his words:
"If you truly are the thane of the King of Glory
Who sits in majesty, as you have said,
then tell the mysteries, how he taught
speech-bearers under the sky. Our journey is long 420
over the fallow flood; comfort the minds
of your servants. There is still a great distance
to voyage over the sea-stream, the land very far
to seek. The sea is stirred up,
the sea-bed against the sand. God easily may 425
offer help to men who fare across the sea."
Then with wise words he began to strengthen
his followers, men filled with glory:
"You all resolved, when you set out on the sea,
that you would risk your lives in a remote nation, 430
and for the love of the Lord suffer death,
give up your souls on the distant shores
of a foreign land. I know full well
that He who shaped the angels shields us,
the strong Lord of hosts. These sea-terrors, 435
the crashing sea, compelled and overcome
by the King of glory, must become gentler.

So we, long ago, over the surging waves
once chanced to venture out in a sea-vessel
riding the swells. Horrible seemed   440
the hostile ocean currents—the high seas
beat upon the ship's planking, the sea cried out,
one wave after another. At times terror arose
over our boat from the bosom of the sea
to the bottom of the hold. And there He abode,   445
the Almighty, radiant Maker of mankind,
in our wave-courser. Then the men became
fearful at heart, asking for peace and mercy
from the mighty One. When many began
to cry out in the ship, the King soon arose,   450
Bringer of blessings to angels—he stilled the waves,
the welling waters, and rebuked the winds.
The sea subsided, the stretches of the stream
were made smooth. Then our minds rejoiced
once we saw under the course of the sky   455
the winds and waves and water-terrors
grow afraid for the fear of the Lord.
Therefore I wish to tell you in truth
that surely the living God never forsakes
any man on earth, if his courage endures."   460
Thus the saintly champion spoke these words,
mindful of his men; the blessed soldier
taught his thanes, strengthened his troops
until sleep came suddenly over them all,
weary by the mast. The sea abated,   465
the rushing of the waves turned away,
the rough sea's tempest. The holy man's spirit,
after a time of terror, was gladdened again.

V

He began to speak, sage in counsel,
wise in wit, unlocked his chest of words: 470
"Never have I met a more skilled sailor,
a better seafarer, than you seem to me,

one braver at the oars or better in counsel,
wiser in words. I would ask of you,
unblemished noble, one new request   475
further, even though I have few rings,
no precious things or decorated treasure
that I might give you. I would obtain,
most glorious prince, if I might,
your good friendship. You will win gifts for that,   480
holy joy in heavenly majesty,
if you would be kind to these worn-out seafarers
and share your lore. I would learn,
kingly warrior, one craft from you,
if you would instruct me, since the King of glory,   485
maker of mankind, has given you might
to steer the wave-floaters, sea-stallions
dashing on the water, across the waves.
I have been on the ocean, early and later,
sixteen times in a seagoing boat,   490
stirring the sea with frozen hands,
the broad ocean streams—and this is one more—
but never have I seen such a man,
no mighty youth to be likened to you,
steering over the stern. The surging stream roars,   495
beats upon the shore. This boat is very swift,
floating foamy-necked, fast as a bird
gliding over the deep sea. I know for certain
that never over the wave-paths have I ever seen
more skill and craft in a seagoing man.   500
It is exactly like standing on dry land
stock-still, where neither storm nor wind
might sway it, nor surge of water
break over the broad sides, yet over the sea
it hastens, swift under sail. You are young,   505
protector of warriors, not old in winters,
yet you have in your seagoing spirit
the answer of an earl. Of every man's word
you have wise understanding in this world."

The eternal Lord answered him:
"Often it happens upon the high sea-path,
in ships among sailors, that when the storm comes,
we bound over the bath-way in our ocean steeds.
At times we meet trouble on the waves
in the sea, although we endure with difficulty, 515
survive the journey. The surging flood
cannot hinder or harm any man
against the Creator's will; He has control of life,
He who binds the seas, compels and rebukes
the dark waves. He will always direct 520
the nations with right, Who raised the firmament
and fixed it fast with his own hands,
shaped and sustained it, and filled the shining
bountiful home with glory—thus He blessed
the angels' homeland through His own might. 525
Therefore it is clear, a truth recognized,
manifest and evident, that you are the favored
servant of the King who sits in majesty—
the expanse of the deep perceived it at once,
the swelling seas saw that you had the favor 530
of the Holy Spirit. The high waves retreated,
the surging sea-swells; the terror was stilled,
the ample waves and welling seas withdrew
when they realized that you were wrapped
in the protection of God, who established 535
with His great might the joys of Glory."

Then the bold-hearted champion exclaimed
with holy voice, revered the King
and Wielder of Glory, and spoke these words:
"Be thou blessed, O Prince of mankind, 540
Lord and savior! Forever live your fame!
Near and far your name is hallowed,
brightened in glory, celebrated for mercy
over all nations. Nor is there any man
of the race of heroes under the vault of heaven, 545
who could relate rightly or know by reckoning

how You gloriously deal out your grace,
Prince of all peoples, Comforter of spirits.
Indeed it is evident, O Savior of souls,
that You have been gracious to this young man   550
and honored him with your gifts in his youth,
wise in his wits and skillful in his words.
I have never met one more wise at heart
or sage of spirit at such a young age."

   Then from the ship the King of glory spoke,   555
Beginning and End, and asked boldly:
"O thane wise in thought, say, if you can,
how it happened to be among mankind
that impious men with evil thoughts,
the Jewish race,[1] raised hateful speech   560
against the Son of God. These unfortunate men,
cruel, bloody-minded, did not believe
that their Lord of Life was God himself,
though he worked many wonders among the people,
clearly and plainly; sinful, they could not   565
know that noble Child, who was born to be
a refuge and comfort for the race of men,
all the dwellers on earth. He grew up nobly
in words and wisdom; but did he ever,
in his glory and power, reveal any part   570
of these great wonders to that worthless people?"

   Andreas gave him an answer there:
"How might it happen among the nations of men
that you have not heard of the Savior's might,
dearest of men, how he made his grace known   575
across the wide world, Son of the all-Ruling God?

---

1   *the Jewish race* Medieval Christians routinely blamed the Jews for the death of Jesus, and
made them into metaphors for stubbornness, spiritual blindness, and other kinds of evil. It
is unlikely that any Anglo-Saxon had actually met a Jew, so the anti-Semitism of this and
other passages in Old English literature is somewhat theoretical in nature, though no less
ardent and no less disturbing for that. See Andrew Scheil, *The Footsteps of Israel: Understand-ing Jews in Anglo-Saxon England* (Ann Arbor: University of Michigan Press, 2004).

He gave speech to the dumb; the deaf could hear;
the hearts of the lame and leprous rejoiced,
who had long been sick in their limbs,
weak and weary, imprisoned in their pain;   580
throughout the cities the blind could see.
Likewise he awoke, by means of His word,
many mortal men of diverse kinds from death
across the earth. In this way, kingly and noble,
he worked many miracles through the might of his skill.   585
For the mighty multitude he consecrated
wine from water, and ordered it to change
to a better nature, for the bliss of men.
Likewise he fed, with two fishes
and five loaves, a full five thousand   590
of the race of men. The ranks of foot-soldiers
sat, sad at heart, and received this food,
weary from their journey they rejoiced in their rest,
men on the ground, as was most agreeable to them.
Now, dearest youth, you might hear   595
how the Lord of glory loved us in his life
with words and deeds, and drew us by his teaching
to that fairer joy, where freely we might
inhabit a blessed home with the angels,
those who seek out the Lord after their death."   600

VI

Their protector on the sea then spoke again,
boldly on the gang-board unlocked his word-hoard:
"Can you tell me—so that I may truly know—
whether your Ruler ever revealed
his wonders, which he had worked on earth   605
at no few times for the folk's consolation,
in the place where high priests and scribes
and elders always came together
in council? It seems clear to me
that they devised their evil deeds for envy   610

in deep heresy; these death-doomed men
too eagerly heeded the devil's teaching,
faithless and full of rage. Fate deceived them,
misled and mistaught them. Soon they must
suffer woe, wearied among the weary,   615
bitter flames in the fiend's embrace."

    Andreas gave him an answer there:
"I will tell you truly that he very often,
before the leaders of the people, performed
wonder upon wonder in the sight of men,   620
and likewise the Lord of men worked in secret
for the people's good, as he sought to protect them."
The protector of princes answered him:
"Can you, wise warrior, tell me in words,
brave-hearted hero, the wonders he worked   625
in secret, bold-minded, when you sat with the Lord,
Prince of the heavens, in private counsel?"
Andreas gave him there an answer:
"Why do you question me in elaborate words,
most beloved lord, when you know the truth   630
of every event through the power of your wisdom?"

    Again their Guardian on the sea gave a reply:
"I do not ask to blame you, nor to rebuke you
on the whale's riding, but my mind rejoices,
flourishes, elated, in your eloquence,   635
your abounding nobility. Nor am I alone in that,
but the heart of every man will be happy,
his spirit comforted, whosoever far or near
remembers in his heart what that hero did,
on earth, the Son of God. Souls were converted,   640
hastened to seek the joys of heaven,
home of angels, through his noble power."

    Quickly Andreas gave him an answer:
"Now I truly perceive that you yourself

are given wise understanding, wondrous skill, 645
and great good fortune—your breast flowers
within with wisdom in radiant bliss.
Now I wish to say to you yourself
the beginning and end, just as I often heard
the word and wisdom of that noble Prince 650
in the meeting of men, from his own mouth.
Often the ample multitudes assembled,
people beyond counting to the Lord's councils,
that they might hearken to his holy teaching.
Then the protector of princes departed again, 655
bright Giver of bliss, to another temple,
where many came to meet him there,
praising God, in that place of assembly,
wise hall-counselors. Always men rejoiced,
happy at heart at the coming of the city's Protector. 660
Thus it befell long ago that the victorious Judge,
mighty Lord, went forth; there were not many
people at his departure from among his own,
except eleven men-at-arms, reckoned among
those blessed with glory—He himself was the twelfth. 665
When we came to that kingly city
where the temple of the Lord was timbered,
high and horn-gabled, famous among men,
glorious and beautiful, the high priest began
to speak insults through inward malice 670
and reviling words, revealed his secret thoughts
in a web of reproaches. Well he knew
that we followed the footsteps of the Righteous one
and kept his words of counsel. Quickly he raised up
a malevolent cry, intermingled with woe: 675
'Lo, you are more wretched than any men!
You wander wide, and weary you travel
troubled paths, and heed the teachings
of an alien man without lawful authority;
deprived of all bliss, you proclaim him your Prince, 680
and say that you dwell, truly, each day
with the Son of God. But it is well known to all

where your leader's lineage arose.
He was brought up within these borders,
born a child among his kindred; 685
those who live in his home, we have heard
through our recollection, are called
Maria and Joseph, his father and mother.
There are in his family two other
children born, brothers and siblings, 690
Simon and Jacob, sons of Joseph.'
So exclaimed the commander of men,
a troop eager for fame, and thought to veil
the Creator's might. That sin came back again,
evil without end, to where it had arisen before. 695

VII

    Then that prince, strong in power, departed
from that assembly with a troop of thanes,
lord of men, to seek a secret land.
Through many wondrous works in that wasteland
He revealed that he was rightful King 700
over middle-earth, strong in might,
Ruler and Creator of glorious majesty,
one eternal God of every creature.
Likewise he made known a countless number
of other works of wonder in the sight of men. 705
On another occasion he went again
with a great troop, so that he stood in the temple,
Lord of glory. In that lofty hall arose
the sound of his words, but sinners would not swallow
the Holy one's teaching, even though he worked 710
so many true signs while they looked on there.
Likewise he saw, Lord of victories,
many wondrous images engraved on the walls
of the temple hall on either hand
in the likeness of his angels, brightly adorned 715
and beautifully wrought. He said these words:
'This is an image of the most illustrious

of the race of angels, who reside in that city
among its citizens; in celestial joy
they are called Cherubim and Seraphim.   720
Before the face of the eternal Lord
they stand stout-hearted, praising in song
and holy hymns the Heavenly king's glory,
the Creator's protection. Here is depicted
their holy image through handicraft,   725
these thanes of glory engraved on the wall.'
The Lord of hosts, holy heavenly spirit
then spoke further before the mighty multitude:
'Now I command that a sign be shown,
a miracle appear among this multitude,   730
that this beautiful image might seek the earth
from its wall, and speak in words,
declare with true speech, so that men in this country
may better believe what my lineage might be.'
It dared not deny the Savior's command,   735
a wonder before the hosts, but from the wall it leapt,
stone from stone, so that it stood on the ground,
ancient work of old. Its voice came after,
loud through the hard stone; its speech thundered,
its words echoed. The stone's actions   740
seemed wondrous to those stout-hearted men.
He instructed the priests with clear signs,
wisely rebuked them and spoke these words:
'You are unfortunate, full of wretched thoughts,
deceived by guile, ignorant of the good,   745
your minds clouded. You call him a man,
God's eternal Son who with His own hands
made land and sea, marked out
heaven and earth and the angry waves,
the salt sea-streams and the sky above.   750
This is the same God, supreme Ruler,
whom your fathers knew in far-off days.
To Abraham and to Isaac
and to Jacob He granted His grace,

honored them with wealth, and to Abraham   755
first foretold in words his noble destiny,
that from his kin would be conceived
the God of glory. Now is that great event
open and obvious among you; with your own eyes
you may behold the Lord of Heaven, God of Victory.'   760

  After these words, throughout the wide hall
the host hearkened—all hushed in silence—
and then the oldest ones, sinful men, began
to speak again, would not see the truth;
they said that it was done through devilish illusion   765
and the sorcery of magic, so that the shining stone
spoke before men. Sin flourished
in the breasts of these men, burning hatred
welled up in their wits, the worm in blazing flames,
a poison most toxic. Their doubting minds   770
were evident there in their hateful speech,
the men's mis-thoughts wrapped up in murder.
Then the prince commanded that mighty stonework
to go forth from its place into the public street,
there to travel out through the ways of earth,   775
the green lands, and by his teaching to lead
the messengers of God among that kingdom
to the land of Canaan, and by the king's word
bid that Abraham and both his sons[1]
arise from out of their earthen graves,   780
leave their rest, gather their limbs,
receive their spirits and their youthful state,
come forth once again, wise ancient counselors,
into the present, reveal to the people
which God they had once acknowledged in His might.   785
Then he departed, as the mighty Prince,
Creator of men, had charged him,

---

1   *both his sons*   Ishmael and Isaac. Mamre is said to be the burial-place of Abraham and his
    descendants in Genesis 25.10 and Genesis 49.29-33.

over the border-roads, until, brightly shining,
he came to Mamre, as the Maker had commanded,
where for a long while the remains of the patriarchs, 790
their bodies, had been buried in the earth.
He swiftly commanded them to stand up,
Abraham and Isaac and Jacob, the third
princely one, from the ground, to meet with God,
quickly from their sound sleep. He bade them gear up
    for a journey, 795
and travel according to the Lord's instruction. They were to
    show the people
Who it was that in that first creation had arranged
the earth, all green, and the heavens above,
and what Ruler it was who established that work.
They dared not delay for any longer time 800
the King of glory's word. These three wise men
bravely went walking across the borderland, left behind
    their tombs,
earth-graves lying open; they wanted at once to make known
the Father of creation. Then all that folk was
struck numb with terror, when the noble men 805
praised in their prayers the Prince of glory.
Then the Shepherd of kingdoms commanded them
to go at once and seek a second journey
in prosperity, in peace, in celestial bliss,
and enjoy it forever after at their own will. 810

    Now, dearest youth, you might hear
how He worked many wonders through His word,
though men, their minds blinded, did not believe
his teaching. I know many more things yet,
great and glorious stories of the Son's deeds, 815
the King of heaven, which you could not endure
or encompass in your mind, no matter how wise."
Thus Andreas, all that day, praised
the Holy one's teaching in resounding speech,
until sleep suddenly slipped over him 820
on the whale's home, near the heavenly King.

VIII

Then the Lord of life commanded His angels
to carry him over the crashing waves,
to bear in their bosom in the Father's keeping
that beloved man with blessing over the vast sea,   825
until sleep overcame those sea-weary travelers.
Lofting through the air he came to land
by that citadel which the king of angels ...[1]

... then arose to resume his journey,
blessed in the sky above, to seek his homeland.   830
They set down the holy man beside the war-road
sleeping in peace under the shelter of heaven,
blithely waiting by the city wall,
near his hated foes, the whole night long,
until the Lord released the day's candle   835
to shine in splendor. Shadows vanished,
dark under the clouds, when shining over the city
came the blazing sun, bright beam of heaven.
The hardy warrior awoke, surveyed the field
before the city gates; steep cliffs   840
and hills soared high, around the grey stone
stood towers and buildings with colored tiles,
and windswept walls. Then the wise man knew
that his journey had reached the regions
of the Mermedonian race, as the Father of mankind   845
had ordered when He appointed his voyage.
There on the sand he saw his young men,
battle-brave, right beside him,
dreaming in slumber. He soon began
to wake the warriors, and spoke these words: 850
"I can tell you the truth, beyond a doubt,
that yesterday, in the depth of the sea,
a noble Lord led us over the broad ocean stream.

---

1   *king of angels* There is no break in the manuscript here, and hardly any narrative is miss-
    ing, but the sense and meter are defective. Perhaps only a line is missing, something like
    "had earlier shown him in Achaia" (as suggested by Brooks).

In that keel was the Glory of all kings,
Ruler of all peoples; I recognized His word,   855
though He had obscured his appearance."

    The noble princes said in reply,
young in speech and in spiritual insight:
"We can easily tell you, Andreas,
of our journey, so that you may yourself   860
wisely understand it in your inward heart.
Wearied by the sea, sleep overcame us;
Then came eagles over the crest of the waves
soaring in flight, exulting in their feathers.
They drew forth our souls as we lay sleeping,   865
and bore them through the breeze in flight,
rejoicing with joyful noise, bright and calm.
They showed their love lightly and lived in praise;
there was endless song and soaring in the heavens,
beautiful throng of hosts and celestial bands.   870
All around that noble Lord the angels stood,
thanes around their Prince, a thousandfold,
praised in the height with holy voices
the Lord of lords, in hope and delight.
We recognized the holy high patriarchs,   875
and no small band of martyrs, singing
righteous praise to the Prince of victories,
a troop eager for glory. There was David
in their midst, blessed champion, son of Jesse,
King of Israel, come before Christ.   880
Likewise we saw you all standing there
twelve in number, eternally noble,
your glory never failing, before the Son of God.
And there, sitting in glory, you were served
by holy archangels. It will be well   885
for those heroes allowed to enjoy that bliss.
The joy of glory was there, warriors in splendor,
noble ceremony, no sorrow or strife.
Exile is ordained and torment lies open
for any who become alien to these joys—   890
they will wander wretched when they go hence."

Then the heart of the holy man was greatly
gladdened in his breast, when he heard the stories
of his young companions, that God would
honor them so much over all other men,   895
and the protector of warriors said these words:
"Now I have understood that you were never far
from us, O Lord God, on the long sea-road,
when I climbed onto the ship, King of glory,
even though, Prince of Angels, I did not perceive it   900
on the sea-voyage, O Savior of souls.
Be merciful to me now, almighty Creator,
O radiant king! On the ocean streams
I spoke a great many words, but now I know
who bore me in honor in a wooden boat   905
across the sea's flood. He is the Spirit of comfort
to the race of men; there is ready help,
mercy from His greatness given to every man,
mighty prosperity for those who seek it of Him."

    Then before their eyes in that same instant   910
the Prince revealed Himself visibly to them,
King of all creatures, in the form of a child.
Then the Lord of Glory spoke these words:
"Be thou well, Andreas, with your willing band,
rejoice in spirit! I will keep you safe,   915
so that these wicked workers of evil,
grim hostile enemies, cannot harm your souls."
He fell to the ground; he sought favor
in words, wise warrior, and asked his dear Lord:
"What might I have deserved, O Lord of men,   920
Savior of souls, sinning against You,
that I could not recognize You as my God
on the sea-voyage, where I spoke many more
of my words before the Creator than well I should?"

    The all-ruling God answered him: 925
"You have never committed so great a sin
as when in Achaia you made refusal,

saying that you did not know how to travel
such distant ways, nor come to this city,
or carry out the task within the course   930
of three nights' time, as I had bid you travel
over the battering waves. Now you know better
that I can easily accomplish any thing
and further the fortunes of any of my friends
in every land, wherever it pleases me most.   935
Arise now quickly, devise a plan at once,
O blessed man, so that the Bright Father
will honor you with gifts of glory forever more,
with skill and might. Go into that city
beneath the citadel gates, where your brother is.   940
Matthew, I know, through wicked men's hands
has been struck by cruel wounds, your close kinsman
beset by subtle snares. You must seek him out,
free your loved one from their fiendish hate,
and all the race of men who rest with him there,   945
enslaved in misery by the evil snares
of an alien race. Soon relief will come
for him in the world, and reward in glory
just as I myself have been saying to him.

IX

Now, Andreas, into the enemy's clutches   950
you must venture at once. War is set for you,
fierce blows in battle, your body battered
and broken by wounds until your blood flows
like water in a stream. They cannot share
your life with death, though you suffer the strokes   955
and blows of sinful men. Endure that sorrow;
do not let the might of heathen move you,
grim spear-struggle, so that you forsake God,
your Lord. Be eager always for glory;
keep in mind how it was made known   960
to many men throughout many lands,
that wretched men mocked and shamed me,

fast in my bonds, bitterly taunted me,
struck and scourged me. Sinful men might not
perceive the truth through their bitter speech.   965
Then among the Jews I was hung on the gallows,
a cross lifted up, where a soldier let
the blood flow forth out of my side,
my gore to the ground. I have suffered
many miseries on the earth—in them I wanted,   970
with kindly intent, to give you an example
of what will be revealed in this alien land.
There are many in this mighty citadel
whom you will turn towards the light of Heaven
through my name, although they have committed   975
many deadly sins in days long past."
Then the Holy one departed to seek the heavens,
King of all kings, joyfully upwards
to that pure home, where mercy is prepared
for every man who might know how to find it.   980

    Then he was mindful, patient in heart,
the battle-hardened warrior hastened to the city,
resolute fighter, with courage renewed,
fierce of heart, faithful to his Creator,
strode upon the street—the path led the way—   985
so that none of the sinful men could see him
or recognize him. The Ruler of Victories
had shielded with the protection of His favor
the beloved prince in that open place.
When the noble champion of Christ   990
had pressed his way inside near the prison,
he saw a host of heathens all together,
seven prison wardens standing at once
by the shuttered door. Death took them all,
they fell ingloriously—a sudden slaughter   995
seized them, blood-spattered. The Holy one
gave thanks in his mind to the merciful Father,
praised to the heights the heavenly King's majesty,
God's great kingship. The door quickly opened

at the hand-touch of the Holy Spirit,   1000
and he, brave in battle, passed within,
a hero mindful of glory. Heathens slept in death,
drunk with gore, stained the killing field red.
He beheld Matthew, bold battle-warrior,
locked in a dungeon in that house of death,   1005
giving thanks to the Lord, and glory
to the prince of angels. He sat alone,
sad and sorrowful, in his prison cell.
There under the sky he saw his dear companion,
one holy man to another—and hope was renewed.   1010
He rose to go to him, and thanked God
that they might ever be allowed to see one another
safe and sound under the sun. Peace and joy
filled anew the breasts of these two brothers,
each clasped the other in his arms,   1015
kissed and embraced him. Both were dear
to the heart of Christ. About them, heaven-bright,
shone a holy light; their hearts within
were welling up with joy. Then with a word
Andreas began to greet his noble companion,   1020
God-fearing man, in his confinement,
and with his speech told of the war to come,
fighting of hostile men: "Now happy are your people,
heroes are here …[1]

*   *   *   *   *

… deed to seek out home."   1025
After these words the thanes of glory,
both the brothers, bowed down to pray,
sending their prayers before the Son of God.
And so the holy man, in that place of harm,
greeted his God and asked for His grace,   1030

---

1   *heroes are here*   A leaf is missing from the manuscript here. Prose versions of the story sug-
    gest the following action: Andreas tells Matthew about their coming trials; he miraculously
    restores the sight and reason of the other prisoners; he and Matthew plan to lead them from
    the prison to safety, and to their own homes.

help from the Savior, before his flesh should fall
before the battle power of the heathens,
Then he led forth from their bondage
in that prison into the protection of the Lord
two hundred men, reckoned rightly,   1035
    ... and forty more[1]
delivered from tribulation—he left no one
in the fortress enclosure locked in his chains—
and the women as well, along with the host,
one less than fifty, ...[2]   1040
he freed from their fear. They were eager to go forth;
quickly they left, and did not linger long
waiting in that house of woe for the war to come.
Matthew went out leading the multitude
in God's keeping, as the holy man commanded him.   1045
He covered that host with clouds on their joyful journey,
lest their evil foes, ancient enemies,
should come to harm them with a hail of arrows.
There those men of courage held council there,
trusty companions, before they parted ways.   1050
Each of the earls encouraged the other
with the hope of heaven, and the pains of hell
they warded away. So these warriors,
brave-hearted heroes, with holy voices
adored the King, proven champions,   1055
praised the God of Fate, of whose glory
there will be no end in all the world.

X

    Then Andreas turned back into the city,
going glad-hearted to where there was gathered,
as he had heard, a great force of hostile foes;   1060

---

1   *and forty more* There is no gap in the manuscript here, but they meter indicates that
something is missing—at least a half-line. Sources do not agree on the number of prisoners
rescued by Andreas and Matthew.

2   *one less than fifty* The verse and grammar are incomplete, but it is not clear what might be
missing.

until he encountered a column of brass,
standing near the street along the highway.
He sat himself down beside it, his heart full of love,
his thoughts ever turned upward towards angelic bliss;
there he awaited under the walls of that citadel   1065
whatever deeds of war would be his lot.
Then mighty multitudes of armies assembled,
the captains of the folk. To that fortress
came a horde of faithless men wielding weapons,
heathen warriors, to where their captives had once   1070
in that dark dungeon suffered such harm.
These evil-minded men expected and hoped
that they might make a meal of the foreigners,
their appointed food—their hope failed them
when these bands of angry spear-bearers   1075
found the cell-doors of the prison standing open,
the hammer's work unhinged, the wardens dead.
Without their booty they turned back again,
bereft of all joy, to bear the bad news;
they announced to the folk that they had found   1080
none of the foreign peoples come from afar,
and no one left alive within that prison;
instead the guards lay spattered in gore,
dead in the dust, doomed lifeless bodies
stripped of their souls. That sudden news   1085
struck fear into many of the folk's leaders,
wretched, downcast, dreading hunger,
that pale table-guest. They knew no better course
than to save their own lives by feasting upon
the bodies of the departed....
       ... All the door-guards,[1]   1090
in a single moment, were stirred
from their deathbeds through brute force.

---

1 *All the door-guards* The manuscript is not defective, but the line does not alliterate, and
Brooks proposes that two half-lines are missing here.

Then, I have heard, in great haste the people
of the city were summoned together. Men came,
a throng of soldiers riding their steeds,   1095
proud on horseback, to the place of assembly,
strong with their spears. When the people
were all gathered together in the meeting-place,
they let the lots decide between them
which of them might first be taken as food,   1100
sacrifice his life to serve the others;
they cast their lots with hellish craft,
reckoned their fate with heathen rites.
Then the lot selected a certain old warrior,
who was advisor to that troop of earls,   1105
in the forefront of battle. At once he was
fast in fetters, hopeless of life.
He cried out boldly, with care in his voice,
said that he would hand over his own son
into their power—his young offspring—   1110
in exchange for his life. They quickly took that gift
with thanks, for the people's thoughts were bloody,
ravenous, craving meat, not rewards or money,
nor hope in precious things. They were oppressed
cruelly by hunger, for the rough beast ruled them,   1115
destroyer of nations. There was many a soldier,
fierce battle-warrior, burning in his breast
for that young life. The combat and conflict
were widely known by woeful sign,
proclaimed through the city to many a man,   1120
so that they sought the boy's death in droves,
old and young alike—each would receive a share
to sustain their lives. Swiftly they summoned
the host, the heathen guardians of the temple
called the city's residents; the clamor rang out.   1125
Then the youth, in chains before the crowd,
began to sing a sorrowful song with mournful voice,
deprived of all friends, begging for peace.
But the wretched boy might find no mercy
or favor from the folk, who might spare his life   1130

and set him free. These fierce attackers
sought their strife—the sword's edge,
sharp, storm-hardened, singed and stained,
in an enemy's hands must demand a life.
To Andreas, that deed seemed shameful to endure,   1135
a great and grievous evil among the people
that such an innocent should so quickly
be put to death. That people's hate
was harsh, cruelly sharp; the crowds rushed in,
proud serving-thanes, bent on slaughter,   1140
they wished at once, valiant warriors,
to break open the head of that young boy,
and gut him with spears. God defended him,
holy from on high, from that heathen people.
He commanded that the men's weapons   1145
melt away like wax in the midst of battle,
lest those evil enemies might harm him,
wicked foes, with the force of their blades.
So the young man was saved from affliction,
hatred and grief. Thanks be to God,   1150
Lord of all lords, Who gives glory
to every one who wisely seeks
His comfort and aid. There will always be
unending friendship for those who may find it.

XI

Then a shout was raised up in the cities of men,   1155
loud lamentation in the host. Heralds cried out,
mourned their lack of meat; they stood weary,
captives of hunger. Their horned halls
and wine-houses stood empty; no wealth
did they have to enjoy in that bitter hour.   1160
Keen-minded men sat apart in secret counsel,
meditating on misery; there was no joy in their land.
One warrior frequently asked another:
"Let him that has good counsel never hide it,
or keep wisdom in his heart! The time has come,   1165

our grievous tribulation; now there is great need
that we should hear the words of men of wisdom."
At that moment, before the multitude, the devil appeared,
pale, unlovely, in the likeness of a criminal.
The dispenser of death, crippled hell-demon,[1]   1170
began there with evil intent to accuse
the holy man, and muttered these words:
"Here has fared from afar, over distant ways,
some noble man into your city,
an alien, whom I have heard called Andreas.   1175
He has harmed you here in your recent injury
when he led forth out of our fortress
far more of mankind than was fitting.
Now you can easily avenge these vicious deeds
on the one who did them. Let your weapons' tracks,   1180
hard-edged iron, scar his life-house,
the doomed man's body. Go forth boldly,
that you may conquer your opponent in combat."

    Then Andreas gave him an answer:
"Lo, you eagerly instruct this people   1185
incite them to battle! You know the bite of flames,
hot in hell, and yet you urge on this army,
foot-soldiers to the fight? Will you feud with God,
Who decides among hosts? You devil's dart!
You multiply your misfortune, whom the Almighty   1190
has humbled miserably, and hurled into darkness,
where the King of kings clapped you in irons,
and then ever afterwards they called you Satan,
those who knew to acknowledge the Lord's laws."

    But still the wicked-minded one spoke words,   1195
urged the people to fight with fiendish skill:
"Now you hear the enemy of heroes,
the one who has worked such great harm to this host.

---

1   *crippled hell-demon*   Old English *helle hinca* "lame one of Hell." The idea that the devil
    limps or is lame appears in later traditions, but is not commonly found in Old English.

That is Andreas, who strives against me
in cunning words before this crowd of men."   1200
Then a sign was given to the city-dwellers;
the bold men leapt up with loud clamor of arms
and the warriors thronged to the wall-gates,
brave under their banners, charging to battle
in a mighty troop with spears and shields.   1205
Then the Lord of hosts, the Maker great in might,
spoke a word, and said to his loyal thane:
"Andreas! You shall do great deeds of courage!
Do not conceal yourself from this crowd, but set fast
your mind against these strong men! The time is not long   1210
before the bloodthirsty men will bind you in torment,
and cold chains. Declare yourself,
harden your mind and set fast your heart,
that they may know My power in you.
These men, guilty sinners, cannot and may not   1215
divide your fleshly body with death
against My will, though you may suffer beatings
and dark evil blows. I will abide with you."

    After these words came a countless host,
shameful counselors, with shield-bearers,   1220
their hearts enraged; they rushed out quickly
and bound the hands of the holy one there,
once that man, delight of princes, was discovered,
and they might see him with their own eyes,
triumphant, in their midst. Many a man   1225
in that killing field was craving battle,
the troop's leaders. Little did they care
what reward they might receive thereafter.
They ordered him, these bitter enemies,
to be led over the land, dragged along   1230
over and over, as harshly as they could devise it.
Cruelly they dragged him through mountain caves,
down rocky slopes, those stony-hearted,
as far as their ways lay over the land,
the ancient works of giants within their cities,   1235

the streets stone-paved. A storm rose up
above the city dwelling, no small din
of that heathen army. The holy man's body
was sodden with sore wounds, soaked in blood,
his bone-house broken. Blood welled out   1240
in waves of hot gore. He had within him
unwavering courage—his noble heart
was free from sin, even though he must suffer
so many sore pains of deep wounding blows.
And so all day, until evening came,   1245
bright with victory,[1] he was beaten. Pain pierced
the warrior's breast, until the bright sun departed,
radiant and gleaming, glided to its setting.
Then the people led their loathed enemy
to prison. Yet he was still precious to Christ   1250
in his mind. His heart was light,
in his soul a holy spirit, his purpose unshaken.

XII

Then the holy man, earl of hardy courage,
was occupied by wise thoughts all that night
in the dark shadows. Snow bound the earth   1255
in winter storms; the skies grew cold
with hard hail-showers, and those grey storm-troopers,
frost and rime, froze up men's homeland,
the folk's households. The land was frozen
with cold frost-icicles, the mighty water shrank   1260
over the river streams, ice stood bridging
the white water-way. The undaunted earl
remained happy in heart, mindful of courage,
fearless and stalwart in his severe need
all the winter-cold night; nor did his heart cease,   1265
chilled by fear, from what it had begun,
so that he ever most honorably praised the Lord,

---

1   *bright with victory*   Old English *sigetorht*. The manuscript reads *sigeltorht*, "bright as the sun."

worshiped in words until the world's jewel
appeared, heaven-bright. Then a band of men
came to that dim dungeon, no small troop;   1270
they came bloodthirsty with the clamor of war.
They commanded the prince be placed at once,
that man of true covenants, into their hostile hands.
Then again, as before, all the day long
he was scourged with sharp blows. Blood welled in waves   1275
from his bone-coffer, swelled in thick streams
of hot gore. His flesh had no rest from pain,
wearied by wounds. Then a sob of weeping
burst from the man's breast, pale tears poured out
streaming in a flood, and he said these words: 1280
"Behold, O Lord my God, Provider of all good,
my suffering! You know and understand
the woe endured by each and every man.
I believe in You, my Lord of life,
that You, so merciful, in your mighty power,   1285
will never forsake me, Savior of men,
or abandon me, eternal and Almighty God.
So too may I do, while my life endures
on this earth, so that I may little forsake
Your beloved counsel, O my Creator.   1290
You are a shelter against the enemy's weapons,
eternal Source of blessings, for all your people;
do not now let the murderer of mankind,
first-born of evil, afflict with reproaches
through his fiendish craft those who bear your favor."   1295

    Then among them appeared the foul fiend,
fierce and faithless—before that armed host
the devil from hell, accursed in his torments,
instructed the warriors, and said these words:
"Strike this sinful man across his mouth,   1300
this foe of the folk! He talks too much."
Then strife was stirred up again
yet another time. Angry hate rose up
until the sun went gliding to its setting-place

under the cloudy headland. Night's covering   1305
spread itself brown-black over the steep mountains,
and the holy man was led to the hall,
bold, glory-bound, in that dim dwelling;
steadfast, all the space of that night, he was forced
to remain in close confinement in that foul abode.   1310

    Then a horrible attacker came to that hall,
along with seven others, intending evil,
evil lord of crimes, cloaked in murky darkness,
the devil, death-greedy, bereft of all good,
began to speak words of shame to the holy man: 1315
"What did you intend, Andreas, coming here
into hostile hands? Where is now the glory
which you raised up in your arrogance
when you ground down the idol of our gods?
Have you now laid claim to land and people   1320
for yourself alone, as your teacher did?
He who was called Christ raised up kingly glory
over middle-earth, while he might do so.
Then Herod[1] came and cut short his life,
overcame in battle the king of the Jews,   1325
stripped him of his kingdom, consigned him to a cross,
so that he gave up his spirit on the gallows.
So I now command my children here,
thanes of great valor, young men in battle,
that they put you down. Let the point of the spear,   1330
arrows stained with venom, strike deep
into your doomed life. Go forth directly,
hungry for war, and humble his pride!"
They were savage, and swiftly rushed on him
with greedy clutches. God protected him,   1335
steadfastly steering with His strong might.
Once they perceived the glorious sign
of the cross of Christ on his countenance

---

1   *Herod*   According to the gospels it is actually Pilate who is responsible for putting Jesus to death.

they were terror-stricken in the attack,
fearful, afraid, and put to flight.   1340

    Again, as before, the ancient foe began,
Hell's captive, to chant a song of sorrow:
"How have you become so bold, my warriors,
shield-companions, that you have prospered so little?"
A wretched one gave him an answer,   1345
wicked arch-fiend, and said to his father:
"We may not easily inflict injury on him,
death by our guile. Go to him yourself!
You will at once find a battle there,
a fierce fight, if you dare go further   1350
and risk your life against this lone man.

XIII

We can easily, dearest of earls,
instruct you better in this sword-play—
before you go at once to make war,
raise the din of battle, beware how you might fare   1355
in the give-and-take of blows. Let us go again
to jeer at him, fast in his chains,
and mock his misfortune. But have your words ready,
all considered, against this monstrous attacker."

    Then he cried out with a loud voice,   1360
weighed down with torments he said these words:
"Too long, Andreas, have you trafficked
in the dark arts![1] Lo, you have mistaught and misled
too many peoples! No longer might you
have power in your work—such grim punishments   1365
are appointed as you deserve. You will suffer,
weary-minded, wretched, deprived of comforts,
and feel the sharp pains of death. My soldiers

---

1   *the dark arts*   Old English *aclæc-cræftum* might mean something like "arts of terror" or
    "magical arts."

stand ready to begin their battle-play;
they will swiftly, in a short space of time,   1370
cut the life from your body with their keen deeds.
Who is so mighty over middle-earth
among the race of men, that he might be able
to free you from these fetters against my will?"

Andreas gave him an answer there: 1375
"Lo, the almighty God can easily save me,
Savior of men, He who many years ago
fastened you in the bondage of fiery chains,
where ever since, bound in agony,
you wait in exile, having wasted your glory,   1380
since you scorned the word of Heaven's king.
There was the beginning of evil, but your exile
will never reach its end. All the rest of your life
you will increase your woe—always and forever,
day by day, your condition grows more dire."   1385
Then he was put to flight, he who had fought
a feud so fiercely against God in ages long past.

There came at dawn, with the break of day,
a heathen mob seeking that holy man,
a host of warriors. They bid them bring out   1390
that long-suffering thane for a third time,
they wanted to try entirely to break the spirit
of that man of courage—it could not be done!
Then their grim hatred was again stirred up,
hard and merciless. The holy man   1395
was beaten sorely, bound with chains,
driven through with wounds, while the day gave light.
Then he began to call on God with a heavy heart,
in his harsh bondage, with a holy voice,
he wept weary-minded, and said these words: 1400
"Never have I borne, beneath the sky's vault,
a more bitter fate by the will of the Father,
where I must go to preach the Gospel of the Lord.
My limbs are broken, my body shattered,

my bone-house blood-stained, wounds welling forth,   1405
sinews gory with blood. O God of victories,
Lord and Savior, in only one day's time
You grew so dejected among the Jews
that from the gallows, Living God,
Lord of all creation, you cried out to the Father,   1410
Glory of kings, and called to Him thus:
'Father of angels, I want to ask you,
Lord of life, why have you forsaken me?'
And now three days I have had to endure
grim savage torment. God of hosts, I ask   1415
that I be allowed, Giver of grace to souls,
to send forth my spirit into your own hand.
By your own holy word you promised us,
when You first started to strengthen the twelve of us,
that the strife of evil foes should never harm us—   1420
no part of our body would be swiftly severed,
neither sinew nor bone would be left behind,
not even a lock of our hair would be lost—
if we would only observe your teachings.
Now my sinews are slack, my blood splattered,   1425
all across the land my locks lie scattered,
my hair on the earth—an end to this life
is far better to me than this bitter woe."

     Then came the voice of the King of glory,
speaking these words to that stout-hearted man: 1430
"Do not weep for your wretchedness, dearest friend,
it is not too harsh for you. I will hold you in peace,
the power of my protection surrounds you.
Power over all ...[1]
and victory are given to Me. Many will make it known   1435
in the gathering place on that great day
that it will come to pass that this bright creation,
heaven and earth, will all pass away,

---

1   *Power over all*   The meter suggests that a half-line is missing, though there is no break in
    the sense or in the manuscript.

before a single word will be shaken
that I have uttered with my own mouth.   1440
See now your tracks—your blood has been shed
from the bloody traces of your broken bones
and your body's bruises. The blows of their spears
will not be able to inflict further injury,
they who have worked the worst of bitter harms."   1445
When the beloved champion looked behind him,
according to the words of the King of Glory,
he saw there standing blossoming bowers
hung with fruit, where he had shed his blood.
Then the protector of warriors said these words: 1450
"Thanks be to you and praise, Protector of nations,
and glory in the heavens forever and ever,
for You have not forsaken me, estranged
and alone in my distress, my Lord of victories."

    So that doer of bold deeds praised the Lord   1455
with saintly voice until the radiant sun,
glory-bright, went gliding under the waves.
Then a fourth time the leaders of the folk,
terrible persecutors, led the prince
to his dungeon cell; there in the dark night   1460
they planned to twist his mind, the great thoughts
of the counselor of men. Then came the Lord God
to that prison hall, Glory of heroes,
Father of mankind, and greeted his friend
with kind words, and spoke comfort,   1465
Guide of life, gave orders that his body
become whole again: "No longer in humiliation
shall you suffer the pain of your armed enemies."
He arose there, courageous, said thanks to the Creator,
whole from the fetters of harsh torment.   1470
His beauty was not blemished, nor the hem
even loosed from his garment, nor a lock of his head;
no bone was broken, no bloody wound
was found on his body, nor any injury
from a driving blow, dripping blood,   1475

but he was just as he had been through that noble power,
lifting up songs of praise, sound in his body.

XIV

Lo! For some time now I have sung his teachings,[1]
praised the holy one's deeds in my poetic songs,
proclaimed in words his well-known fate.   1480
It is beyond my power, too much to say,
tedious to tell what he endured in his life,
all the way in order. A wiser man on this earth
than I esteem myself might find that story
in his heart, might know all the hardships   1485
he suffered so bravely from the beginning,
the grim battles. Yet briefly we must
further recount in a few verses
some small portion. It is said of old
that he suffered a great many grievous torments,   1490
hard battles in that heathen city.
He saw by the wall, made wondrously fast
within the vast courtyard,[2] huge columns,
pillars standing battered by storms,
old work of giants. To one of these   1495
he made address—mighty, stalwart,
wonderfully wise, raised up these words:
"Hear, marble stone, the Maker's decree,
before Whose face all created things
will be afraid, when both heaven and earth   1500
will behold the Father with a mighty host
seeking out the race of man on middle-earth.
Let now streams surge forth from your pedestal,
a rushing river! Now the almighty Ruler,
heaven's King, commands that you quickly   1505
send forth upon this perverse folk
wide-running water, a raging sea,

---

1   *I have sung his teachings*   This first-person disclaimer by the narrator, which serves to move
the action along to its climax, is not found in any of the surviving sources.
2   *vast courtyard*   MS *sælwange* "hall-plain" (?) has been variously interpreted.

to bring death to men. Lo! Dearer are you
than gold and precious gifts! On you the King,
God of glory, inscribed, set forth in words   1510
his awesome mysteries, and marked out
righteous laws in ten lines,[1]
the Maker strong in might. He gave it to Moses,
and so since then righteous men held it,
courageous thanes, his own kinsmen,   1515
god-fearing men, Joshua and Tobias.[2]
Now you may know that the King of angels
adorned you in former days more greatly
with gifts of grace than any kind of gemstone
by His holy command; you shall quickly show   1520
if you have any understanding of Him."

   There was then no more long delay in reply
but the stone split asunder and a stream welled out,
flowing over the ground. Foaming waves
enfolded the earth at the first light of dawn,   1525
the sea-flood swelled. After the feast-day
was the mead all spilled;[3] the armored men
were torn from slumber. The sea swallowed the ground,
disturbed the deep. The host was terrified
by that sudden flood. Death found the doomed—   1530
the onslaught of the sea drowned those young men,
the salt waves. That was a sorrowful brew,[4]
a bitter beer-feast. The cupbearers and serving-thanes
did not delay; for each there was enough

---

1 *righteous laws in ten lines* I.e., the Ten Commandments, said to have been carved on stone
   tablets.
2 *Joshua and Tobias* These names appear to be taken more or less at random from the catalog
   of righteous figures; they are probably just cited as examples of people who kept God's com-
   mandments.
3 *the mead all spilled* Old English *meadoscerwen*, apparently coined on the model of *ealuscer-
   wen* in *Beowulf* 769, which is only slightly less obscure. Both words mean roughly "panic"
   or "distress," and seem to imply something like "a bitter drink" (though mead, made from
   honey, is in fact not all that bitter when drunk in moderation).
4 *sorrowful brew* Taking MS *sorgbyrpen* "sorrowful burden" as *sorgbrypen* "sorrowful brew,"
   as in Brooks's edition. This continues the ongoing metaphorical description of the flood as
   a kind of wild drunken feast.

drink soon ready from the dawn of day. 1535
The water's might grew; the warriors wailed,
old spear-bearers. It was their intention
to flee the fallow flood and save their lives,
seek a shelter in the mountain caves,
a dwelling in the earth. An angel stood before them 1540
who overspread the city with a gleaming flame,
hot fire surging. Within was the fierce tempest
of the beating sea; the band of warriors
could not make their escape from that fortress.
The waves waxed, the flood roared, 1545
sparks of flame flew, the flood-waves surged.
There inside the city it was easy to find
lamentations sung and sorrow mourned,
many a desperate heart, many dirges chanted.
The violent flames were readily visible, 1550
savage devastation, shrieks of terror.
Ascending through the air the blasts of flame
encircled the walls; the flood swelled.
There the wailing of men was widely heard,
their wretched turmoil. Then one began, 1555
a desperate man, to draw the folk together;
downcast, sad-minded, weeping, he spoke:
"Now you can know the truth for yourselves,
that we have unrighteously restrained
the alien man within our prison 1560
in bonds of torment. Fate rebukes us,
hard and hateful—that is here evident!
Far better it is, as I figure the truth,
that we free him from his binding fetters,
all of us resolved—and the sooner the better— 1565
to ask the holy man for his help,
his comfort and consolation. Peace will come
for us soon after sorrow, if we seek it of him."

Then the disposition of the people
was obvious to Andreas in his heart, 1570
that the power of their pride was humbled,

their warrior's glory. The waters were spreading,
the mountain streams flowed, the flood at its full,
until the welling waters rose above their breasts
up to men's shoulders. Then the noble man bade   1575
the flowing streams be still, the storms rest
around the stony cliffs. Bold, courageous,
swiftly he strode out from his prison cell,
wise in mind, dear to God. A way was soon
made ready for him through the rushing torrent.   1580
Fair was that field of victory, the earth already
dry after the flood wherever his foot trod.

   The city-dwellers grew glad at heart,
rejoicing in spirit, for relief had come
after their affliction. The waves receded   1585
at the holy man's command, the storm grew silent,
the sea stood still. The mountain gaped open,
an awful cavern, and there in its embrace
drew in the flood, the fallow waves,
the earth swallowed the grinding surge of the sea.   1590
Nor did he sink the waves by themselves,
but also the worst members of that war-band,
fourteen guilty persecutors of the people
departed with the waves, thrown into destruction
in the abyss of the earth. Then many men   1595
were frozen in fear among those left behind;
they expected the slaughter of women and men,
more savage suffering, a more wretched time,
when stained with sin, guilty of murder,
those battle-players were plunged under the earth.   1600
They all cried out with one accord:
"Now it is clear that the true Creator,
King over all beings, governs with might,
Who has sent this messenger among us
as a help to our nation. Now there is great need   1605
that we eagerly heed this most excellent man."

XV

Then the holy one began to cheer the heroes,
comfort the troop of warriors with kind words:
"Be not overly afraid, though these sinful men
have chosen death; they suffered destruction,   1610
torment for their deeds. The dazzling light of glory
is revealed to you, if you think rightly."
He then sent his prayer before the Son of God,
asked the Holy one to give His help
to those young men among them who, in the sea,   1615
had lost their lives in the flood's embrace,
that their spirits, destroyed in torment,
deprived of all good, shorn of all glory,
might not be brought to the hands of enemies.
When by the sweet discourse of the Holy Spirit   1620
that message was made acceptable to almighty God,
pleasing to the Lord of all peoples,
He commanded the young men to rise up whole
from the dust, whom the sea had drowned.
Then up they stood, all speedily there,   1625
as I have heard, in the assembly, many
youthful boys, there was body and soul
joined together, though they had just before
laid down their lives in the rushing flood.
Released from torment, they received baptism,   1630
the covenant of peace, the pledge of glory,
the Maker's protection.

                              Then that mighty man,
the high King's craftsman, bade them build a church,
raise a temple to God where the young men rose
by their father's baptism, and the flood sprang forth.   1635
Then throngs of men gathered together
from far and wide throughout that wine-city,
earls of one accord, and their wives with them;
they said that they faithfully wished to follow,
receive the bath of baptism devoutly,   1640

as it pleased the Lord, and put aside completely
their old idolatry and heathen temples.
Then baptism was brought to that people,
nobly among nobles, and God's law
and righteous decrees were raised up in the land   1645
among the citizens, and a church hallowed.
Then the envoy of God ordained a man
wise in words and fast in learning
as a bishop for the people in that bright city,
and hallowed him before the host   1650
in apostolic office for the nation's need.
His name was Plato; he earnestly asked
that they eagerly attend to his teaching
and achieve salvation.

        He spoke his mind,
said he was eager to leave that city of gold,   1655
the hall-joys of men and treasure-hordes,
the bright ring-hall, and he would seek
a ship for himself at the sea's shore.
That was hard work for the host to endure,
that the people's leader no longer wished   1660
to remain with them. Then the God of glory
appeared to him upon that journey,
Lord of hosts, and spoke these words:[1]

      *　　*　　*　　*　　*

"... this folk from their sins. Their souls are eager,
they go about groaning, grieving and mourning,   1665
men and women alike. I have heard their weeping,
their lamentations ...[2]
        ... hasten before me.
You shall not forsake your flock
in their new-found joy, but firmly and securely   1670

---

1 *spoke these words* Something is missing here, probably only a few lines in which God asks
    Andreas why he is abandoning his people before his work is done.
2 *lamentations* Another line may be missing here, though the sense is not notably broken.

establish My name in the depths of their souls.
Dwell in the wine-city, protector of warriors,
in the treasure-laden halls, for seven nights' time.
After that you may go with My grace."

Then the stalwart man went out a second time,   1675
bold in strength, to seek the city
of Mermedonia. The word and wisdom
of the Christians increased when they laid eyes upon
the thane of glory, herald of the heavenly King.
He taught the people in the path of faith,   1680
greatly encouraged them, guided to glory
a measureless host of bright-blessed men,
to a holy home in the heavenly kingdom,
where Father and Son and the Spirit of Comfort
rule triumphant in majestic Trinity   1685
forever and ever in those halls of glory.
Likewise the holy man destroyed heathen shrines,
drove out idolatry and dispelled error.
That was sore for Satan to endure,
great sorrow of mind, when he saw the multitude   1690
turn glad-hearted from their houses of hell,
through the kindly teaching of Andreas,
to a fairer joy, where there will never be found
any fiends or fierce-minded spirits walking in the land.

Then the full number of days was fulfilled,   1695
as the decree of the Lord had commanded,
that he should remain in that stormy city.[1]
He began to hasten and prepare for his voyage,
eagerly rejoicing; he wished once again
to seek out Achaia in a ship,   1700
there to abide his death in battle
and his life's end. That would be no cause for laughter
for his killer, but he set his course

---

1   *stormy city* The compound *wederburg* is found only here; its meaning is obscure. Brooks
translates "pleasant city."

into the jaws of hell, and since that hour,
guilty, friendless, he has never found comfort.   1705
Then I have heard that a host of people
led their beloved teacher to the stern of a ship,
with mournful spirits; in many a one
the heart was welling hot within him.
Then they brought to the ship's wave-board   1710
at the sea's headlands the hastening warrior;
they stood on the shore weeping after him
as long as they could see over the sea-waves
that joy of princes across the seal-path.
And the God of glory they honored,   1715
cried out in chorus, and said these words:
  "There is one, eternal God of all creation!
His might and dominion over all middle-earth
are greatly blessed, and His glory shines over all
His holy ones in the majesty of heaven,   1720
eternal with the angels for ever and ever,
in splendor and glory. This is a noble king!"

The Fates of the Apostles

Listen! Weary of life, worn out at heart,
I found this song, assembled it from far and wide,
how those noble lords made their valor known,
bright and blessed with glory. There were twelve,
famed for courageous deeds, chosen by the Lord,   5
dear in the days of their loves. Their fame spread far,
their might and splendor over middle-earth,
the Lord's thanes, no little glory.

Lots gave guidance to that holy company
where they should preach the law of the Lord,   10
recount it among men. To Rome some went,
brave, bold in battle, and gave up their lives
through the close clutches of Nero's cruelty,
Peter and Paul. Their apostolic authority
is honored far and wide among all people.   15

Likewise Andreas in the land of Achaia
laid his life on the line before Egeus.
No worldly king could shake his courage
anywhere on earth, but he chose eternal
and immortal life, unfailing light,   20
when, hardy in battle, he hung on a cross
amid the roar of armies, after his war-play.

Lo! We have also heard men wise of counsel
recount the noble character of John.
He was, as I have heard, of all   25
the generations of the human race,
dearest to Christ, when the King of glory,
Leader of angels, sought the earth
through a maiden's womb, Father of mankind.
In Ephesus on every occasion   30
he taught the people, then on the path of life

he sought his journey to the joy of heaven,
bright home of glory.

          His brother was not late
nor slow on his journey, but by a sword's bite
among the Jews, Jacob was forced   35
to lose his life before the throne of Herod,
sever soul from flesh.

          Philip was
Among the Assaeans when he sought out
eternal life by death on a cross,
when on a gallows in Gearapolis   40
he was hanged with a small band of warriors.

Indeed, the destiny was widely known
that Bartholomew, battle-crafty man,
made his way to the men of India;
then in Albania, Astrias commanded,   45
heart-blind heathen, that he be beheaded,
because he would not worship at heathen temples,
honor their idols. For him the bliss of Heaven
was dearer by far than their false gods.

    And Thomas, too, boldly took his way   50
among the men of India in other parts,
where the minds of many were enlightened,
and hearts strengthened, by his holy word,
after he awakened, with wondrous craft,
the king's brother before the host, bold in spirit,   55
so that he arose from death, young and ready for battle,
through God's might—his name was Gad—
and then he handed over his life to that people,
taken by the sudden thrust of a sword in strife
in a heathen hand. There the saint collapsed,   60
wounded before the host; his soul went from there
to seek radiant glory as a reward for victory.

Lo! We have heard in holy books
that the truth was made known to the Ethiopians,
the noble law of the Lord. The dawn awoke,   65
the light of faith dawned; the land was cleansed
by the mighty teaching of Matthew.
Then the fierce king Irtacus, with angry heart,
commanded that he be killed with weapons.

We have heard how Jacob in Jerusalem   70
was put to death before the priests
by the stinging scourge; he fell stout-hearted,
blessed, for their envy. He has eternal life
with the King of glory as a reward for his combat.

Nor were those other two slow to battle,   75
the play of shields; Simon and Thaddeus
eager to depart, sought out the land of Persia,
men bold in battle. To both together
there came a single end-day. Through anger and arms
those noble men were forced to endure affliction,   .   80
seek out a reward of triumph and true joy,
delight after death, once their lives were torn
from their bodies; fleeting treasure
and idle wealth they scorned entirely.
Thus these noble men met their end,   85
twelve kind-hearted ones, thanes of glory;
they bear in their hearts unbroken honor.

Now then I pray the person, whoever might enjoy
the course of this song, that he pray to that holy
company of men for help in my misery,   90
comfort and consolation. How greatly I need
gentle friends along the way, when I will
seek out alone the long home, unknown dwelling,
and leave behind my body, this bit of earth,
to be a spoil of slaughter and solace to worms.   95

Here a man wise in forethought may find,
one who loves to listen to songs and poems,
who wove this verse.[1] Wealth (F) stands at the end—
men enjoy it on earth, but they cannot always
stay together in the world; Joy (W) will slip away,   100
ours (U) in the land,[2] and then afterwards fades
the body's fleeting treasure, trickling away like Water (L).
When the Torch (C) and Horn (Y) ply their trade[3]
in the night's narrow hours, Need (N) compels them
in the service of the King. Now you can know   105
who was unknown to men in these words.

Let the man be mindful, whoever might enjoy
the course of my song, that he ask for comfort
and aid for me. I must journey far away,
go forth alone to seek a foreign land,   110
set out on a journey, I myself know not where,
away from this world. Its houses are unknown,
the land and realm, as it will be for every man
unless he have a share in the Spirit of God.

---

1   *who wove this verse*   Here Cynewulf inserts an anagram of his name into his poem—he is
    able to do this because the name of each rune is also a word, e.g., the rune ᚠ (for the sound
    f) was called *feoh* or "wealth," ᛚ (for the sound *l*) or *lagu* means "sea" or "water," and so
    on. The rune ᛟ (for the sound *e*) or *eþel* "homeland" is used in other manuscripts as an
    abbreviation for the word. The interpretation of the lines is not simple; in some cases the
    names are not known, and once in a while Cynewulf seems to use the rune-name only as a
    homophone, e.g. ᚢ (for the sound *u*) *ur* "aurochs" or "ox," used here to stand for the Old
    English word *ure* "our." But anyone reading the manuscript would see the runes as letters
    spelling out the word F W U L C Y N, which can be rearranged to spell "Cyn(e)wulf."
    Knowing his name, the reader can now pray for the poet's soul. Cynewulf does the same
    thing, with different verses, in *Elene*, *Christ II*, and *Juliana*. He is the only Anglo-Saxon poet
    to sign his work.
2   *ours in the land*   Or "strength on earth." The rune *ur* literally means "ox"; the name may
    have been metaphorically extended to mean "strength." The translation here follows the
    interpretation in Brooks's edition.
3   *When the Torch and Horn ply their trade*   No one is really sure what these runes represent;
    the translation follows a plausible guess proposed by Brooks. The idea, apparently, is that
    the poet, working late into the night with his torch and inkhorn, is, through his moral
    poems, doing God's work ("the service of the King").

So let us ever more eagerly cry out to God 115
to send us His blessing in this bright creation,
that we may have a place in those halls,
homes on high, where is the highest bliss,
where the King of angels crowns pure souls
with an imperishable reward. His praise stands forever, 120
great and glorious, and His might abides,
eternal and ageless, over all creation.

Finit.

Judith

TRANSLATED BY STEPHEN O. GLOSECKI

This poem survives in the manuscript that also contains *Beowulf* (London, British Library, Cotton Vitellius A.xv). As with most Old English poems, its author is unknown, and the poem is untitled in the manuscript. It is commonly referred to as *Judith* because it takes its subject from the Book of Judith, a text found in the Greek and Latin versions of the Bible and accepted as canonical in Catholic traditions, but placed among the Apocrypha in the Protestant Bible. The book and the poem tell the story of a pious Hebrew widow, Judith, who rescues the people of the besieged city of Bethulia by beheading the Assyrian general Holofernes as he attempts to seduce her.

The beginning of the poem has been lost, and the story begins in mid-sentence just before the drunken feast in which Holofernes orders Judith to be brought to his tent. It is not known how much is missing prior to the first surviving line of the poem. The first numbered section is X, implying that nine previous sections (perhaps some thousand lines) have been lost, but some have suggested that this is misleading, and that the surviving poem is nearly complete. Like other Old English Biblical poems, they argue, *Judith* condenses and adapts the biblical story to a poetic one, a heroic ode that focuses on the crucial episode of the story, the slaying of Holofernes and the rout of the Assyrian army.

Judith is metrically unusual, especially in contrast to the precise meter of its manuscript neighbor *Beowulf*. The poem abounds in hypermetric lines (lines with more than the four stresses normally found in lines of Old English poetry), in irregular alliteration, and in rhyme, a very rare feature in Old English poetry. This relatively unusual meter has suggested to some scholars that the poem was composed fairly late in the Anglo-Saxon period, but the relationship between metrical strictness and date of composition has not been established with any certainty. The poem may instead reflect a different approach to meter, or different audience expectations about metrical precision; the difference between the meter of *Beowulf* and of *Judith* may be stylistic, not chronological, in origin.

Poetically *Judith* blurs the distinctions between ancient and contemporary, Biblical and Germanic, which is a characteristic of many other Old English poems such as *Exodus*—Hebrew warriors rage into battle clad in helmets and byrnies (coats of mail), carrying linden shields and ancient swords, while around them circle the traditional Germanic "beasts of battle," the wolf, raven, and eagle. Accuracy of historical details mattered less to Anglo-Saxon poets than fidelity to the spirit of the story and the dramatic deployment of their traditional poetic motifs. In contrast to *Exodus*, however, the poem focuses on heroic action rather than complex allegorical interpretation. The choice of a female character as the subject of a heroic poem indicates the relatively high status of women within the Anglo-Saxon nobility prior to the Norman Conquest of 1066; the poem subtly alters its source to stress the heroine's wisdom and courage rather than the allure of her beauty or the cunning of her plot to seduce Holofernes. Judith is portrayed as a woman of power, and may have been seen by audiences not only as a figure from the Biblical past, but also as a contemporary hero; the homilist Ælfric, who wrote his own prose paraphrase of the Biblical Book of Judith, sees a connection between her time and his own. At the time Ælfric was writing, the Danes were carrying out frequent raids along the English coast; in Ælfric's retelling Judith is not only a Hebrew fighting against the Assyrians but also a saintly Christian queen defending her homeland against pagan invaders. We should therefore not be surprised that, although the poem is set in pre-Christian Israel, Judith prays to the Trinity of Father, Son, and Holy Spirit to give her strength to assassinate Holofernes, nor that many of the poem's most dramatic moments seem drawn as much from Christian hagiography as from Old Testament history.

Translator's Note: I am grateful to Roy Liuzza and Broadview's four anonymous readers, whose suggestions vastly improved this translation. As far as possible, I follow Classical Germanic rules of prosody (rules equally apparent in Old English, Old Norse, Old Saxon, and Old High German heroic verse). I discuss my alliterative approach in "Skalded Epic (Make It Old)" in Beowulf *in Our Time: Teaching* Beowulf *in Translation*, ed. Mary K. Ramsey, *OEN Subsidia* 31 (Kalamazoo: Medieval Institute Publications, 2002), 41-66. I rely upon the original as edited in E.V.K. Dobbie's *Beowulf and Judith* (Anglo-Saxon Poetic Records 4, New

York: Columbia University Press, 1953). Dobbie's introduction cites the poem's numerous hypermetric halflines. Though unable to preserve their original distribution, I include some long lines to suggest the poem's remarkably ornate versification. But I have simplified its equally ornate syntax. This is unavoidable, since, for instance, verb-final periods, though still grammatical in German, disappeared from English centuries ago (along with a powerful suspended effect, a sort of semantic "crack the whip" when the closing verb clinches the action and the preceding phrases fall into place). The original also includes a surprising amount of end rhyme (a feature Dobbie notes, with line references; this flourish suggests a late date of composition). I therefore take my own liberties with the rhyme, using it to mark pivotal passages in a translation dedicated to my wife Karen Anne Reynolds, *idese alf-scinre minre.*

– August, 2005

SOURCE

London, British Library MS Cotton Vitellius A.xv, fols. 202r-209v.

EDITION

E.V.K. Dobbie, *Beowulf and Judith*. Anglo-Saxon Poetic Records 4. New York: Columbia University Press, 1953.

FURTHER READING

Chickering, Howell D., Jr. "Poetic exuberance in the Old English *Judith*." *Studies in Philology* 106 (2009): 119-36.

Garner, Lori Ann. "The art of translation in the Old English *Judith*." *Studia Neophilologica* 73 (2001): 171-83.

Griffith, Mark, ed. *Judith*. Exeter: University of Exeter Press, 1997.

Lochrie, Karma. "Gender, Sexual Violence, and the Politics of War in the Old English *Judith*." *Class and Gender in Early English Literature*. Ed. Britton J. Harwood and Gillian R. Overing. Bloomington and Indianapolis, IN: Indiana University Press, 1994. 1-20.

Magennis, Hugh. "Gender and Heroism in the Old English *Judith*." *Writing Gender and Genre in Medieval Literature: Approaches to Old and Middle English Texts*. Ed. Elaine M. Treharne. Cambridge: Cambridge University Press, 2002. 5-18.

... nor ever upon earth's broad surface[1]   could she be
                                    brought to doubt
the grace of God   who gave favor—
renowned Ruler—   when she needed it most:
protection came from the primal Power   against pure terror,
help from the highest Judge   when our heavenly Father   5
in glory bestowed   an outstanding gift,
thanks to her full belief,   her faith in the Almighty forever.
I've heard that Holofernes   then heartily called
for a wine-swilling   with wonders served
to senior thanes,   each sweet delight;   10
and the master of men   commanded them come.
Shield-fighters rushed   to their ruling prince—
all his folk-leaders.   That was the fourth day then
since she'd first arrived—   since the radiant lady,
elf-lovely[2] Judith,   ingenious had come.   15

X

Then to the feast they fared   and found their seats.
Wine-drinkers reveled,   wretched henchmen
in byrnies bold.   Time after time were bowls so deep
down benches borne   brimful to hall-guests,
shield-warriors keen.   Likewise were cups and jugs   20
for the fated filled,   though their fell ruler,
the fierce warlord,   didn't know fate was near.
Old Holofernes,   heroes' gold-friend,
sunk in wine-joy,   screamed with laughter,
roared and ranted,   raged and chanted,   25
so no man afar   could fail to hear
him storm with pride   while plunged in mead,
demanding brave war-deeds   from bench-sitters.

---

1   *nor ever upon earth's broad surface*   The opening of the poem is imperfect, and the transla-
    tion is conjectural. The manuscript reading is "... doubted the gifts in this wide world."
2   *elf-lovely*   The Old English compound *ælf-scinu* may mean "wonderfully bright"; *Ælf-* is a
    common element in Old English names (such as Alfred and Ælfric), so it presumably had
    a positive connotation. The word appears elsewhere in Old English poetry only to describe
    Sarah in *Genesis A*.

Treacherous schemer!   For the entire day he
drenched his band   with drafts of wine,   30
arrogant ring-breaker,   until his band all swooned
as drunk as death—   doughty veterans
drained of virtue.   So he kept the drink flowing,
poured for hall-thanes,   prince of warriors,
till dark of night   dropped down on men.   35
Festering with evil,   he ordered her fetched—
brought to his bedstead—   blessed maiden,
in circlets rich   all ring-adorned.

     The appointed thanes   as their prince ordered—
byrnie-troops' chief—   charged off boisterous   40
and grabbed Judith   from the guest-house there.
Then with the wise lady   they went promptly,
linden-shield[1] troops   leading her forth—
the bright maiden—   to the mighty tent,[2]
towering pavilion   where the tyrant slept   45
inside at night   by our Savior loathed—
old Holofernes.   There flowed round his bed
a fair curtain,   fly-net all golden,
wrought so fine that the folk-leader—   fiercely lethal
prince of warriors—   could peer through it   50
to see whomever   therein might come—
whichever heroes' sons;   but at him not a one
from the tribe of men   might take a look
unless that arrogant lord   should issue commands
for counselors to come   from his keen warband.[3]   55

---

1   *linden-shield*   With shields made of lime-tree wood.
2   *the mighty tent*   The poet uses the unusual word *træf* for "tent" rather than the more com-
    mon *geteld*, perhaps because the latter could also mean "tabernacle" and had a more positive
    connotation.
3   *There flowed ... keen warband*   The biblical source only mentions that Holofernes' bed
    had a *canopeum*; the poet adds the apparently original detail that it functioned as a sort of
    two-way mirror, an appropriately sinister detail that aptly reflects the paranoia of those who
    wield the power of evil.

Straight to his bed they brought   the brilliant lady.
Sturdy warriors   strode to tell him
they'd brought the holy maid   to the high tent then.
The famous fort-prince   felt fiendish glee:
with filth and vice he'd ravish   the radiant lady!   60
But the Guardian of Hosts,   glorious Judge,
our Lord on high   wouldn't allow this thing:
He stopped outrage;   He restrained evil.
Spawn of devils,   his spirit lustful,
he strode toward the bed   with his band of men.   65
Before that night elapsed   he'd lose honor,
reach the unhappy end   he'd earned before.
Evil-doer!   On earth he'd dwelt
a cruel prince,   oppressing men
under the clouds' rooftops.   Then the king collapsed   70
in midst of bed so drunk on wine   that his wit-locker
was of sense empty.   Off went his soldiers,
wine-glutted troops,   once they'd led that troth-breaker—
loathsome tyrant—   to his last resting.
Then the Savior's handmaid,   hearty and strong,   75
astutely sought   the most certain way
to end that besotted life   before the sinner woke.
Her locks entwined,   she took a sword—
razor-sharp blade,   battle-hardened:[1]
the Shaper's maid   from its sheath drew it   80
with her right hand then.   Heaven's Defender
she addressed by name—   Redeemer of all
in this world dwelling—   and these words then spoke:[2]
"Source of all, great God on high,   and Spirit of holy help,
Son of the Almighty: mercy I need now,   85
Trinitarian strength!   Intensely now
is my heart inflamed: Lord, fierce sorrow
oppresses my soul.   Prince of heaven:

---

1   *battle-hardened* As in the climactic dragon-fight in *Beowulf*, there is a considerable dra-
matic gap between the drawing of the sword and its use.

2   *these words then spoke* Judith's prayer to the Trinity makes her more like a Christian saint
than a Hebrew heroine, but her prayer for vengeance and courage in battle makes her a
warrior rather than a martyr.

give me triumph and true belief;   let me take this sword
and cleave this murder-monger!   Mankind's Ruler,   90
grant me health and grace: I've never had greater need
for your mercy before.   Almighty Lord,
bright-minded Glory-Giver,   grant me vengeance;
let my mind's fury   inflame my heart!"

    Then supreme Justice   promptly filled her   95
with strength and zeal,   as He still will do
for everyone who dwells down here   seeking help for himself
with true faith and much counsel.   Thus her mind was filled
with hope renewed.   She took that heathen man
by the hair fast then   and with her fists tugging   100
stretched him deftly   in deep disgrace,
wielding control   of the wicked man,
that hapless wretch.   Then with her hair knotted
she hacked fearsome foe   with fateful blade,
carved halfway through   his hateful neck,   105
so that he lay in a drunken swoon   with a deadly wound
though as yet unslain,   with his soul elsewhere.
So she swung the sword   a second time then—
the brave lady   lashed in earnest,
and that heathen hound's   whole head unwound—   110
rolled forth on the floor,   leaving the foul carcass
empty behind it.   Elsewhere the soul went:
under the cliff of death   cast down below,
ever thereafter in torment tied,   to torture bound,
with worms wound round   rank under ground: 115
leashed in hellfire!   lost in darkness!
Never a hope of leaving hell—   hall of serpents!
Throughout endless time   eternally slow
his soul shall stay   enslaved below
in that darkest home   no joy to know!   120

XI

Thus she won foremost fame   as a fighter there:
God gave Judith   glory at war—

the sky's Chieftain   let her achieve triumph.
Into her bag at once   the brilliant maid
put the army-hunter's   head all bloody—   125
in the supply pouch that   her companion had brought
with food for both   when they'd first set out—
fair-faced maiden,   filled with virtue
and astute judgment.   Judith gave her
the bloody head   to bear homeward.   130
She and her young helper—   high-born ladies,
boldly daring,   brave in spirit,
blessed with triumph—   both left quickly,
steadfast maidens,   to steal right through
the hostile camp   till they could clearly see   135
the gleaming walls   of the gorgeous town,
Bethulia indeed!   Adorned with rings,
they hastened forth   on the footpath then,
until, glad-minded,   they made it through
to the wall's gateway.   Warriors sat there   140
holding watch then,   wakeful guardsmen
at the mighty fort—   just as, with mournful heart
but good judgment,   Judith had ordered
before setting forth   filled with courage.
Lady so brave!—   back at last now,   145
famed for valor,   to her folk so dear:
at once the clear-minded woman   called for someone
to come towards her   from the tall fortress
to help them in   with utmost haste
through the wall's gateway;   and these words she spoke   150
to the victory-folk: "I can confirm for you
something to make us all grateful   and end grieving:
mourn no longer: the Measurer exults!
Toward you the Wonder-Prince   is well-disposed:
over the whole wide world   it's well-known now: 155
to you is glory given   and great honor
instead of the dire torment   you've endured so long."
All those city-dwellers   knew sudden bliss then,
once they'd heard her speak,   the holy maid,
over the high wall there.   The host rejoiced.   160

To the fortress-gate   all the folk hastened,
men with women   in multitudes.
The host in hordes   all hurried and thronged,
by the thousands pressed   toward the Prince's maid—
the young and old,   each uplifted—   165
all their minds hopeful   in that happy city
where they rejoiced to hear   of Judith's return
to her own homeland.   Humble, reverent,
with utmost haste   they helped her in.
Then the deep-minded maid   adorned with gold   170
bade her servant—   resourceful companion—
to unveil the man-hunter's   head before them—
show the bloody trophy   to the townspeople
so all could see   her success at war.
Then spoke the fine lady   to the folk-gathering: 175
"Victory-famed troops,   valiant commanders:
here you can see   the heathen warrior's
head before you.   Yes, Holofernes
now lies lifeless.   Our most loathsome foe,
who committed more murder   than any man on earth,   180
caused us grievous pain   and had plotted more
grief than before,   but God refused
him longer life—   didn't let him commit
more atrocity: for I took his life
with the help of God.   Now, each good man here   185
in this town dwelling: I tell you all,
shield-bearing men: you must make haste now
and gird for war.   When our glorious King,
God the Creator,   from the east sends high
His shining light,   then bear linden shields forth,   190
boards before breasts   and byrnie-jackets
under gleaming helms   to the host of the foe!
With flashing swords   fell folk-leaders,
their doomed chieftains.   Death is allotted
to all your foes   and honor to you,   195
glory in battle,   as God in his might
through this hand of mine   has made clear now."

Then the eager host   became all ready
to contend bravely.   Thence bold as kings
veteran companions   bore victory-flags   200
forth to the fight—   forth for the right!
Heroes under helmets   left the holy town
at dawn of day   to din of shields
loudly resounding.   And so the lean one rejoiced,[1]
the wolf in the woods,   with the wan raven,   205
corpse-hungry bird.   The beasts both knew
the local troops   would allot them the fated,
let them feast their fill.   There flew in their tracks,
all prey-driven,   the dew-feathered
brown-coated eagle,   who sang battle songs   210
through horn-hooked beak.   The host advanced,
bear-troops[2] to battle   by boards covered,
by the curved linden—   those who not long before
had suffered outlanders'   lashings of scorn,
heathen insults.   But that was all repaid—   215
and repaid fiercely!—   when play of spears
found the Assyrian host   once the Hebrews came
to wage battle   under war-banners
in the invaders' camp.   Keenly they launched
arrow-showers   shooting forward   220
from horn-curved bows—   battle-adders,
stout-headed darts!   Storming loudly
furious warriors   flung forth spears then
into the hardy throng.   Heroes went raging:
against that loathsome tribe,   the land-dwellers   225
stepped stern-minded,   stout in spirit,
unsoft to wake up   old opponents,
all mead-weary.   With mighty hands
thanes pulled from sheath   the patterned sword
with sturdy edge   to strike and slay   230
Assyrian foes,   fearsome warriors.

---

1   *the lean one rejoiced* The "beasts of battle" (the raven, wolf, and eagle) are a traditional motif in Old English poetry, signaling the beginning of a scene of slaughter.

2   *bear-troops* Literally *beornas* or "warriors," but the animal imagery is not inappropriate here.

Their spirits frenzied,   they spared no one
in that army's ranks,   neither rich nor poor,
no man alive   they might subdue.

XII

And so in those morning hours   the mighty thanes   235
fiercely assailed   the foreign troops
until the chief leaders   of that large army
were forced to find   fury drove them!
They showed their strength   with stout sword-swings,
Hebrew fighters.   Their foe brought word   240
to the eldest ranks   of ruling thanes:
to their flag-bearers   they brought fierce tidings:
they woke warlords   with wild stories—
told the mead-weary   of the morning kill,
deadly swordplay.   Then soon I'm told   245
death-fated troops   tossed aside sleep,
and, heavy-hearted,   they huddled round
the mighty tent   of their murderous prince,
old Holofernes.   They'd hoped quickly
to warn their lord   that war was near   250
before the attack itself   brought terror down
with all the armed Hebrews.   They all still thought
the bear-troops' chief   and the bright maiden
in the lovely tent   still lay together—
Judith the regal   and their corrupt leader   255
wickedly lusting.   But of his lords not one
would dare to wake   the war-chief there
or try to find   how the flag-warrior
had behaved himself   with the holy woman,
with God's handmaid.   The host approached,   260
Hebrew folk all   fighting briskly
with their hard weapons,   with haft requiting
old offenses   when the flashing sword
answered old slander.   Assyria watched
glory's downfall   in the day's work there—   265
her pride toppled!   But troops still stood

round the lord's tent then,   intensely alarmed,
their spirits darkening.   Drawn together
they began to murmur, moan,[1]   lament aloud,
and grind and gnash: they showed no virtue,   270
gnashing teeth in fear.   Thus did they forfeit honor,
glory and valor.   They wanted to go waken
their beloved leader—   which would do little good!
Sooner or later   someone would have to.
So a ring-warrior went   right to the tent—   275
undaunted enough   when need drove him.
On the bed he found—   blanched, sprawling—
his gold-giver: gone his spirit—
his life taken.   Then he tumbled flat—
to the earth frozen;   with frantic mind   280
he ripped his hair,   rent his garments,
and wailed out words   to warriors around,
unhappy all,   outside waiting:
"Here it's plain to see   ourselves all doomed:
we have clear token   our time has come,   285
evil upon us: now we all must lose,
assailed by strife: here lies sword-stricken—
our lord!— beheaded!"   Thus heavy-minded
they cast down weapons   and went with weary hearts
in flight trembling.   But they were attacked from behind   290
by the mighty host   until most who ran
with that force all lay   felled in battle
on the victory-field,   hacked flat by swords
as wolves would wish   and war-birds too,
all corpse-hungry.   Yet they kept fleeing,   295
shield-foe survivors.   Vying in foot-tracks
came the Hebrew force,   flushed with triumph,
honored with glory: God the Ruler,
our almighty Friend,   gave His full support.
With bloody swords   they boldly went: 300

---

1   *murmer, moan* Or (more comically) "cough," "clear their throats"? The Old English word
cohhetan appears only here and its meaning is not known. The discreet hesitation of the
retainers—they assume Holofernes is still in bed with Judith—is presumably meant to be
ironic and bitterly comical.

headstrong heroes   hacked a pathway
through the thronging foe.   They thrashed linden;
they slashed shield-wall—   those soldiers raged
with war's frenzy—   furious Hebrews.
Those thanes lusted   with a long thirst then   305
for the spear-thrusting.   There lay spent in dust,
by head-tally,   a high number
of slain nobles,   Assyrian lords,
the chief liege-men   of the loathsome tribe.
Few survived to go home!

                     Valiant as kings then   310
the warriors returned,   tearing through carnage,
reeking corpses.   They found room to loot—
land-dwellers there—   their most loathsome foe,
their old enemies,   all unliving.
They took bright booty,   bloody trappings,   315
board and broadsword,   burnished helmet,
much precious wealth.   Thus they won glory
on the battlefield   when they beat enemies,
the land-guardians: they'd laid to sleep
old foes with swords.   In swaths they sprawled,   320
those whom they loathed the most   among living tribes.
Then the whole nation   of noble clans—
foremost families—   took a full month there,
proud, hair-knotted,   to hoist and cart
to Bethulia the bright   beautiful city   325
helm and hip-sword,   hoary byrnies,
men's war-trappings   all tooled with gold:
they took more treasure   than any man living,
no matter how clever,   could recount fully—
all taken by troops   with true valor,   330
brave under banners,   battling in strife,
thanks to the wise counsel   of the keen Judith,
bold-minded maid.   From their mighty quest
spear-brave they gave   gifts of esteem
in her high honor: old Holofernes'   335
gory helm and broadsword   beside his byrnie so wide,

arrayed in gold so red,   with goods that the ring-warriors'
                        prince
in pride and power had owned: his heirlooms and riches
                              and gems,
all his glittering wealth and his rings: this to the radiant lady,
to the one so ingenious they gave.   And Judith devoted it all   340
to the glorious God of high hosts   who'd given her honor
                              on earth,
renown in the worldly realm,   with reward in heaven to come,
triumph in splendor on high,   thanks to her true belief,
her faith in the Almighty forever.   In the end there could
                              be no doubt
about the reward she'd cherished so long.   For this to our
                              Lord so dear   345
be there glory forever arrayed.   Air and the lofty wind He
                              made,
rolling sky and roomy ground,   rushing streams all tumbling
                              down,
and, through His bounty of merciful love,   bliss in His
                              heaven above.[1]

---

1   *For this ... above*   These last four lines are written in a hand dated to around 1600; they
    may have been copied from a now-lost final page in the manuscript. The scholar Franciscus
    Junius reported these lines as part of *Judith* in the seventeenth century, but it is not at all
    clear what relationship they have to the rest of the poem.

4. Fame—Heroes and History

The Battle of Maldon

During the reign of King Æthelred "the Unready" (978-1016) England experienced a renewed campaign of Viking attacks, which increased in strength and effect until the Danish king Cnut became king of England in 1016. Æthelred apparently lacked the resources, financial and otherwise, to repel the Vikings, and sources such as the *Anglo-Saxon Chronicle* depict his nobles and advisors as a treacherous, fragmented, and demoralized gang (the king's nickname, which may be a later invention, is in Old English *Un-ræd*, "no counsel," a pun on the name *Æthel-ræd* "noble counsel").

The last decade of the tenth century was a period of remarkable literary creation by writers such as Ælfric, Wulfstan, and Byrhtferth of Ramsey; it also saw the production of many *de luxe* manuscripts and works of art. But it is also remembered for the abysmal failure of Æthelred's policy of Viking appeasement. This began with the payment of £10,000 in 991, followed by £16,000 in 994, £24,000 in 1002, £36,000 in 1007, £48,000 in 1012, and finally the king's forced exile to Normandy in 1013. The idea of buying off the Vikings with "Danegeld" was apparently inspired by the arrival in August 991 of a fleet of 93 Viking ships; according to the *Anglo-Saxon Chronicle* the Viking army sacked Ipswich, sailed up the river Blackwater (called *Panta* in Old English) to Maldon in Essex, and defeated the English army led by Byrhtnoth, ealdorman of Essex. This battle may have been regarded as the turning-point in Anglo-Danish relations; this poem was presumably composed to commemorate the brave destruction of the English army and their leader.

The manuscript of *The Battle of Maldon* was already missing its beginning and end before the remaining pages were destroyed in the fire which devastated a portion of the Cotton library in 1731. Fortunately a transcript had been made before the fire, and this transcript is now the only source for the poem. 325 lines survive, and while we do not know how much has been lost, the main action of the battle is clear and fairly complete. The Vikings have beached their boats on a spit of land that is cut off from the shore at high tide, but accessible via a causeway at low tide. The English army, ranged on the shore opposite the Vikings, is depicted as being composed of Byrhtnoth's own troops—his "retainers"—and a local militia, drawn from all ranks of society and only partly trained; a Viking messenger cannily tries to exploit potential differences in class or status among the troops, but the narrator portrays the English army as united by loyalty to their leader and a desire for honor.

The poem's attitude towards its hero, however, is not entirely celebratory; Byrhtnoth is praised for his bravery and strength, but his decision to allow the Vikings passage across the causeway (so that they might have more room to fight) is said to arise from his *ofermod*, a word which can mean either "great courage" or "pride." This proves to be a disastrous tactical error. Byrhtnoth and his men fight well but the battle quickly turns against them; Byrhtnoth dies with a desperate prayer on his lips. Upon his death the treacherous retainer Godric leaps on Byrhtnoth's horse and gallops away; the men further away from Byrhtnoth assume that it is their leader who is fleeing, so they do the same, and the shield-wall—the linked line of armed men that was the key to the English defense—falls apart. The rest of the poem depicts the brave speeches and noble deaths of the men who remain.

Byrhtnoth's loyalty to his king Æthelred and his ringing refusal to pay tribute to the Vikings must have had provocative resonance in the last years of the king's reign, assuming the poem was written shortly after the battle. But *The Battle of Maldon* is not a news report, but rather a reflection on the complex relation between military victory and moral triumph; it draws on the conventions of heroic poetry to give motive and meaning to the historical facts, and turns the humiliation of Byrhtnoth's death and defeat into a celebration of other virtues such as courage and steadfastness. The poem may idealize the voices and actions of ordinary soldiers facing certain death, but it does not glorify their leaders or their cause; though the Vikings are by no means depicted as heroic, or even as individuals, the poem's moral absolutes are not arranged as an English "us" against a Viking "them," but as a personal choice between courage and cowardice, loyalty and treachery, which is only made clearer by the impossibility of victory.

SOURCE

The manuscript, London, BL Cotton Otho A.xii, was destroyed by
fire in 1731. A transcription by David Casley survives as Oxford,
Bodleian Library MS Rawlinson B 203, fols. 7r-12v.

EDITION

Bruce Mitchell and Fred C. Robinson, eds., *A Guide to Old English*,
8th edition. Oxford: Wiley-Blackwell, 2011.

FURTHER READING

Cooper, Janet, ed. *The Battle of Maldon: Fiction and Fact.* London
and Rio Grande, OH: Hambledon Press, 1993.
Niles, John D. *Old English Heroic Poems and the Social Life of Texts.*
Studies in the Early Middle Ages 20. Turnhout: Brepols, 2007.
Robinson, Fred C. "God, Death, and Loyalty in The Battle of Mal-
don." *J.R.R. Tolkien, Scholar and Storyteller: Essays in Memoriam.*
Ed. Mary Salu and Robert T. Farrell. Ithaca, NY, and London:
Cornell University Press, 1979. 76-98. Reprinted in *The Tomb
of Beowulf and Other Essays on Old English.* Oxford: Blackwell
Publishers, 1993. 105-21.
Scragg, Donald, ed. *The Battle of Maldon AD 991.* Oxford and
Cambridge, MA: Blackwell, with the Manchester Centre for
Anglo-Saxon Studies, 1991.

… was broken.
Then he[1] ordered every young soldier to send off his horse,
drive it far off and go forward,
pay heed to hands and high courage.
When the kinsman of Offa first discovered   5
that the earl would not suffer slackness,
he let fly from his hands his favorite hawk
off to the woods, and advanced to the battle;
by that you knew that the young warrior
would not weaken at battle, when he took up weapons.   10
Likewise Eadric wished to support his leader,
the lord in the fight; forward he went
with his spear to battle. He had a stout heart

---

1   *he*   Though the beginning of the poem is lost, this "he" refers to Byrhtnoth.

as long as he might hold in his hands
board and broad sword; he fulfilled his boast   15
when he had to fight before his lord.

    Then Byrhtnoth began to array the troops,
ordered, instructed, and showed the soldiers
how they should stand and hold the field,
told them to hold their shields securely,   20
firm in their fists, and never be afraid.
When he had properly organized all those men,
he dismounted among the men where he most wanted
to be, where he knew his retinue most loyal and brave.

    Then on the riverbank, stoutly shouting,   25
stood a Viking messenger who made a speech,
broadcast the boast of the seafarers
to the earl where he stood on the shore:
"Bold seamen have sent me to you,
commanded me to say that you must quickly   30
send us rings for protection; and it is better for all of you[1]
to buy off this spear-storm with tribute
than for us to share such a hard battle.
We needn't ruin one another, if you all are rich enough;
we will call a truce in exchange for gold.   35
If you, the richest one here, agree to this,
to pay ransom for your people,
give to the seamen all the money they want
in exchange for peace, and take a truce with us,
we will go back to our ships with the gold coins,   40
sail off on the sea, and hold you all in peace."

    Byrhtnoth spoke out, raised his shield,
shook his slender spear and made a speech,

---

1   *for all of you* Old English preserved distinct forms for the singular and plural second-person pronouns *þu* and *ge* (*thou* and *you*); these seem to be deployed very deliberately by the poet to portray the messenger as trying to drive a wedge between Byrhtnoth and his army, sometimes speaking harshly to him alone (with the singular *þu*) and sometimes more kindly to the whole army (with the plural *ge*). The translation tries to indicate some of this distinction with plurals such as "you all" or "all of you."

angry and resolute, he gave this answer:
"Do you hear, seafarer, what this people says?   45
They will give you spears for your tribute,
poisoned points and ancient swords,
the heriot[1] that will not help you in battle.
Messenger of the sailors, take back a message,
tell your people much more hateful news: 50
here stands an undisgraced earl with his army,
who will defend this homeland,
the land of Æthelred, my own lord,
the folk and the fields. Fated are heathens
to fall in battle—it seems too shameful to me   55
to let you go with our gold to your ships
without a fight, now that you have come
this far into our country.
You shall not get your treasure so easily;
points and blades will settle this business,   60
grim war-play, before we pay tribute."

    Then he commanded his men to carry their shields
until they all stood on the river's edge.
The water kept each troop from the other
when the flood came flowing after the ebb,   65
locking the water-streams.[2] It seemed too long
until they could bring their spears together.
They stood arrayed on the shores of the Panta,
the East-Saxon vanguard and the Viking army;
neither side could strike at the other,   70
unless one might fall from an arrow's flight.
The tide receded; the sailors stood ready,
a great many Vikings eager for battle.
The protector of heroes[3] ordered a hardened warrior
to hold the causeway; he was called Wulfstan,   75

---

1   *heriot* Old English *here-geatu* was a kind of estate tax which required that a nobleman, on his death, give his king some quantity of weapons, armor, and other military equipment.

2   *locking the water-streams* The Blackwater (Old English *Panta*) is a tidal river; when the tide came in the island on which the Vikings have landed was cut off from the shore. Later, at low tide, a stone causeway connects it to the shore.

3   *protector of heroes* Byrhtnoth.

the son of Ceol, brave among his kinsmen;
he shot with his Frankish spear the first man
who stepped most boldly across the bridge.
Beside Wulfstan stood fearless warriors,
Aelfere and Maccus, two valiant men   80
who would not take flight at the ford,
but stoutly defended themselves against the foe
as long as they might wield weapons.
When they perceived this, and clearly saw
that they would meet bitter bridge-wardens there,   85
the hateful visitors hatched a plot—
they asked if they could have access
to lead their footsoldiers across the ford.

    Then the earl in his overconfidence[1] began
to allow too much land to that hateful people.   90
Over the cold water he called out then,
the son of Byrhthelm, while the soldiers listened:
"Here's room enough—now come quickly to us,
bring on the battle; God alone knows
who will hold this place of slaughter."   95
On came the slaughter-wolves, not minding the water,
the Viking troop went west over the Panta,
carried their shields over the shining water,
the seamen bore their linden shields to land.

    Against the attackers Byrhtnoth and his men   100
stood ready; he ordered them to raise
the battle-wall with their shields, and stand
fast against the foe. The fight was near,
glory in combat; the time had come

---

1   *overconfidence*   The Old English word *ofermod* is notoriously ambiguous in this passage—
literally it means "too much *mod*" (spirit, courage), implying a degree of reckless excess in
what might still be an admirable quality, but in later Old English prose it often translates
Latin *superbia* "pride," a deadly sin. It is difficult to argue that the hero of the poem—if that
is what Byrhtnoth is—is guilty of a deadly sin in deciding to engage the Vikings in battle
where they stood; but part of the poem's enduring interest is its undertone which qualifies
the moral absolutes in which battles are usually recounted. Whatever the precise meaning
of the word *ofermod*, and whatever the military necessities under which Byrhtnoth reaches
his decision, his act proves to be a fatal error, as even he seems to recognize.

when fated men should fall.
The cry was raised, ravens circled,
the eagle longed for prey, and panic was on earth.
They let fly the file-hard spears,
grimly ground spearheads from their grip;
the bows were busy, the shield-boards took the arrows. 110
The attack was bitter, on either hand
warriors fell, young men lay dead.
Wulfmar was wounded, chose his bed of slaughter;
the kinsman of Byrhtnoth, savagely cut
to pieces with swords, his sister's son. 115
Payback was brought to the Vikings for that:
I heard that Edward struck one fiercely
with his sword—not stingy with strokes—
until at his feet fell the doomed soldier;
his leader gave thanks for that 120
to his chamberlain when he had the chance.

And so they stood their ground, stouthearted
young men at war, eagerly worked
to see who might be the first to win
the life of a doomed man with his spear, 125
soldiers with weapons; slaughter fell on earth.
They stood steadfast; Byrhtnoth encouraged them,
ordered each young warrior to give thought to war
if he hoped to earn fame from the Danes in the fight.

Then came a tough warrior, weapon raised, 130
his shield for protection, and stepped toward him.¹
Just as firmly went the earl to the churl;
each of them thought to harm the other.
The sailor sent off his southern spear
so that the lord of warriors was wounded; 135
he shoved with his shield so that the shaft broke in two,
and sprung out the spear when the point sprang back.
The warrior was furious—he stabbed with his spear
the proud Viking who gave him that wound.

---

1   *him*   I.e., Byrhtnoth.

The battle-leader was bold—he let his spear go forth,   140
his hand threaded it through the young man's neck
and he took the life of his attacker.
Then without waiting he stabbed another
so his armor burst; he was wounded in the breast
through his ring-mail, a deadly point   145
stood at his heart. The earl was the happier;
he laughed, brave man, and thanked his Maker
for the day's work the Lord had allowed him.

Then one of the Vikings threw a spear from his hand,
let it fly from his fingers so it went too far,   150
through the noble thane of Æthelred.[1]
By his side stood a half-grown young warrior,
a boy in the battle, who very boldly
drew out the blood-drenched spear from the man—
Wulfstan's son, Wulfmar the young—   155
and sent the hard spear flying back again;
the point went in, so he lay on the earth,
the one who had grievously wounded his lord.
Then an armored man went to the earl;
he wanted to plunder the warrior's gear,   160
his robes and rings and decorated sword.
Byrhtnoth drew his sword, broad, bright-edged,
from its sheath, and swung at his mail-coat.
Too soon one of the seafarers stopped him
with a wound in the earl's arm.   165
The gold-hilted sword fell to the ground;
he could no longer hold the hardened blade,
or wield a weapon. But still the old warrior
said what he could, encouraged the young men
and bade them go forth as good companions.   170
He could no longer stand steady on his feet;
he gazed up to heaven:[2]

---

1   *noble thane of Æthelred* Byrhtnoth again.
2   *he gazed up to heaven* This half-line has no match, but the dramatic quality of the speech
    introduction is so starkly effective that few critics have tried to improve it by inventing one.

"I give Thee thanks, O Lord of Nations,
for all the joys I have had in this world.
Now, gracious Maker, I have most desperate need   175
that Thou grant grace to my spirit,
so that my soul may journey to Thee
into Thy keeping, King of Angels,
and depart in peace. I implore Thee
that the fiends of Hell may not harm it."   180
Then the heathen savages hacked him up,
and both the men who stood beside him,
Ælfnoth and Wulmær both lay dead,
and gave up their lives with their lord.

Then some unwilling ones bowed out of the battle: 185
the sons of Odda were the first in the flight,
Godric left the battle, and abandoned the good man
who had often given him many horses;
he leapt on the horse that belonged to his lord,
in his riding gear—which was not right!—   190
and his brothers with him both ran away,
Godwine and Godwig didn't care for battle,
but turned from the war and took to the woods,
fled to safety and saved their lives,
and many more beyond any good measure,   195
if they had remembered all the rewards
he had given them for their services.
So Offa had said, earlier that day
in the assembly, when he held a meeting,
that many a man spoke bravely there   200
who later would not stand firm at need.

Then the people's leader lay fallen,
Æthelred's earl; all the house-troops
saw that their lord lay dead.[1]
Then forward pressed the proud thanes,   205

---

1   *saw that their lord lay dead*   That is, the troops closest to Byrhtnoth (cf. lines 23-5) see that
    he is dead; those further away mistake the fleeing Godric for their leader (lines 239-40).

uncowardly men hastened eagerly;
they all wanted one of two things—
to give up their lives or avenge their dear lord.

So the son of Ælfric urged them forward,
a warrior young in years spoke his words,   210
Ælfwine spoke, and bravely said:
"I remember the speeches we made over mead
when we raised our boasts on the benches,
heroes in the hall, about hard struggle;
now he who is bold has to prove it.   215
I will make known my noble descent to all:
I come from a famous family among the Mercians,
my ancestor was called Ealhelm,
a wise nobleman, and prosperous in the world.
Thanes will not mock me among my people,   220
that I would go away from this army,
seek my homeland, now that my lord lies
cut down in battle. Mine is the greatest grief:
he was both my kinsman and my master."
He went forth, remembering revenge,   225
until with the point of his spear he struck one
of the seamen so that he lay dead on the ground,
cut down by his weapon. He urged his comrades,
friends and companions, to go forth.

Offa spoke, shook his ashen spear: 230
"Indeed, Ælfwine, you have reminded all
the thanes at need, now that our lord lies dead,
the earl on the earth. Each of us
needs to encourage every other
warrior to war, as long as he can have   235
and hold his weapon, the hard blade,
the spear and the good sword. Godric,
wretched son of Odda, has betrayed us all.
When he rode off on that horse, that proud steed,
too many men thought that it was our lord;   240
and so our forces were divided on this field,

the shield-wall broken. Shame on his deed,
by which he caused so many men to flee!"

Leofsunu spoke and raised his shield,
his board for protection, and replied to him: 245
"I hereby promise that I will not from hence
flee the space of a single foot, but will go further,
avenge in the battle my beloved lord.
The steadfast men of Sturmer need not
mock me, now that my lord has fallen,   250
saying I would go home without my lord,
turn away from war—instead weapons shall take me,
point and iron." Full of anger he went forth,
fought tenaciously; he scorned flight.

Dunnere then spoke, shook his spear,   255
a humble churl, cried out over all,
urged each man to avenge Byrhtnoth:
"He must never weaken, who hopes to revenge
his lord on this people, nor care for his life!"
Then they went forth, not fearing for their lives;   260
the retainers set about fighting fiercely,
the grim spear-bearers, and asked God
that they might avenge their dear lord
and bring about the downfall of their foe.
The hostage[1] began to help them eagerly;   265
he was from a strong family of Northumbrians,
the son of Ecglaf—his name was Æscferth.
He never weakened at the war-play,
but he shot forth arrows ceaselessly;
sometimes he struck a shield, sometimes a man,   270
again and again he gave one a wound,
as long as he was able to wield weapons.

---

1   *The hostage* Hostages were often exchanged for diplomatic purposes in Anglo-Saxon Eng-
land; noble children might be sent to the courts of neighboring kings as a way to guarantee
peace agreements. The point here is perhaps that even a Northumbrian hostage, who had no
ties of blood or land to Byrhtnoth or to Æthelred, nor any particular reason to fear a Viking
conquest, was caught up in the heroic moment and fighting bravely alongside his comrades.

Still in the front stood Edward the long,
brave and eager, spoke boastful words
that he would not flee a single foot's space, 275
or turn back now that his better lay dead.
He broke through the shield-wall and did battle
with the seamen, until he had worthily avenged
his treasure-giver, then took his place among the slain.
Likewise Ætheric, excellent comrade, 280
eager, death-ready, fought earnestly.
Sibyrht's brother and many another
split banded shields,[1] boldly defended themselves—
the shield-rim burst, and the byrnie sang
its grim horrible song. Then Offa struck 285
a seafarer in the fight[2] so that he fell to the earth,
and there Gadd's kinsman sought the ground.
In the heat of battle Offa was hacked up,
but he had lived up to his promise to his lord—
he had boasted before his ring-giver 290
that they would ride together into the stronghold,
get home safely, or fall in the slaughter,
die of wounds on the field of war:
he lay like a thane at his lord's side.

Then shields were shattered, the sailors advanced, 295
enraged by battle; spears broke open
many a doomed man's life-house. Then Wistan went forth,
Thurstan's son, and fought with them;
he was the killer of three in that crowd,
before Wigelin's son[3] lay down in the slaughter. 300
There was keen conflict; the men stood

---

1   *banded shields*   The precise meaning of the Old English adjective *cellod*, translated "band-ed," is not known; the word appears only here.

2   *a seafarer in the fight*   The Old English specifically says "*the* seafarer," as if some particular opponent had already been pointed out; there may be a line or two missing, indicating that Offa stepped forward, fought against an attacker, etc.

3   *Wigelin's son*   It is not clear how Wistan can be the son of both Thurstan and Wigelin, unless (of course) Wigelin is his mother. Matronyms (names derived from or referring to the maternal parent) are virtually unknown in Old English, but this may be a rare instance of one.

firm in the struggle, warriors fell,
weary with wounds. Slaughter fell on earth.
Oswold and Eadwold all the while,
two brothers, exhorted the troops, 305
bade their band of brothers with their words
that they had to stand steady there at need,
use their weapons without weakness.

　　Byrhtwold spoke, raised his shield—
he was an old retainer—and shook his ash-spear; 310
he most boldly gave the men a lesson:
"Spirits must be the harder, hearts the keener,
courage the greater, as our strength grows less.
Here lies our lord all hacked to pieces,
a good man in the dust. He will mourn evermore 315
who thinks to turn back from this war-play now.
I'm an old man; I will not leave,
but by the side of my lord—by such
a beloved man—I intend to lie."

　　So also the son of Æthelgar urged them all, 320
Godric, to the battle. Often he let go a spear,
sent a slaughter-shaft whirling to the Vikings,
as he advanced foremost among the folk,
hacked and laid low, until he fell on the field.
That was not the Godric who turned away from the battle....[1] 325

1　*turned away from the battle*　The poem ends as it begins, fragmented. Perhaps not much is
　lost—the rest of the battle (a complete rout by the Vikings) is easy to imagine, though one
　wonders what sort of moral, ideological, political, or spiritual point the poet would have
　made of it.

The Battle of Brunanburh

The *Anglo-Saxon Chronicle* originated in the West-Saxon kingdom during the reign of Alfred the Great. There scholars and church-men compiled a year-by-year record of important events from the birth of Christ to their own day, based on Bede's *Ecclesiastical History*, other written sources, some local traditions, and the annotations (called "annals") made in monastic Easter tables to record the most memorable events of each year—the death of a king or bishop, a major battle, the appearance of a comet, a notably bad famine. From these bits and pieces the authors of the *Chronicle* assembled an essentially coherent narrative which tells a story of England from the time of the Romans to Alfred's struggles against the Vikings. The completed record was sent to various places across England around 892. Each copy was supplemented, added to, and continued, sometimes annually as events were unfolding, and each resulting version tends to represent the interests and narrow views of the place in which it was written. Some copies include records of local events, often no more than a line or two; others have lengthy continuations which preserve elaborate histories of the monasteries in which they were kept. Scholars have discerned several different threads of continuations, interwoven in various ways (surviving manuscripts are often copies of copies of the originals, and a great deal of cross-borrowing and collating has taken place in the history of the *Chronicle* texts). A version from Peterborough was continued by two different scribes well into the twelfth century, providing an invaluable witness not only to the period of transition from English to Norman rule but also to the gradual shift of the English language from Old to Middle English.

Some tenth-century and eleventh-century entries in the *Chronicle* are in verse—poems were written alongside or in place of annals for major events. Some of these poems were probably composed by the same people who wrote the prose annals; others may preserve works originally composed elsewhere. Examples include *The Capture of the Five Boroughs* (942), *The Coronation of Edgar* (973), *The Death of Edgar* (975), and *The Battle of Brunanburh* (937). Among these poems *Brunanburh* is notable for its length—it is nearly twice as long as the others—and its highly artful use of the traditional language of heroic poetry. The poem commemorates a military victory by King Athelstan of Wessex (ruled 924-39) and his brother Edmund against a combined army of Norsemen, Scots, Irish, and Britons led by Anlaf (Olaf), the Norse king of Dublin; the site of the battle is said to be *Brunan-burh*, but this place cannot be identified today. The battle was the high point in the West Saxon push against the Vikings begun by Alfred the Great (ruled 871-99), and its significance is reflected in the triumphant language of the poem. Heroic epithets and synonyms abound; within a few lines (48-51) a battle is called *beaduweorca, cumbolgehnastes, garmittinge, gumena gemotes,* and *wæpengewrixles,* "the work of war, the clash of banners, the tangle of spears, the meeting of men, the exchange of weapons." The English heroes earn *ealdorlangne tir* "eternal (*or* lifelong) glory" when they *heowan heapolinde hamera lafan* "hacked at shields with the hammer's leavings (*i.e.,* their swords)" (line 6). The humiliating defeat of the enemy is vividly celebrated, and the greatness of the English and their king is joyfully proclaimed. But at the end of the poem the narrator slips back into the language of the chronicle; we are told that there was never a greater battle on the island since the arrival of the Saxons in Britain, *þæs þe us secgað bec, ealde uðwitan* "as books tell us, old wise men (*lit.* historians)" (lines 68-69). This acknowledgment of written sources and a specific historical framework—imagined perhaps as Bede's *Ecclesiastical History,* or quite possibly the *Chronicle* itself—never occurs in a heroic poem like *Beowulf;* it is a hint that the tone of martial celebration is ultimately a nostalgic exercise in heroic mythmaking, promoting Athelstan and his army as the heirs of the ancient heroes of legend, and the real sources of authority and truth are no longer the songs of praise in the halls of kings and heroes, but the books and manuscripts of scholars and churchmen supporting the ideological apparatus of state formation.

SOURCE

Found as the entry for the year 937 in the *Anglo-Saxon Chronicle* MSS A (Cambridge, Corpus Christi College MS 173, fols. 26r-27r), B (London, British Library, MS Cotton Tiberius A.vi, fols. 31r-32r), C (London, British Library, MS Cotton Tiberius B.i, fols. 141rv), and D (London, British Library, MS Cotton Tiberius B.iv, fols. 49r-50r).

EDITION

John C. Pope, *Eight Old English Poems*. 3rd revised edition by R.D. Fulk. New York: W.W. Norton, 2001.

FURTHER READING

Foot, Sarah. "Where English Becomes British: Rethinking Contexts for *Brunanburh*." *Myth, Rulership, Church and Charters: Essays in Honour of Nicholas Brooks*. Ed. Julia S. Barrow and Andrew Wareham. Aldershot and Burlington, VT: Ashgate, 2009. 127-44.

Livingston, Michael, ed. *The Battle of Brunanburh: A Casebook*. Exeter Medieval Texts and Studies. Exeter: University of Exeter Press, 2011.

Scragg, Donald. "A Reading of *Brunanburh*." *Unlocking the Wordhord: Anglo-Saxon Studies in Memory of Edward B. Irving, Jr.* Ed. Mark C. Amodio and Katherine O'Brien O'Keeffe. Toronto: University of Toronto Press, 2003. 109-22.

Trilling, Renée R. "Poetic Memory: The Canonical Verse of the Anglo-Saxon Chronicle." *The Aesthetics of Nostalgia: Historical Representation in Old English Verse*. Toronto Anglo-Saxon Series 3. Toronto: University of Toronto Press, 2009. 175-213.

Here[1] Athelstan the King, lord of warriors,
bestower of rings, and his brother also,
Edmund the prince, won eternal glory
with the blade of their swords in battle
around Brunanburh. They split the shield-wall,　　　5
hacked at shields with the hammer's leavings,[2]
Edward's sons, as suited their noble descent
from royal ancestors, that they often at battle
should defend their land against all enemies,
their hoard and homes. Their attackers fell,　　　10
Scottish men and seafarers,

1　*Here*　Entries in the *Old English Chronicle* begin with the word *her*, meaning "in this year" (but also "at this place on the page").
2　*the hammer's leavings*　A condensed metaphor or *kenning* for a sword—what the hammer leaves behind on the anvil.

fated to die. The field flowed[1]
with the blood of warriors, from when the sun rose
shining in the morning, the glorious star
glided over the earth, God's bright candle,   15
the eternal Lord, until that noble creation
sank to its seat. There many a man
lay spattered by spears, men of the North
shot over their shields, and Scotsmen as well,
weary, dazed with war.

           All day long   20
the West Saxons pressed on, their best troops
pursued that hostile people, hacked at
the retreating troops fiercely from behind
with swords whetstone-sharp; the Mercians
did not refuse hard hand-play to any warrior   25
who sailed with Anlaf over the tumbling sea,
sought land in the bosom of a ship,
doomed in their battle. Five lay dead
on the field of battle, five young kings
put to sleep by swords, and seven more   30
of Anlaf's earls, and countless soldiers,
seafarers and Scots. Put to flight
was the North-men's chief, forced by need
to the prow of a ship with a small troop,
he drove his *cnearr*[2] afloat; the king escaped   35
on the shadowy flood and saved his life.

  There too the old man, Constantinus,[3]
fled in flight to his northern land,
old grey-bearded warrior. In that great meeting
he had no cause to rejoice—he was cut off from kinsmen,   40

---

1 *flowed* The meaning of the Old English word *dennade*, here translated "flowed," is not
known. Many editors have emended to *dynode* or *dynede* "resounded, rang out" for a strik-
ing use of figurative language.

2 *cnearr* This is a borrowing of the Old Norse word for "ship."

3 *Constantinus* Constantine II was king of the Picts and Scots. He abdicated his throne in
943 and died in a monastery in 952.

friends felled on the field of action,
slain in the struggle, and he left his son
on the killing field, ground down by wounds,
a young man in battle. That grey-bearded soldier
had no reason to boast of that sword-slaughter,   45
old deceiver, any more than Anlaf did;
their shredded scraps of an army could not laugh
that they were better in the work of war
on the battle-field, the clash of banners,
the tangle of spears, the meeting of men,   50
the exchange of weapons, when they took the field
to play against the sons of Edward.

The Northmen departed in the nailed *cnearrs*,
dreary spear-leavings,[1] on Dinges mere,[2]
sought Dublin[3] over the deep water,   55
back to Ireland, ashamed in their spirits.
Likewise the two brothers together,
King and Prince, sought their kin,
the West-Saxon land, elated from the battle.
They left behind them to divide the corpses   60
the sallow-coated ones: the dark raven
with crooked beak, and the dusky-coated one,
the white-tailed eagle, to enjoy the carrion,
the greedy war-hawk, and the gray beast,
the wolf in the woods.

There was never a greater slaughter   65
on this island, nor ever yet so many
people slain by the sword's edges
before this, as books tell us,
old wise men, since from the east

---

1   *dreary spear-leavings* Old English *dreorig daroþa laf.* The first word might also mean
    "bloody." The expression *daroþa laf* is another kenning—in this case, what the spear leaves
    behind are wounded and defeated enemies.
2   *Dinges mere* This name, otherwise unknown, probably refers to some part of the Irish Sea
    between England and Ireland, perhaps the estuary of the River Dee in the Wirral.
3   *Dublin* Old English *Dyflin* was the capital of Anlaf's Viking kingdom of Ireland.

the Angles and Saxons came up
across the broad sea to seek Britain,
proud war-smiths; they overcame the Welsh,
and those men of glory gained a land.

The Fight at Finnsburh

This poem was already a fragment—just one manuscript leaf—when it was printed in the English antiquarian George Hickes's 1705 *Linguarum Veterum Septentrionalium Thesaurus Grammatico-Criticus et Archæologicus*. The manuscript leaf, presumed to have been originally from London, Lambeth Palace 487, is now lost, so Hickes's printed version, of dubious accuracy, is the only surviving record of the poem. Not quite 48 lines of the poem survive; the beginning and end of the poem are lost.

The little that does survive of *The Fight at Finnsburh*, however, is enormously important. Not only does it provide important background information for an episode in *Beowulf* (and evidence that the stories told digressively or alluded to in passing in that poem were already familiar to its original audience), but it offers a glimpse into a genre of poetry—short heroic narratives or "lays"—that might otherwise be completely unknown except for the *Battle of Maldon*.

The "Finnsburh Episode" to which this poem corresponds is found in *Beowulf*, lines 1063-1160. In the celebration that follows Beowulf's fight against Grendel, a story is told to entertain the Danes. The story tells of a visit by the Danes Hnæf and his right-hand man Hengest to the hall of Finn, king of Frisia (Finn is married to Hnæf's sister Hildeburh). At some point the festivities turn sour and the Danes are attacked at night in their guest-hall. The story in *Beowulf* focuses on the aftermath of this attack—the uneasy truce, the devastation of Hildeburh, who loses both her brother and her sons in the battle, and the revenge of Hengest on Finn. The *Fight at Finnsburh* takes place squarely in the middle of the first fight, when the Danes, under attack by Frisians and Jutes, are trapped in the hall and must defend the doors. The action is direct and vivid, moved forward by first-person speeches and impressionistic flashes of imagery. When it was complete the poem must have been a powerful one; the short surviving fragment packs in many of the familiar narrative elements of heroic battle, including repeated images of fire and flame, grim boasts, the roar and din of battle, and the ominous circling of birds awaiting their chance to devour the corpses of the slain.

SOURCE

The poem survives only in a transcript in George Hickes, *Linguarum Veterum Septentrionalium Thesaurus Grammatico-Criticus et Archæologicus* (Oxford, 1705).

EDITION

R.D. Fulk, Robert E. Bjork, and John D. Niles, eds., *Klaeber's Beowulf and the Fight at Finnsburh*. 4th ed. Toronto: University of Toronto Press, 2008. 283-85.

FURTHER READING

Fry, Donald K., ed. *Finnsburh: Fragment and Episode.* Methuen's Old English Library. London: Methuen; New York: Harper and Row, 1974.

Hill, Joyce, ed. *The Old English Minor Heroic Poems.* 3rd ed. Durham Medieval and Renaissance Texts 2. Durham: Center for Medieval and Renaissance Studies; Toronto: Pontifical Institute of Mediaeval Studies, 2009.

North, Richard. "Tribal Loyalties in the *Finnsburh Fragment* and Episode." *Leeds Studies in English* n.s. 21 (1990): 13-43.

Tolkien, J.R.R. *Finn and Hengest: The Fragment and the Episode.* Ed. Alan Bliss. London: Allen and Unwin, 1982.

"... are burning."

Then Hnæf spoke, the battle-young king:
"This is not the eastern dawn; no dragon flies here,
nor are the gables of this hall aflame,
But they bear forth here ...
... birds are singing,   5
the gray-coated one howls, the war-wood resounds,
shield echoes to shaft. Now this moon shines
wandering under the clouds; now woeful deeds arise
which will make enemies for our people.
But awake now, my warriors!   10
take up your shields, think of valor,
fight in the fore, and be firm of mind!"
Then many a gold-laden thane arose, girded his sword;

then to the door went the noble warriors
Sigeferth and Eaha, drew their swords,   15
and at the other door Ordlaf and Guthlaf,
and Hengest himself was at their heels.
—Meanwhile Garulf exhorted Guthere
that he should not risk so precious a life
at the first attack on the hall-door,   20
since a hardy warrior wished to take it away,
but he asked over all, openly,
the bold-minded hero, who held the door.
"Sigeferth is my name," said he, "I am a prince of the Secgan,
a well-known exile; I have survived many woes,   25
hard battles, and here there is appointed to you
whatever fate you wish to seek from me."

                    Then in the hall was the sound of slaughter:
the hollow shield, the body's guard, was to shatter
in the hands of the brave; the rafters rattled,   30
until in the battle Garulf fell,
the foremost of all the men of that country,
the son of Guthlaf, and around him a host of good men,
the corpses of the brave. The raven wheeled,
dark and dusky. The gleam of swords shone   35
as if all Finnsburh were on fire.
I have never heard of sixty more worthy warriors
bearing themselves better in the clash of foes;
nor ever was the sweet mead better repaid
than those young companions paid to Hnæf.[1]   40
They fought five days, so that none fell
among those retainers, but they held the door.

                    Then a wounded hero took himself away,
said that his mail-coat was broken,

---

1   *nor ever was … paid to Hnæf* The meaning of these lines is disputed and the text corrupt.
    They seem to refer to the idea that warriors who drank at their lord's table incurred an
    obligation to repay his generosity with their loyalty in battle. The mead is sweet, but the
    battle is bitter.

his armor useless and his helmet pierced; 45
then the ruler of the people quickly asked him
how those other warriors endured their wounds,
or which of the two young men ...

Widsith

Widsith is similar to *Deor* in being written in the voice of a poet or performer. But while *Deor* is a personal lament—or perhaps a bid for patronage in the form of a lament—*Widsith* is a kind of boasting poem, a catalogue of legendary possibility, a jagged outline of heroic history and a request for reward for a poet whose trade is in fame and memory. The speaker is a *scop* or singer of tales named Widsith (the name means "far-traveler"). His homeland is among the Myrgings, presumably a sub-group of the continental Saxons (but otherwise unknown outside this poem), but he claims to have traveled widely in time and space to have been among many tribes and nations, including the Huns, Burgundians, Scots, Franks, Greeks, "Hebrews and Indians and Egyptians" (83), and above all the Goths, at the court of the legendary king Eormanric (who also figures prominently in *Deor*). Wherever brave kings rule great peoples, it seems, Widsith has been there, or at least knows how to tell the tale. Much of the poem, apart from its introduction and conclusion, is in the form of a simple paratactic catalogue—"Attila ruled the Huns, Eormanric the Goths, / Becca the Banings and the Burgundians Gifica" (18-19). Some of these are real, some are legendary, some are a bit of both; a few of the names are found in other poems like *Beowulf.*

The appeal of this sort of list-making may be hard for the modern reader to understand; many of the people and places on these lists are no more than names to us today, and may have been little more than that to the poem's original audience. More than a century of scholarly ingenuity has gone into tracking down the owners of these names and the stories behind them; a casual reader of the poem can feel overwhelmed by footnotes and background information. But the catalogue of names serves to advertise and demonstrate the breadth of heroic memory and the depth of the poet's repertoire. The fact that these names are singled out for remembrance is a sign of their greatness; it is also, importantly, a sign of the power of poetry, and of the people who make poetry, to confer memory or consign to oblivion. Time and again the singer reminds us that generosity—specifically the sort of generosity that rewards a good poet or singer—

is the true mark of a great king and the surest path to a good memory. *Widsith* is a begging poem, asking for payment while showcasing the poet's confidence, proclaiming his wide knowledge and experience, and demonstrating his poetic skill.

SOURCE

Exeter, Cathedral Library, Dean and Chapter MS 3501, fols. 84v-87r.

EDITION

Kemp Malone, *Widsith*, rev. ed. Copenhagen: Rosenkilde and Bagger, 1962, and Bernard J. Muir, Jr., *The Exeter Anthology of Old English Poetry*, 2nd ed., 2 vols. Exeter: University of Exeter Press, 2000.

FURTHER READING

Hill, Joyce. "*Widsið* and the Tenth Century." *NM* 85 (1984): 305-15.
Niles, John D. *Old English Heroic Poems and the Social Life of Texts.* Studies in the Early Middle Ages 20. Turnhout: Brepols, 2007.
Rollman, David A. "*Widsith* as an Anglo-Saxon defense of poetry." *Neophilologus* 66 (1982): 431-39.

Widsith spoke, unlocked his word-hoard,
he who had wandered most widely over the earth
among the races of men; he had often received
precious treasures in the hall. His noble people
sprang from the Myrgings. He was with Ealhhild,   5
beloved peace-weaver,[1] on her first journey,
when she sought the country of the victorious king

---

[1] *peace-weaver* Women were sometimes called "peace-weavers" because marriages were supposed to settle feuds and cement alliances between tribes. In literary examples this seldom seems to have worked out; Ealhhild is presumably the same woman as Swanhild, the wife whom Eormanric murders in the Old Norse *Poetic Edda*.

Eormanric,[1] east among the Angles,
the scourge of traitors.[2] He began to speak many things:

"Much have I heard of men who wield power!   10
Every prince must practice virtue,
each nobleman guide his land like others,
if he wishes his princely throne to prosper.
For a while, Hwala[3] was the best of these,
and Alexander the most powerful of all   15
the race of men, and he prospered the most
of all those I've heard of on the face of the earth.
Attila ruled the Huns, Eormanric the Goths,
Becca the Banings and the Burgundians Gifica.
Caesar ruled the Greeks and Caelic the Finns,   20
Hagen the Holmrugians and Heoden[4] the Glomman.
Witta ruled the Swaefe, Wada the Halsings,
Meaca the Myrgings, Mearchealf the Hundings.
Theodric ruled the Franks,[5] Thyle the Rondings,
Breca[6] the Brondings, Billing the Werns.[7]   25
Oswine ruled the Eow and Gefwulf the Jutes,
Finn Folcwalding[8] the race of the Frisians.

---

1   *Eormanric* The historical Eormanric was king of the Ostrogoths, defeated by the Huns
    in the fifth century. Old English *hreðcyninges*, here translated "victorious king," could also
    mean "king of the Hreths," i.e., the Goths. He is also mentioned, less flatteringly, in *Deor*,
    lines 21-26.

2   *the scourge of traitors* Old English *wrapes wærlogan* could also mean "the cruel oath-break-
    er," an allusion to Eormanric's legendary slaying of his wife. The reading here is that of
    Kemp Malone.

3   *Hwala* This name is found in the genealogy of the West-Saxon kings in the *Anglo-Saxon
    Chronicle*, but nothing is known of him.

4   *Heoden* The manuscript reads *Henden*, but the connection with *Hagen* makes it likely that
    this the same as the king Hedinn (ON *Heðinn*) in the Norse *Skáldskaparmál* and the Middle
    High German *Kudrun*.

5   *Theodric ruled the Franks* This is the Merovingian son of Clovis rather than the legendary
    Germanic hero; he ruled the Salian Franks from 511 to 534.

6   *Breca* Breca is mentioned in *Beowulf* 499-606, where, depending on whom you believe, he
    either wins or loses a swimming contest against Beowulf.

7   *Werns* Probably the same as the *Varini* mentioned by Tacitus in his *Germania*, a tribe
    connected to the Angles.

8   *Finn Folcwalding* This is the Finn of the Finnsburh episode in *Beowulf* and *The Fight at
    Finnsburh*.

Sigehere for a long time ruled the Sea-Danes,
Hnæf the Hocings, Helm the Wulfings,
Wald the Woings, Wod the Thuringians,   30
Sæferth the Secges, the Swedes Ongentheow.[1]
Sceafthere the Ymbers, Sceafa the Langobards,
Hun the Hætwera and Holen the Wrosns.
Hringwald was called the king of the War-farers,
Offa ruled the Angles, Alewih the Danes;   35
he was most brave of all these men,
yet he did not overcome Offa in noble valor,
for Offa won, while still a boy
in his first manly fight, the greatest of kingdoms.
No one in his day could equal him in valor   40
on the field of battle. With a single sword
he redrew the map of the Myrgings
around Fifeldore; afterwards the Angles
and Swedes[2] held their land just as Offa had won it.
Hrothulf and Hrothgar held peace together   45
for a long time, uncle and nephew,
after they had wrecked the race of vikings
and humbled Ingeld's battle-array,
hacked down at Heorot the pride of the Heathobards.[3]

   Since I have sojourned in many strange lands   50
across the wide world, where I have come to know
good and evil, cut off from my home,
wandered wide, far away from my kinsmen,
therefore I can sing and tell a tale,
make known before many in the mead-hall   55
how my noble patrons chose to reward me.
I was with the Huns and with the Ostrogoths,[4]

---

1 *'Ongentheow* The Swedish king Ongentheow appears as a terrifying enemy in *Beowulf.*
2 *Swedes* Old English *Swæfe.* This may in fact be the Swabians rather than the Swedes; while
   present-day Swabia is in Bavaria, the original Germanic homeland of the *Suebi* was on the
   Baltic Sea. If so, they may be the same tribe as the narrator's Myrgings.
3 *hacked down ... the Heathobards* These events are alluded to in *Beowulf,* though not de-
   picted there.
4 *Ostrogoths* Old English *Hreðgotum.*

with the Swedes and the Geats and the South-Danes.
With the Wendels I was, and the Wærns and the vikings,
with the Gifthas I was, and the Wends and the Gefflegas,   60
With the Angles I was, and the Swedes and the Ænenas,
with the Saxons I was, and the Secges and the Swordsmen.[1]
With the Hrones I was, and the Deans and the Heathoreams,
With the Thuringians I was and the Throwends,
and with the Burgundians, where I was given a ring;   65
Guth-here gave me a gracious treasure there
as my song's reward—that king was no miser!
With the Franks I was, and the Frisians and the Frumtings,
with the Rugians I was, and the Glomman and the Romans.
I was also in Italy with Ælfwine,   70
who had, to my knowledge, the readiest hand
of any man for earning praise,
the most generous heart for giving our rings,
bright circlets, the son of Eadwine.

With the Saracens I was and with the Syrians,[2]   75
with the Greeks I was, with the Finns and with Caesar,
who had possession of the cities of wine,[3]
riches and beauty and the realms of the Walas.[4]
I was with the Scots and the Picts and the Scride-finns,
with the Lid-vikings[5] and the Leons and the Langobards,   80
with heathens and heroes and Hundings.[6]
I was with the Israelites and the Assyrians,
the Hebrews and Indians and Egyptians;
I was with the Medes and the Persians and the Myrgings,

---

1   *Swordsmen*   Old English *sweordwerum*. A tribe called the *suardones*, which may be the same thing, is mentioned in Tacitus's *Germania*.

2   *the Saracens … and with the Syrians*   Old English *Sercingum … ond mid Seringum*. These may be the names of some unidentified or imaginary Germanic tribes, but since the narrator appears to broaden his scope of reference in this passage, this translation is preferred.

3   *cities of wine*   Old English *winburga* could also mean "cities of joy."

4   *realms of the Walas*   Old English *wala rices* may be a way of referring to the riches of the inhabitants of Rome.

5   *Lid-vikings*   These are probably the *Letavica* of Brittany.

6   *with heathens and heroes and Hundings*   Old English *mid hæðnum ond mid hælepum ond mid Hundingum*. It is not clear whether the first two of these are proper or common nouns.

and the Ongen-Myrgings and the Mofdings,   85
and with the Amothings.[1] With the East-Thuringians I was
and with the Eols and the Ists and the Idumings.
And I was with Eormanric all the while,
where the king of the Goths did good for me;
he gave me a ring, that ruler of cities,   90
whose worth was reckoned at six hundred shillings
of pure gold, counted out in coins;
I gave it over as a gift to Eadgils,
my lord and protector, when I returned home,
a reward for my dear lord because he gave me land,   95
the lord of the Myrgings, my father's homeland.
And then Ealhhild, daugher of Eadwin,
gave me another, noble queen.
Her praise spread long and far in many lands,
whenever I could say in my songs   100
that I knew where, under the skies, was the best
of gold-laden queens giving out gifts,
when Scilling[2] and I raised up a song
with a clear voice for our victorious lord,
loud with the harp the happy noise rang,   105
when many men, proud of heart,
said in words what they knew well,
that they had never heard a better song.

    Then I passed through all the land of the Goths,
always seeking the best companions: 110
such was the household of Eormanric.
I sought Hehca[3] and Beadeca and the Herelings,
I sought Emerca and Frindla and East-Goth,
the wise and good father of Unwen.
I sought Secca and Becca, Seafola and Theodoric,   115
Heathoric and Sifeca, Hlitha and Incgentheow;
I sought Eadwin and Elsa, Ægelmund and Hungar,

---

1 *the Ongen-Myrgings ... with the Amothings*   The text here is corrupt and something may be
   missing, miswritten, or out of order.
2 *Scilling*   This is apparently the name of his harp.
3 *Hehca*   The manuscript reads *heðcan*. Hehca may be the father of Eormanric.

and the proud warriors of the With-Myrgings.
I sought Wulfhere and Wyrmhere, where war seldom ceased,
when the army of Hræd with hard swords   120
had to defend around Vistula-wood
the old ancestral home from the people of Attila.
I sought Rædhere and Rondere, Rumstan and Gislhere,
Withergild and Frederic, Wudga and Hama;
that band of comrades was by no means the worst,   125
though I must name them last in my song.
Often from that throng flew hissing
the singing spear among an angry people;
those exiles over the earth, Wudga and Hama,
ruled by wound gold over men and women.   130
Thus I have always found in my journeys
that he is most beloved to land-dwellers
to whom God gives power over men
into his hands while he lives here on earth."

   And so, wandering as their fate unfolds,   135
the singers of men among many lands,
speaking at need, saying words of thanks,
always south or north where they meet some one,
wise in songs, not stingy with gifts,
who would build up his fame before his men,   140
do honorable deeds until it all fades away,
light and life together; he earns glory,
and has high-towering fame under the heavens.

From the Publisher

A name never says it all, but the word "Broadview" expresses a good deal of the philosophy behind our company. We are open to a broad range of academic approaches and political viewpoints. We pay attention to the broad impact book publishing and book printing has in the wider world; for some years now we have used 100% recycled paper for most titles. Our publishing program is internationally oriented and broad-ranging. Our individual titles often appeal to a broad reader-ship too; many are of interest as much to general readers as to academics and students.

Founded in 1985, Broadview remains a fully independent company owned by its shareholders—not an imprint or subsidiary of a larger multinational.

For the most accurate information on our books (including information on pricing, editions, and formats) please visit our website at www.broadviewpress.com. Our print books and ebooks are also available for sale on our site.

broadview press
www.broadviewpress.com

This book is made of paper from well-managed FSC® - certified forests, recycled materials, and other controlled sources.

PCF

PERMANENT